# VOICES OF THE GODDESS

# VOICES
## OF THE
# GODDESS
### A Chorus of Sibyls

EDITED BY
CAITLÍN MATTHEWS

THE AQUARIAN PRESS

First published 1990

The illustrations in chapters 2, 3, 4, 5, 7, 8 and 10 are by Stuart
Littlejohn. The other illustrations are drawn by the writers in
whose chapters they appear.

British Library Cataloguing in Publication Data

Voices of the goddess.
1. Goddesses
I. Matthews, Caitlín
291.2114

ISBN 0-85030-965-4

*The Aquarian Press is part of the Thorsons Publishing Group,
Wellingborough, Northamptonshire, NN8 2RQ, England.*

Typesetting by MJL Limited, Hitchin, Hertfordshire.
Printed in Great Britain by Woolnough Bookbinding Limited,
Irthlingborough, Northamptonshire.

1  3  5  7  9  10  8  6  4  2

# Contents

*Acknowledgements*                                                              7
*Author's Note*                                                                 8
*Introduction*                                                                  9

*Chapter*
  1 **The Rebirth of the Goddess**  Olivia Robertson                 29
  2 **Priestess and Witch**  Vivianne Crowley                         45
  3 **The Voice of the Bitch Goddess**  Margaretta D'Arcy            67
  4 **The Testament of Rhiannon**  Caitlín Matthews                  85
  5 **The Goddess as the Way of the Land**  Helene Hess            109
  6 **Tested by the Dark/Light Mother of the Other**
     **World**  Monica Sjöö                            123
  7 **The Path of the Solar Priestess**  Sunflower                   151
  8 **The Search for the Beloved**  Vivienne Vernon-Jones           175
  9 **Consecration**  Diana L Paxson                                 197
10 **The Garments of Isis**  Naomi Ozaniec                                    217
*Oracle For a New Priestess and Blessing For all Who*
 *Seek Her*                                                               231
*Bibliography*                                                                 233
*Useful addresses*                                                            239

# Dedication

To the memory of Dion Fortune, whose own mediation and priestesshood laid the foundations for women of my generation and who has enabled us to journey ever deeper into the greatness of the Goddess. Also to all who sing Her song and weave Her web: the makers and shapers of Her voice.

# Acknowledgements

To all the priestesses and priests with whom I have worked over the years, by their example I was trained and inspired. I hope that my own mediation may mirror their faithful and compassionate devotion.

To all my readers and students who have given me opportunities to mediate and learn more about the Goddess.

To John and Emrys Matthews, husband and son in my household temple — both of you are my special blessing. May you continue to tolerate my activities with your usual goodwill, love and chuckles!

To Philip Clayton-Gore, my spiritual brother, who gladdened my heart with poetry and buoyed up a sinking priestess more than once.

To Bob Stewart, true mediator of the ancestral earth, for ritual companionship and expert guidance.

To Felicity Aldridge, sister shamanka on the native trail, through whom the ancestral and Goddessly voices also speak. She miraculously combines the elements in a way that gives me faith in this strange muddled New Age.

To Katherine Kurtz-Macmillan whose experience of priestess-hood is an inspiration to those walking the mystical Christian path.

To Stuart Littlejohn, whose sensitive artistry enhances this book.

To Chesca Potter, thanks for permission to reproduce her work on page 43.

To Eileen Campbell, whose foresight and inspiration have been a beacon in the world of New Age publishing. Her skilful wisdom and warm friendship are much valued.

# Author's Note

Around each of us there are webs of women and men who help weave our unfolding lives. Mine has been interwoven with some wonderful people, some of whom appear in this book.

In choosing to make this a book solely for female contributors, I have done a lot of heart-searching, for I like mixed company and I am aware that there are already a lot of books on the market that go out of their way to exclude men.

The role of priestess, sibyl, wisewoman and mediator, however, is such an unusual one in our era, that this collection must stand as an attempt to review the priestly role of women. It may be that I shall write another book or edit another collection in which a wider dialogue can take place, for this is also an age where a man can be a priest of other than orthodox religions. Indeed, it was not from want of knowing men who are themselves voices of the Goddess that they were excluded: this ancient role, little understood, deserves wider attention as does the role of women as mediators of the energies of the Divine Masculine. However, I hope that this book will be read by both men and women who may find within themselves greater access to the heart of the Goddess.

The views expressed in this book are particular to each individual writer and are not necessarily shared or endorsed by the editor. Such is the diversity of opinion and approach to the Goddess that Her voices encompass the full range of sound. Naturally, we each gravitate to the note that best pleases our individual taste. May you find harmonious notes within in this chorus that resonate with your own song.

Caitlín Matthews
Midsummer's Eve 1989

# Introduction

## Sibyls

'Foremost among the ladies of sovereign dignity are the wise sibyls, most filled with wisdom ... They were born in different countries of the world and not all at one time, and all foretold a great many things to come'.

Christine de Pizan, *The Book of the City of Ladies*, 1405

The function of a sibyl is to be a mediator, or a pure channel for the voice of the gods. She is also an earth-speaker — sensitive to the subtle energies of the land and its indwelling spirits. Within our own time, the earth, the Goddess and women themselves have had no voice.

In ancient Rome, Amalthaea, the Cumaean sibyl, was the keeper of the Sibylline Oracles — oracular sayings of a lineage of sibyls that were preserved in nine books. According to the Roman historian, Livy, the sibyl offered these for sale to Tarquin, who rejected her offer, so she burned three of these books. A year later, she offered the remaining six at the same price, was refused and again burned three. After another year, the same offer was repeated for the remaining three books, which was accepted. Amalthaea then vanished from the earth. The books were kept underground in the temple of Jupiter Capitolinus, under the strict custodianship of high priests. Emperor Augustus expunged some of the verses as spurious and they subsequently perished when Rome burned during the reign of Nero.

Since the demise of the Sibylline Oracles, we have seen a correspondingly unfortunate decline in the female exercise of spiritual ministry. This has gone hand in hand with a curious absence of the Divine Feminine principal from Western spirituality. Discovering the reasons for this lack of the Goddess' real presence, has been at the core of woman's search for empowerment and meaning — a long quest that is not yet over.

In the twentieth century, women have begun to explore the myriad ways of mediating the Goddess, for they have discovered that when they have contacted Her they also find their own voice. Significantly, since this search began, the voice of the Goddess has been heard in the land. It is as though countless women have become oracles of the Goddess, that leaves from the sibyl's bonfire have blown through time to land in our laps.

This book is a collection of such leaves. As one would expect from prophetic writing consigned to the flames, some of it is fragmentary. The nature of these fragments, mediating the voice of the Goddess, is necessarily obscure, requiring skilful interpretation. Correspondingly, in nearly every chapter in this collection, there is a hesitancy, a cautious grasping towards a mediator's ethic. However, this is also balanced by a sure confidence and trust in the Goddess and the unfailing wisdom that can only come from personal experience. For the voice of the Goddess to be heard in our age, each woman had to find access to her own personal note and practise it until true harmony resounds.

The women here assembled are only a few of the voices of the Goddess now being heard all over the earth. They speak with urgency and love, with bitterness and bewilderment, with joy and courage. Each is a sibyl, in the true sense, though many would define themselves in other, more personally appropriate ways.

Unlike the often obscure prophecies of the ancient sibyls, this medley of sibylline voices sounds a clear call for women everywhere to discover their vocation and join the chorus.

## Guardians of the Goddess

'I found God in myself
and I loved her
I loved her fiercely'.

Ntozake Shange, *For colored girls who have considered suicide when the rainbow is enuf* (Macmillan, 1976)

There is no respected title for a woman exercising a spiritual ministry in the English language. 'Priestess', 'witch', 'prophetess', 'medium' and 'sibyl' all carry atavistic or perjorative connotations in popular usage. Some women prefer not to use the feminized masculine nouns, such as prie*ss* and prophe*ss*, at all, calling themselves instead 'priests of the Divine Feminine', or even, 'prophets of the Mother God'. Mary Daly, the American feminist thealogian, has actually laid the foundations of a restored language in which women can define their own meanings and verbal values in her *Wickedary* (Women's Press, 1988). She has coined or re-fashioned meanings for titles that express female spiritual ministry, such as, Webster, Weird-Sister, Archelogian — one who augurs pasts and futures veiled by archetypes — and Nag-Gnostic — 'Elemental Feminist Philosopher'. Whether such titles will be commonly adopted by women is yet to be seen. For the rest of us, we are driven to re-vision and re-empower by example the titles that our language has for 'priestess'.

Throughout this book, the word 'Goddess' is employed in the sense of the standard usage commonly understood world-wide for the Divine Feminine principle. Similarly, I have employed 'priestess' as an honourable title by which women may call themselves. I have also used the word 'mediator' quite a lot. A mediator is a person, fulfilling a conscious mediumistic or sibylline vocation. This title also encompasses the direct mediation of the Goddess' energies by a priestess within rituals and life-situations. Since the female personal pronoun is frequently employed in these pages, I have referred to the Goddess throughout — reverentially by giving the pronouns a capital letter.

There are many forms of priestesshood. Medicine women, shamankas, healers, therapists, mediums, diviners, prophetesses, mediators of all kinds throughout our world. They have exercised a hidden function for hundreds of years, although they have carried the stigma of being referred to as hysterical females or passed over as being mere housewives dabbling in paganism. Western dualistic thought usually assigns a lower status to women, even to the extent of denying them a spiritual vocation.

The way in which women's spiritual vocation has been denied has far-reaching consequences for society today. While the small number of women operating as Christian ministers may increase and their role become more acceptable as the years go on, it is still considered unusual at the time of writing. As for women fulfilling a spiritual ministry outside the broad framework of orthodox religions, there is as yet no common consciousness of their existence or of it being an option.

It is quite obvious to anyone taking a head-count in churches, for example, that the predominant gender of congregations is female. Enter any church during the day and the people at prayer will be women. This is but one indication that women have a natural capacity for spirituality, a fact that was recognized in Tibetan Buddhism, even during its most patriarchal phase. As Guru Pema said to the mystic Lady Yeshe Tsogyel,

'The gross bodies of men and women are equally suited (as temples of the Yidam [personal deity]) but if a woman has strong aspiration, her potential [for existential realization] is greater.'

Keith Dowman, *Sky Dancer* (Routledge & Kegan Paul, 1984)

Such pronouncements, however, have not been anything other than theoretical exhortations for, as Yeshe Tsogyel herself later remarked,

'Whatever we do, the lot of a woman on the path is a miserable one. To maintain our practice is virtually impossible, and even to stay alive is very difficult.'

(Ibid)

Despite these problems, currently a great reappraisal of the Divine Feminine is taking place, even within Judaism, Buddhism and Christianity.

The problem of spiritual training is one that each of the women contributing to this collection has had to face head-on. Although there are great developments in the field of women's studies and a greater consciousness of Goddess spirituality, we are a long way from having public Goddess temples or universities. (There are, of course, notable exceptions to this rule. Ritual training is given by many Goddess associations and networks. The Fellowship of Isis, for example, has a series of lyceums run by its members, offering training and a yearly series of rituals, as well as study-groups for all matters concerning the Goddess. See page 239 for addresses.

The social expectation has been to find a spiritual niche within an established religion as a lay-woman, so many women have been confused when presented with strong spiritual vocations. Some of our best contemporary exponents of the Goddess are ex-nuns, for example. In the case of these women, one may say that it was not so much that they mistook their spiritual direction, but that they lacked opportunities for spiritual exposition. What does one do if one is receiving the Goddess on all channels? Perhaps a careers advisor might suggest a degree in comparative religion to serve as a springboard to a university post where one could propound one's personal doctrine through a laudable academic mouthpiece. No one would expect one to set up as a shamanka or prophetess as a matter of course.

The Old Religion — sometimes called witchcraft, Wicca or simply the Craft — has been a major factor in helping women train as priestesses. The revival of the native European traditions of spirituality has opened the way for the Goddess and boasts some of the most spiritually empowered women in its ranks. Alongside the Old Religion and various unassociated pagan circles, many Goddess-oriented groups have been established that have a semi-esoteric basis. Yet again, only in parts of the United States do female witches function as professional priestesses. Perhaps, like Buddhist nuns, the rest of us will be supported by what we can beg!

Of course, this century has seen a proliferation of therapies and esoteric disciplines in which women have become foremost exemplars: notably psychoanalysis — especially of the Jungian variety. However, although 'analyst and 'astrologer' may be thought of as marginally respectable professions, we have yet to see the role of priestess become an 'official' or funded profession.

For most women, the discovery and expression of their spirituality is enacted wherever they happen to be — whether this be at home, at work or at college. It manifests itself in the daily ecstasies of life and, if they have the self-confidence and empowerment to exercise it, it can spill out in all directions and make the world a really holy place where joy and beauty become reality.

The female experience of spirituality is extraordinarily simple: it is as basic as the homing instinct. It is a recognition of that primal configuration of elements which constitutes our soul. Once we are aligned with that configuration, the rest of our life constellates in subtle and satisfying patterns of enrichment. When a woman has found her spiritual home, the blunted, blinded, desperate look goes out of her eyes and is replaced by what William Blake called 'the lineaments of gratified desire'. This phrase is a telling one, for it evokes images of sexual desire being assuaged at a deep level.

Sexuality and spiritually are intertwined — a fact that the monotheistic religions have ignored or played down. Women, for whom sexuality plays a natural part of their spiritual life, have been excluded from expressing their ecstasy. Needless to say, it has been siphoned into slightly more acceptable channels such as mysticism. It is a little known fact that some female and male religious experience orgasm at the moment of receiving communion: that this is an appropriate ecstatic response to their religion cannot be doubted — the absence of duality affirms that they are truly aligned with their spiritual home. 'Mysticism is not disguised sex', wrote the philosopher E. I. Watkins. 'Sex is disguised mysticism'.

Sexuality is the primal power to create. This wonderful gift of life, which we are freely given, finds its fullest expression in the spirituality of the Goddess, for here it is not denied, ignored or distrusted. The fact that many women experience the Goddess as a result of their own awakening sexuality is not surprising, for She is life and we are Her garments. This sexual awakening is experienced even within times of celibacy or a lifetime of celibacy. The dynamo is running and it gives us great power to fulfil the Goddess' work. The Goddess has never excluded anyone from her dispensation so that, regardless of sexual orientation, women and men of all conditions have found and rejoiced in her loving bounty.

If we feel good about our sexuality, which, after all, is rooted in the very experience of being women, we will also feel confident about our creativity. It is not for nothing that women have always petitioned the Goddess for the gifts of fertility, whether this be physical or creative fertility. If we are unhappy about being sexual beings functioning in female bodies, then we are likely to feel less confident about our achievements. In such a case, our ideas are never free to grow by themselves, in the light of our own experience of the Divine, but are constantly searching for a source of light to validate them.

Recognition of our intrinsic beauty, richness and grace is a basic necessity for all women. This is the truest truth, but you are the only woman who can affirm it for yourself.

One of the wonderful gifts of the Goddess is the way in which we find the freedom to create our world anew. Observing and living through the tides and seasons of our life, we find moments of repose when the meaning is made clear: the ecstasies of blinding vision when the created nature of our world reveals its spiritual reality to us. When we are able to trust in that underlying spiritual beauty, we find the space to follow our homing instinct: this may mean taking up an evening class or self-improvement programme that we had long dreamed of doing, of arranging a shrine to manifest our inner vision of the Goddess, discovering new songs, new ways of playing an instrument. Following the creative curve of the Goddess, we find ourselves and Her as well. Too often we bar our own way to our heart's desire, which is a prophetic vision of the Goddess' treasures.

Political feminism has largely ignored real commitment to the Goddess and attempted to get there on its own merits. It has acknowledged the power of the Goddess and sought ways to wield her gifts, but this wholesale acquisition has to be balanced by thanks and committed dedication to manifesting the Goddess among us. It is the priestess, sibyls and mediators of the Goddess who carry a great responsibility to inform and transform the spiritual desert that the post-religious phase of feminism has created in its first iconoclastic demolition of former patriarchal spiritualities.

This duty is one that all women have, for we are each a garment of the Goddess, and the way we wear Her matters.

## Vocations and Training

'This is the Goddess . . .
This is She whom we are seeking still,
in the bright face of the world,
in the dark face of our hearts.
How shall we call Her?
Shall we find Her here?'

*Liturgy of the Maiden*, Fellowship of the Spiral Path.

Many women reading this collection may ask themselves, 'Am I or could I be a priestess, mediator, sibyl?' In the great desert of spiritual opportunity that constitutes the Western world, the need to make formal acknowledgement of our spirituality is urgent. Yet, lying between us and the achievement of our desire, lies a great abyss excavated by loneliness, lack of emotional and spiritual support, ignorance, uncertainty, fear and the very real need for affirmation. However, there are other qualities that we all possess and can call upon for help.

Chief among these is our faith in the Goddess to help us. Never mind the aching hollowness of our need, She reaches down to the very depths of it and answers it: we have only to ask. Even if we can only begin by behaving *as though* the Goddess existed, we will find her help at hand. This 'as though' proviso is very important to all spiritual transformation. For all of us, however, at some point, faith becomes certain knowledge. No one who has experienced the Goddess' help personally can ever doubt Her presence again.

What then does being a priestess entail? Fundamentally speaking, a priestess is one who mediates the Goddess by making Her power available to all creation. A priestess guards the mysteries of the Mother and helps initiate other travellers on the road to the spiritual home. A priestess changes things, concepts, people.

Most women in this collection have rather fallen over their vocation in the search for spiritual enlightenment. Discovering the core of one's priesthood is mysterious, circuitous work. It unfolds, patching in gradually until most, through rarely all, of the picture is revealed.

At the beginning it is rather like being in the front row of the cinema watching a wide-screen film: the angle is all wrong, the images are too large, the perspective unclear, the sound woolly. This initial confusion is borne out by several of the writers in this book. Many readers may think that, considering the roundabout way in which some have travelled, it is little short of miraculous that any arrived at an understanding of the Divine Feminine at all. The need to try every possible source of spituality available first, is one that frequently needs to be satisfied before the hidden possibilities are discerned.

Throughout the last three to four decades when women were seeking for spiritual empowerment and training, they found a complete dearth of training material. They were forced to train themselves in their chosen devotion to the Goddess via many means, usually the techniques and disciplines of other spiritual traditions. A great deal has also been derived from straight esoteric sources, from the Western magical tradition — both from its native and its hermetic poles. This haphazard training has given Goddess spirituality great strength through diversity of means; it has also given it a diffuse, decentralized and problematic heritage that it will be up to our daughters to cope with. With faith in the Goddess and love in our hearts for all created beings, however these problems can be overcome.

One of the most remarkable things that Goddess seekers find is the power of metamemory — the 'Deep, Ecstatic Memory . . . of participation in Being Spiraling into the Past, carrying Vision forward' (Mary Daly with Jane Caputi, *Websters' First New Intergalactic Wickedary of the English Language*, Women's Press, 1988). Whenever a woman is touched by the fire of the Goddess, a corresponding spark is ignited within her, re-kindling the old memories, casting lightenings ahead of the path so that she can see her way forward.

So how can a woman begin to explore her potential spiritual vocation on her own? We each begin from where we are, in whatever circumstances we find ourselves, however situated along life's road. We respond to the call of the Goddess now, and now, and now. There is no right or perfect moment in which to affirm our commitment. If you suspect the Goddess is calling you to a recognition of your spiritual vocation, put this book down and

ask Her help in clarifying it in your own words, silently ar
faith. Many of the writers in this collection have been following
their vocation for over twenty or thirty years, but none of them
have yet arrived at a definitive idea of the Goddess or a set pattern of response to Her voice. In every case, their chapters are
sketches from lives that are continuing, evolving. Where the Goddess will each lead us to next, we do not know, but we all had
to start somewhere, to consciously affirm our commitment and
resolve to clarify the next step. I have suggested a few basic ways
of beginning work with the Goddess in *The Elements of the Goddess* (Element Books, 1989).

Discovering our priestesshood requires an objectivity, a neu-
tral perspective. Sometimes, though, it is only when we are cast
up on the slopes of solitary grief, joy or shock that we really see
into the heart of things and see where we belong within them.
It is frequently as a result of breakdown, illness or despair that
some of the priestesses in this book have come to this realization. Yet, we also see into the heart of our vocational relationship with the Goddess through the ecstasy of creation, whether
it be giving birth to a child or to a new poem.

The mediation to which we are best suited lies already waiting
in our heart. Each woman is drawn to one or more aspects of
the Goddess. She will naturally choose the one that reflects her
own personal qualities most clearly. Finding the resident archetype is hard work, but the resonances can be found.

The way of establishing contact is very simple. Review your life
and ask yourself these questions.

- What has been the guiding principle of my life?
- Where and in what have I found spiritual sustenance?
- What is my creative source?
- What are the most vulnerable areas of my make-up?
- When I am asked for help by others, what qualities are they
  drawing upon?

The answers to these and similar questions will illumine your
resonance.

When one particular aspect of the Goddess has been worked
with and assimilated, then it is time to continue the journey into
the vastness of the Divine Feminine, to find other, less accessible
aspects to broaden our experience. For, if we remain cosily within
one archetypal boundary, our life's framework becomes limited
in scope, so lessening our helpfulness to others. Such an exercise

may sound very theoretical, but the Goddess does not trade in theories. If She determines that we need to change, then life itself begins to throw up events that shake us out of complacency into confrontation. For example: you may have settled down to a nice, safe mediation of the Goddess in her aspect of Bountiful Mother only to find that your personal resources are stripped from you one by one until *you* become the one in need. You must learn to accept the taking hand of the Dark Mother and personally learn what it is to have nothing, to be disempowered and reduced to basics.

The way we work with our chosen mediation may not be very dramatic at first. Those women who have no contact with their sisters in any spiritually supportive way will find that solitary work is their only method: meditation, lone rituals, study and worship. The difficulties of solitary work are immense, but the rewards are likewise worthwhile. Self-discipline and lethargy seem to go hand in hand whenever we decide to follow a spiritual programme. When we work alone, the dangers of a bloated ego and over-cherishing our achievements must ever be borne in mind.

Self-confidence is slow to manifest within us without the affirmation and support of our sister and fellow beings. And, perhaps because there is no official body to ratify our priesthood, we find that confirmation and support tend to come from those whom we help.

The problems of group working are different: humour, sharing, the realization that we are not alone, more than balance the little disharmonies that being with other people throws up. We learn from others, as they learn from us. We gain a more balanced perspective of the work in hand and appreciate the immense richness and diversity of human nature.

In the last analysis, however, priestess training is found in the course of our lives as much as in formal esoteric studies. As with all life-disciplines, we cannot opt out of existence while we train for it. Our own problems and those of other people will show us profitable ways of practising our theory. We must always be open to the ways in which the Goddess wants us to be active in Her work, to find the flow and the ebb.

To make our vows adequately, we must be always available to mediate the help of the Goddess to all and yet, to be always mediating also means that we must always be communing with Her. The times of practice need to be balanced by the times of communing or we end up operating according to our own directions, drawing on our *own*, not *Her*, energies. Rapid depletion of our resources and subsequent disablement of our natural abilities are the results of such rash behaviour.

To be a priestess in practice is to follow a vocation stripped of its glamour. The mundane occurrences of life are near to hand to remind us that life is to be lived *now*. It means finding the appropriate ritual response to being woken at night by a sick baby, knowing what to say and do when your best friend contracts a life-threatening disease, how to continue a ritual at a sacred site when a coach-load of tourists descends. Poise, presence and humour are essential: especially, the latter. We take ourselves far too seriously. Being a priestess of Demeter and being initiated into several high-sounding orders won't stop you looking a fool when you stub your toe on the cauldron.

One of the joys of sharing one's spiritual tradition with others is the release of laughing kindly at that tradition. Only insiders together can do this without offence, however. Try cracking jokes at someone else's tradition if you like, but prepare to duck!

If you believe yourself to be a priestess of the Goddess, take stock of your resources and abilities. Question yourself about your motives. Does 'priestess' spell power to you? Are you able to cease manipulating situations and relationships in order to let the energy of the Goddess work freely? Does the title 'priestess' make you feel important? Are you prepared to help every created being, regardless of their appearance, status or gender? Look at the problems around you, your friends, your environment and locality. Next look at your mediation of the Goddess. What practical ways can you find to connect one to the other?

There is a short list of useful addresses on page 239 that may put you in touch with others who are working along similar lines.

## Some of Her Voices

'I am spiralling, I am spinning,
I am singing this Grandmother's Song.
I am remembering forever where we
Belong'.

Alma Luz Villanueva's 'Song of the Self: the Grandmother' in *She Rises Like the Sun*, edited by Janine Canan (Crosing Press, 1989).

The contributors to this collection are extraordinary in many ways. They combine many skills, disciplines and approaches. The sheer range and variety of their perspectives is a reflection of the many-coloured mantle of the Mother. Each woman, within her field, represents a separate voice. Collectively, they form a chorus that

is far more powerful than its individual voices. Further there are
countless more voices than appear in this collecton all spinning
out the song.

In attempting to discover the Goddess, we need to listen to our
elder sisters, for though age is not a significant factor in this field,
in every generation there have been women who found ways
through the difficult spiritual terrain with both grace and effectiveness. Every woman feels that the women of her own generation are more dynamic and skilful than those of previous
generations: we too easily belittle the experience of age in our
Western culture. In all other parts of the world, the grandmother
is a woman of power, a matriarch who speaks authoritatively,
whose word is heeded and obeyed for it echoes the speech of
the Goddess. The Goddess tradition also reverences the Grand-
mothers, both those long-dead and those who are still living.
Theirs are guiding voices. In this collection we have two grand-
mothers who have lived lives fully committed to the principles
of the Goddess. Significantly, the chapters of both Margaretta
D'Arcy and Monica Sjöö are the most challenging in this book.
It is upon the wisdom and endurance of such women that we
have built. As Mary Daly rejoices with Jane Caputi in their outra-
geous *Websters' First New Intergalactic Wickedary of the English Language* (Women's Press, 1988):

> 'The Mediumship of trancing, prancing Websters enables us to
> Con-Quest, Con-Question, Consort, and Cavort with the Living.
> Among our lively Boon-Companions are Fore-Familiars and Fore-
> Crones who Live in Archaic Time'.

The status of woman, her place in the lifecycle has, perhaps, been
a guiding factor in the unfolding revelation of the Goddess. This
was recognized in the ancient world as much as within modern
Goddess tradition. Pythagoras wrote:

> 'Women give to each successive stage of their life the same name
> as a god: they call the unmarried woman Maiden (*Kore*), the
> woman given in marriage to a man Bride (*Nymphe*), her who has
> borne children Mother (*Meter*) and her who has borne children's
> children Grandmother (*Maia*).

> Jane Harrison, *Prolegomena to the Study of Greek Religion* (Merlin
> Press, 1961)

The experience of motherhood opens many doors to priestesshood. Many of the contributors to this book are mothers: not only
of their own children but also, in the broader sense, of their stu-

dents and clients. It is an esoteric truism to say that whenever a ritual is worked, the participants are bonded in a family tie deeper than any blood relationship. Within the sphere of the priestess, however, the vocation is frequently so strong that a woman will remain single, a virgin of spirit. For women living in this century, this role has been one of the hardest to maintain because of sheer economics. The solitary woman with a priestessly vocation had, in past centuries, the option of becoming a nun, an anchoress or had to wait until she was left a wealthy widow to pursue her heart's desire. Financial dependency upon family or spouse is still a factor in the assumption of a priestessly profession today. Many women have chosen to become financially independent by pursuing a craft or exercising a therapy. In this collection we have writers, artists, therapists, astrologers, and professional counsellors: these roles are often adopted so that the vocation can find its practical manifestation.

The work of a priestess is mostly unpaid, though it is hardly unrewarding for all that. The untold hours of sitting with friends and strangers in trouble or crisis, of preparing for a public meeting or Goddess ritual, of study, meditation and attempting to integrate one's domestic life into a workable framework of spiritual ministry have necessitated massive reorganization of the schedules of all the writers of this book. There have doubtless been times when they cursed their involvement for getting in the way of personal pursuits, as I have frequently done, but somehow the Goddess has persuaded us all to carry on.

There are many solitary women who wonder how they shall ever come to find the Goddess, but it is not until they open themselves to Her — as Sunflower, Vivianne Crowley and Naomi Ozaniec have done — that they will find the answer to that question. The Goddess stands close to us and we have to first acknowledge Her and work hard to find our hidden vocation. As Dion Fortune wrote in *The Sea Priestess* (Aquarian Press, 1989) where the reincarnated Atlantean priestess, Morgan le Fay, leaves her advice to an untrained woman.

'If you can make yourself a priestess of the great spiritual principle which is behind womanhood you will be able to help . . . Meditate upon the Moon. She will awaken your womanhood and lend you power. May the Great Goddess bless you and help you'.

The Moon has become one of the central images of Goddess spirituality. Its mutability and changing phases remind women of their own cyclical nature. The Moon illumines the darkness of unconscious, unfocused spirituality. However, when we have realized it, we need to examine its contra-imaginal potency — the Sun. If the Goddess is to be fully represented in our society, She must also be the guiding light and warmth of our conscious lives. Sunflower reveals the path of the solar priestess as a balancing factor in our spiritual training. The Sun is not to be regarded solely as an unreclaimable patriarchal symbol, but one that presents the life and joyous delight of the Goddess.

The Earth has another symbolic potency for Goddess spirituality, a factor that is revealed in Helene Hess' chapter where we see the shamanka, the native earth priestess, in action. Ecological responsibility begins on the inner planes, from our initial contact with the Goddess of the Land.

Many priestesses discover who they are by first finding the shadowy, hidden side of the Goddess — the Dark Mother. In the chapters by Monica Sjöö, Vivienne Vernon-Jones, Naomi Ozaniec and in my own chapter, this need is clearly manifest. It almost seems as though the Dark Mother (the *Cailleach*,* or Old Woman, as she is reverently called in Gaelic tradition) needs to be experienced by many priestesses within this time. For many women, the last centuries have been a full manifestation of the *Kali Yuga* — the last, chaotic age of Hindu speculation. I believe that we must see the twentieth century as a time of clearing out, a time of tearing down the imposed structures that have obscured the Goddess. The work of the *Cailleach* is not evil: it is necessary and catabolic. We praise the work of creation, but we are less lyrical about the process of dissolution. Without decay, the world would be a rubbish heap miles high. Without the *Cailleach*, the Dark Goddess, there would be chaos. As in the myth of Midas whose touch turned all to gold, including his food and his own daughter, we cannot preserve what we love inviolate. It must pass from us. We need to learn the just necessity of death and re-making: lessons that the Goddess teaches us plainly as She shows us the joys and skills of creation. Monica Sjöö has written about the painful reality of bereavement, while Sunflower stresses the joy at the heart of the mystery of death, of returning to the Mother and being re-born of Her. Both comprehend that such realizations are a mystery that each heart has to discover for itself.

Many figures of spiritual authority are regarded as strange semi-humans who can abscond from life's realities behind the mantle

*Pronounced Kal'yak

of the Goddess. Vulnerability is a factor that potential priestesses and sibyls should not overlook. None of us is the Goddess incarnate, however well we may mediate Her. We are each human and vulnerable and, as such, open to receiving or imparting compassion. Our humanity is a great gift when it comes to helping others.

When inviting women to write for this collection, I asked for rituals, dreams, blessings or poetry. Poetry and invocations there are in good measure. The Goddess grants her gifts of creativity in many ways, but the personal invocation, the inspired lyrical utterance is always nearest to the surface. This poetic wellspring is part of the sibylline legacy and there is no denying it. It speaks the language of the blood and belly as well as the language of the crystalline stars. It is a weaving song that meshes heaven and earth with the underworld. Poetry is the mouthpiece of the metamemory, the deep, ecstatic memory of an oral tradition that remembered the Goddess daily in domestic and tribal rituals. Since there are no Goddess rituals or liturgies from former times, we have written our own, often drawing directly upon the raw material of personal experience. (See page 236 for contemporary Goddess liturgies and rituals.) Poetry can both bless and uproot, it can extol or refute. It is the true voice of the Goddess speaking through her sibyls. Personal or prophetic, poetry is communication with a deeper level of understanding. It is a gateway for the Goddess to pass through.

Sunflower reveals the intimacy of the relationship that evolves between the priestess and her inspiriting Goddess. The service of the priestess, faithfully maintaining her shrine by prayer and meditation, naturally flows into a liturgical expression where the priestess becomes the voice of the Goddess Herself, as well as uttering petitions on behalf of Her people. Such records of devotion are especially precious in a world that has no memory or experience of reverencing the Goddess.

Within this collection, there are many different approaches to the problematic question of gender roles and relationships. One of the chief features of feminism that has been most remarked upon has been its devaluation of the male species, a side-effect of its reaction to 'patriarchy' and a world where male values have ruled supremely along with masculine-imaged deities. Both Vivianne Crowley and Naomi Ozaniec stress the need to balance and acknowledge both sexes of our species. This is an esoteric concept that is not commony upheld within the wider spectrum of feminism, though both Margaretta D'Arcy and Monica Sjöö acknowledge the worth of men, at the same time decrying the patriarchal attitudes that have brought our culture to a near stand-still. The religion of Wicca, unlike many spiritual systems that recognize the Goddess, actively encourages the polarity of the sexes. Many women discovering the Goddess and re-learning the nature of feminine empowerment do not feel ready to share this with men. These diversities represent the two poles of opinion and approach within Goddess spirituality.

Within this collection also, you will find the warrior-priestess, the one whose inner vision must correspond to an outer reality: and for which reality she will battle.

For many people, politics is the only form of power. However, esotericism — in its broadest sense — is a form of inner politics. Without inner change there can be no outer change. Esotericism is not about exercising 'power over', as Starhawk calls it, it is matter of alignment with natural wisdom, with earth currents, with the great harmony of the created and uncreated worlds.

The warriors of the Mother are many: some people find it unacceptable or inappropriate for women to wield the Goddess' power. Without the courage and endurance of our sisters throughout the ages, however, and most particularly within the last hundred years, we would not now have the leisure to exercise anything like a priestessly vocation. It would be good to see the political and esoteric halves of feminism united, working together for the common end of full integration of both woman and Goddess within our culture — but that day has not yet dawned.

Monica Sjöö expresses doubts about this very factor in her chapter. She realistically faces the prospect that radical feminism's adoption of ritual power is often unbalanced and frequently dangerous for the participant. Truly, without proper guidance and training, the forces invoked can bring horrific repercussions on those women who have not counted the cost of combat. Such wounds are sustained by our contemporary Amazons and furies: the Erinnys of our century who camp at Greenham and at nuclear stations. The Greenham struggle is represented in Margaretta D'Arcy's challenging chapter. The urgent issues of our century will not go away or be conveniently tidied up by the Goddess. She enjoins responsible action upon Her daughters, exhorting them to resist the complaisance of the herd, to speak loudly and prophetically in the accents of Cassandra and the sibyls. It is good that such women are to be found among us. Their voice is often harsh in our ears, yet it speaks urgently and challengingly to us all.

There are many kinds of vocation, some hardly touched upon in this book, but, for all women, the extent to which mythic or archetypal patterns recur in our lives is often a telling factor in fixing upon a vocation. The nature of esoteric work and the dearth of good teachers, leaves many people confused and often prey to self-delusion. Vivienne Vernon-Jones has presented her own spiritual journey through the agency of Psyche, while I have chosen to write about my experience of one Goddess form, that of the British Goddess, Rhiannon.

Making good use of our indwelling myth is perhaps one of the ways that twentieth-century people must employ in default of formal training. This may seem unglamorous advice, but spirituality already has more than enough of its own scintillating diversions that lead to the seemingly safe practice of spiritual materialism, where esoteric glamour can rule our lives, if we let it, while we remain under the impression that we are wonderful, spiritual people. What we all need more of in terms of training, is reality. The challenging lessons that life throws at us may be viewed as initiations into the mysteries. Yearning for robed initiators, theatrical rituals and past-life scenarios is seriously out of line with real mediation of the Goddess: these are merely fantasies.

It will not go unnoticed that the Fellowship of Isis receives a good deal of mention in these pages. This is not without reason. For many women and men throughout the world, the Fellowship has performed great work in bringing together diverse groups and individuals who share a love of the Goddess. Olivia Robertson and her brother, Lawrence Durden-Robertson, have inspired and guided many people seeking the Goddess. Many women within this collection have been ordained priestesses in the Fellowship of Isis, retaining a warm link with the mother temple in Ireland. Such associations are rare as I write, though, before the Aquarian Age is out of its infancy, I prophesy that we may see many more federated groups and a growing network of scattered individuals who come together to practise and study. Both Diana Paxson and Naomi Ozaniec are actively involved in bringing a solid priestessly training to women in search of their spiritual ministry. That great search, pursued by women all over the world, must eventually find expression. The lonely, the enthusiastic, the bold, the cautious, the wonderful variety of sibyls will emerge from their separate caves and start to sing a song that will sweep over the land. Then, even the most unregenerate will hear the voice of the Goddess.

## Her Webs So Wide

> 'Unattainable and Only lady, over your great loom
> and weave me according to design. Guide me
> through chaos, and though I cannot find You,
> be with me, as any creature in the field.'

Janine Canan, 'Our Lady', *She Rises like the Sun*
(Crossing Press, 1989)

Many wise people in the world look to the re-emergence of the Goddess as a redemptive factor. The Goddess' second coming among us — or rather, our recognition of Her continued existence among us — will bring many new challenges and insights, not least of which is the immediacy of Her presence as a source of help. The religion of the Goddess is a hands-on spirituality, not one that keeps its devotees at arm's length. The old channels have become devalued for women who have no time for theology or an intervening sacerdotal caste.

The priestesshood that is envisaged in this book is not one based upon the hierarchical lines of orthodox religions, but rather, it is localized to the environment of each mediator, it is accessible to the community at large. To flourish, it must find a relevant role in the market-place. Of course, many women are already operating as professional therapists, dealing with the problems and crises of clients, without vouchsafing the fact that they are inspired by the Goddess, that they are priestesses of Her cult. They already operate as medicine women, shamankas, and healers, working with dreams, discerning significant patterns that are obscure to the client, bringing the wisdom of the Goddess into lives which are fragmented and disjointed.

Analyst Esther Harding wrote in the early 1970s:

> 'Today, the goddess is no longer worshipped. Her shrines are lost in the dust of ages while her statues line the walls of museums. But the law or power of which she was but the personification is unabated in its strength and life-giving potency.'

*Women's Mysteries* (Harper & Row, 1971)

The first part of this statement is no longer true; the last half has never ceased to be so. Many bedroom shrines and living-room temples exist all over the Western world as women and men seek to bring the Goddess into their homes and lives. For the Goddess has found her way into many hearts and, in the interregnum between the Classical era of the sibyl and the twentieth century, individual hearts have been her only and living shrines.

There will always be the need to mediate the Goddess ritually to those who are orphaned of Her love. We need temples where people can come to heal broken spirits, where direct experience of the Goddess is given by experienced mediators of Her power. These temples are slowly being built, offering alternative rites of passage, seasonal rituals and personalized encounters with the Goddess whose energy to empower is unfamiliar to most people living in this century. This work continues secretly, often without reference to or association with any other organization or group. Such is the power of the Goddess to act as a catalyst to change that it takes only a few individual women to turn the wheel of the times.

In the veneration of the Goddess, all people are potentially Her priests and priestesses, every house a temple for Her worship, every occupation a ritual in Her honour.

All who seek the Goddess and do not know where to begin might follow the advice of Sophia in the Gnostic *Secret Book of John* where She says: 'Follow your root which is myself, the compassionate'. You can be certain that you will find Her and be sustained by that compassion.

May Her love come into your hearts and bring you to blessedness.

# 1
# The Rebirth of the Goddess

## Olivia Robertson

Anyone who has venerated the Goddess and walked Her ways will know already the great liberation of spirit and expansive creativity that results. Self-empowerment is the key, but few women boldly unlock the prison of their own limitations and see how far the Goddess leads them. It is indeed rare to find a woman whose audacity extends to bringing about the focalization of a religion. Yet that is what Olivia Robertson has done. The Fellowship of Isis has brought to thousands of people world-wide companionship and an unhierarchical framework in which lovers of the Goddess may worship. Its co-founder, writes about this daring venture and charts her own spiritual journey in a world that had never heard of the Goddess.

Olivia Robertson was born in London in 1917. With her family she went to live in their family home, Huntingdon Castle, Clonegal, County Carlow in 1925. She was educated at Heathfield School, Ascot, and the Grosvenor School of Modern Art, London. She gained the Purser-Griffith Scholarship and Diploma in European Art History in the National University of Dublin, and held her first exhibition of illustrations when she was 21. She has published six books with an Anglo-Irish background in Britain and the USA and her illustrated novel, Field of the Stranger (Peter Davies and Random House) was Book Society Choice (in London). She worked for the Corporation City Playgrounds in Dublin for four years after a period as a VAD in Britain during the Second World War. With her brother, the Reverend Lawrence Durdin-Robertson, Baron Strathloch and his wife Pamela, she founded the Fellowship of Isis in 1976. By September 1989 it had gained 9,100 members in 62 countries. She has published, through Cesara Publications of which she is Director, eight Fellowship publications and co-edits Isian News.

# The Rebirth of the Goddess

All beings are born of mothers and so it is that humans can attain mystical rebirth through the Goddess. My own experience of this was unexpected and total. I was awakened by the God. I became the Goddess. In my experience of the God I was totally feminine and receptive. I was in that state of being where my surroundings were permeated with a divine beauty while yet retaining their individuality. Their true selves showed through the tenuous veil of that we call reality — a hedge was a true hedge; a flower, a real, eternal flower. In that receptive state I understood that the physical world was but a symbol for the innate, eternal reality hidden behind physical matter. In this open, receptive state, which you could call 'astral' or psychic, however, I was still open to duality. That is, there was also present the anti-good, the ugly, the wrong and my only defence was to ignore it, to withdraw from it. This state of mind lasted for about eight hours and I was so relieved to have my consciousness extended in this way, into a great sphere of mind in which I was active and had power, that evil did not matter and so did not exist for me. It was only a distorted shadow.

It was in this expanded state of consciousness that I became aware of a silver figure of Light and from Her head emanated two streams of white power that looked like giant stag's antlers or lightning. This figure gave me the name of Isis and I felt I had a new identity.

These experiences, which took place in one evening, came in great waves, after which I was back in ordinary, separated consciousness. However, throughout I never lost my everyday awareness of my earthly name, address and surroundings.

During one of these waves I awoke entirely out of earth consciousness for a few seconds, though I was also still my earthly self, for I could think. I was seated cross-legged on sun-parched earth and I thought I was Hindu man. I had my hands clasped behind my head to form a pentagram. I awakened into the Light, which was like being within the sun, and I knew there were others in this state. Then I returned to ordinary consciousness.

The final wave found me, like the Hindu Goddess Lakshmi, seated by Vishnu. She is a sun figure and round my head I was aware of a curious golden mesh radiating, like the Phoenix headdress I had seen round the heads of Chinese figures. This again only seemed to last a few seconds of earthly time. I returned to my smaller self.

These experiences took place back in 1946 and, in the intervening years, meditation has helped me to understand what happened. Only when I acknowledge the Goddess and God in all beings can I describe such happenings without any suggestion of self-advertisement. The final test of mystical experiences after all comes when the mystic faces isolation. At first, loneliness brings with it a desire to communicate with others, to share. The danger when the mystic is isolated is that this may lead to fanaticism. It is easy to think that only one's own religion is the true one because it led to the experience, that one has somehow attained more than other people. So, when many people write to me describing similar experiences — that they are God, Goddesses, Extra-terrestrial, Avatars, Leaders, Prophets — I take care in my replies to stress to them that in no way are they superior to anyone else. They have attained rebirth, yes, but one day this process will be natural for everyone. It will be those who have *not* been reborn who will be looked upon as odd, handicapped, needing extra care and attention. After all, a person who has been 'reborn' may be a very old soul who has had many incarnations incurring failed initiation. Others who appear very materialistic and unevolved, may, in reality, be specializing in this very materialism through scientific studies or other earthly paths. They may choose to leave their spirituality for heaven.

To continue with my story, however, I was gradually drawn to helping others to awaken. At first I hoped to enter the spirit world. I wrote a book and felt that when it was published I could die and enjoy the other world, but I lived and, as time passed, I became aware that I had the gift of helping people attain other states of consciousness. I have never used drugs myself, but I noticed that young people were using them to induce the same state in which their more gifted contemporaries were experiencing mystical adventures. I felt that a new humanity could be growing up around me, with extra-sensory gifts. This did not surprise me because when a race is faced with annihilation, meaningful mutation may take place.

In the past, people who showed telepathic, clairvoyant, levitational and other such gifts were apt to be offered three choices: a convent or monastery, prison or lunatic asylum! In all these cases their gifts could not be passed on to their offspring. Parents then also discouraged the so-called paranormal. When a very young William Blake came running up to his mother saying he had seen the Prophet Elijah sitting under a tree, she smacked him! Later he became one of Britain's most honoured prophets, a visionary, artist and poet. However this acclaim did not stop his widow —

under guidance from a religious minister — from burning a vast
quantity of his writings and drawings.

Further, we know there are intermediaries between the incomprehensible Eternal Being we call Absolute Deity and ourselves.
This used to be called the whole Company of Heaven and I enjoyed
the old Anglican invocation to Angels, Archangels and the whole
Company of Heaven and reading of Seraphim, Cherubim, Thrones,
Principalities and Powers, Archangels and Angels. In this hierarchy our own humble race came next and further down the evolu-
tionary ladder came amoeba, plants and rocks. One of the tragedies
of the secularization of religion is the removal of humanity's age-
long connection with this heavenly company. In the ancient
religions of Egypt, China, India and Babylon these Gods and Goddesses gave laws, teaching and succour, they appeared in varying
forms to prophets and visionaries and instructed their priests
through those gifted with clairaudience and clairvoyance, they
bestowed oracles on the sibyls of ancient Rome and taught priests through the Delphic priestesses. It is true that when religions
became decadent or evil, *false* teachings and oracles were invented
by priests devoid of spiritual or psychic gifts, but, none the less,
a rich harvest of reborn humanity was gained who either remained
in other spheres to progress or returned to earth in order to serve
the divine plan through repeated incarnations.

As humanity began developing the left side of the brain — the
part concerned with thought, logic, technical skills — this old
communion with the world of Spirits began to wither. Yet man
was unwilling to give up priestly power altogether. For the last
three thousand years or so, we have the situation that women —
who have the greatest gifts for psychic awareness — were slowly
but surely pushed out of the priesthood, while men, their inner
founts of inspiration dried up by logical education, took control
of the world's religions.

The result of this over-emphasis on the brain was the cessa-
tion of spiritual evolution. Mankind was climbing energetically
down one branch of the tree of life, as it were, completely ignoring the main trunk. Divine inspiration, no longer available to a
new race of male priests, was relegated to the past, and the priesthood were the total custodians of historic revelation. Hence any
inspirations, teachings, or oracles not embodied in the Bible, the
Koran or other holy scriptures were unacceptable to them. Yet
what prophet would wish to repeat himself?

The repetition of previously given laws and teachings was tedi-
ous and finally brought its own destruction. Obviously if *man*

were to decide what was true and what was not, ignoring any contemporary visions or relevations from the Deity, then the Deity
became some kind of abstraction. So in Christianity a clergyman
could preach a Godless Christianity and communists could reject
religion as 'the opium of the masses'. True inspiration, even in
countries where churchs still prevailed, dried up and so mind
games as to which faith was closest to written scriptures tore
believers apart, both from each other and from the Deity.

Possibly this was all a necessary part of human progress. First
humanity faces an altar, a picture, a holy image, adores the Deity
thus symbolized and receives guidance and support. Like a child
first attending school, however, the cleverer devotee wishes to make
his own decisions, to think and do things on his own. He wishes
to be free of his mother — especially his mother, the Mother Goddess, because the ties of affection are the hardest to endure when
total freedom is longed for. The father can teach skills and ideas.
Possibly, therefore, it is the most advanced of humans who, becoming richly gifted themselves, have appropriated the divine and
turned away from the Deity altogether. Woman, though, gazes
despairingly at all he has accomplished — the mighty works of
Michaelangelo, Beethoven's music, scientific discoveries. What was
*she* doing? 'It is a man's world' became an aphorism among women,
and, up until the middle of the twentieth century, it was so. Her
innate gifts of homemaking, understanding people, caring for children, received no real appreciation, save for some sentimental
praise at Christmas or anniversaries. The very ideals of *Homo
sapiens* exclude women's dreams and cherished qualities. Efficiency,
success in commerce, skills in technology, scientific analyses of
nature including vivisection, medical skills and so on revolted
many women. This natural disgust, a passive repudiation, became
horror when the danger this way of carrying on posed to the whole
earth was gradually recognized in the Fifties. The dangers of atomic
warfare, holes in the ozone layer, pollution of air, seas and plant
life suddenly jerked thousands of women into the realization that
they had to do something — but what? I joined various pacifist
groups but realized that we could get nowhere when the majority
of humankind would fight for their countries and families,
whatever the consequences. When I thought of World War Two
and the horrors of Nazi-occupied countries, death seemed better
than defeat.

The answer for me came through the whole Company of Heaven.
We are not an isolated race, a clever breed of monkeys about to
destroy our own species and all others. We, like monkeys and

the species we threaten, are all part of a tremendous universe full of meaning and purpose. We ourselves are part of the whole Company of Heaven. But why was there evil? Evil was only the outcome of wrong choices may by a very simple, young race learning through mistakes. This world is only a shadow of the real world where we learn through experience. When we progressed beyond this world, we left what we had learned also. The animals and plants are of the same evolution as ourselves and so are prey to our own wrong-doing. I do not see evil as a result of free will, for I see that we do not have much will — that is our problem — but we do have free choice. We *could* choose to develop our willpower. One thing I know — we need help, we are never self-sufficient. Self-sufficiency would be wrong, as total isolation is total selfishness. We have to have mother and father, brothers and sisters, cousins, friends. We need animal friends, plants, trees, all of nature around us. We were not separate from nature and we did not need to conquer it — we *are* nature.

As we are more developed, older, than animals, so there are Beings more advanced than we are. So our ancestors were not as superstitious or as ignorant as sceptics have told us. These Beings were on a brighter, more powerful wavelength than ourselves. As they existed at a faster rate of radiation from a more advanced sphere, we could not see them, unless our own spiritual Being quickened. An essential part of my own spiritual adventures was my discovery that these bright Beings existed at all. The watered-down religion that I had been taught exempted me from 'having' to believe in angels. Having seen and heard an Angel — a God — I remember asking a Church of England bishop what the church taught about angels. He said that I did not have to believe in them! I felt, he didn't and so I sadly abandoned the hope of confiding in him, feeling that he would be incapable of understanding my experience. On the other hand, another clergyman of the same church told me for no particular reason that once, while celebrating Holy Communion he had experienced the Beatific Vision. It was then that I realized that it did not matter what religion or path a man or woman claimed to follow it was the fruits that counted, what had happened to them. However, it is also true that there are saints who have never experienced the miraculous, but who have done much good by helping others.

My contacts with the Shining Ones were simple and seldom. They never gave names. They communed absolutely clearly with me through telepathy. They communicated so clearly that their speech did not sound like it was 'in my head', but as if they were stood in front of me. Yet their words were presumably translated by my brain as they always spoke in my own accent. What struck me was their total clarity of thought and concentration. I realized that our human brains are very backward. I was taken aback by Goddesses and tried to find words to describe Them but failed. 'Saints', 'faeries', 'Them', did not describe the authority, the clear understanding, the beauty and the astonishing power these ladies possessed. It was power of which we have little or no inkling. I expected such power from Gods but not from Goddesses and there was nothing in my previous experience to help me. The only idea I had of God was male. The Virgin Mary was theologically denied Deity and was always portrayed as earning her importance solely through her humble worship of her own Son. She was only entitled, I was told, to veneration, not to 'latria' or divine worship. Hence the only names I could think of as being suitable for the Goddesses were Juno, Demeter, Isis, Dana and Lakshmi. To offer Adoration of Deity to any Being is to acknowledge the Deity as manifesting through that Being, not to deny the universality of God/Goddess. Thus the Holy Spirit came to Christ through Mary, so surely it is not inappropriate for Christians to adore the Divine Sophia through her (she is still not entitled by any church to have a capital H! I give all Gods and Goddesses the capitals usually given to Christ and He gets them too — the God in Christ-Dionysos-Eros).

Having received communion with the Deities, what was I to do? What I did was to read up about them. The Royal Dublin Society has a magnificent library and I read my way through The Bacchanals, Apuleius, the Upanishads, the Baghavatgita, the Bible, the Buddhist Sutras, the Ramayana, James' 'Varieties of Mystical Experiences', Yogananda, Gurdjieff, Ouspensky, Steiner, Mrs Besant — in fact everything and anything dealing with religion. I was quite willing to embrace any path that tallied with my own experiences. I still remained in communion with the Church of England but also attended mass, Society of Friends Meetings, Theosophical lectures, Anthroposophical meetings, and my favourite Spiritualist seances at the Spiritualist Association in London. I made copious notes. The result of this was that all these paths tallied with my own adventures! I concluded that people just used separate terms and descriptions. I read lots of books about the worlds' ancient faiths and found the same thing. Why then are there so many doctrinal disagreements?

My brother had religious experiences in which he, a Minister and one-time Rector of the Church of England, became converted to the religion of the Mother Goddess. His experience was very different to my own and he was far more matriarchal in outlook. I was, by this time, so eclectic that I was effectively disqualified from every regligion — I could reconcile Sufis and Shiites and Sunis in my own mind, I could be Catholic *and* Protestant, Theravada *and* Mahayana Buddhist, I was Norse and Hawaiian and Babylonian and Egyptian and Wiccan. Such liberalism had none of the focused tension of the fanatic. I had become more feminine than ever and, like Dion Fortune's Priestess of the Moon, was veiled. My career as an Anglo-Irish writer was fading away with my lack of interest. I liked best to meditate to music and, working in Huntingdon castle, I was in an ideal situation to do so. I would lie flat on an ancient couch, hair over my eyes, classical music on, floating off in day-dreams. However, I could never recapture what I had already enjoyed. Heaven was not there — I was wasting my time.

It is the experience of many that once the Deities have manifested themselves to you, you are expected to work. Admittedly I was willing, but could not think of how to do this. I was never one of the brave rain-coated women walking up and down outside embassies, carrying anti-nuclear banners. I have never protested, I dislike writing indignant letters, avoid arguing and do not get up on platforms and lecture people, so what did They want of me?

I look back on visions I had been given thirty years ago: I had been shown our castle from the air, radiating forth rays of white Light, I saw thousands of people coming to our home, which I was told was holy. It lies encircled by hills and Mount Leinster and is built over an ancient pre-Druid well between two rivers, the Slaney, river of health (*slainte*) and the river of the oak, the Derry. I dislike the word 'workshops' because I don't like the words 'work' or 'shop', but in 1963 I began to hold weekly groups along with others for people from various paths, many who came from England, and called these 'seminars' — I like that word. We — my brother, sister-in-law Pamela and I — called the place 'The Huntington Castle Centre for Meditation and Study'. It was here that I discovered I had a talent for getting people into a trance. Indeed, I found that some people were far more interesting in trance than they were awake! I had not heard of 'regression' then, but these people were doing this when they were in a state of trance. I found that gently pressing someone on the nape of the neck could make them unconscious or that in making movements with my hands or lightly touching the person's forehead I was using my magnetism of Mesmer, rather than hypnosis. I did not want anybody to become unconscious because I wanted my 'percipients' not only to remember but also to choose what they did. This is the Goddess approach: you are not 'mesmerist' and 'patient', but co-equal and co-operating in a mutual adventure.

What adventures we had! (I described them in 1974 in my book *The Call of Isis*, Cesera.) I learned of the various stages a soul enjoys when it is out of the body. I would start the percipient off by moving him or her to the etheric plane, which is part of the physical sphere, the matrix about which matter is built. I would do this by describing their vital bodies with psychic centres and an aura. When I had safeguarded them by auric cleansing and seen that they had a half-way house, a safe 'temple' to return to if a hasty exit from some scene was required, I would send them off on their adventure. I noticed that the gap between the physical-etheric sphere and the psychic-astral realm was divided by a long dark tunnel of some sort, with light at the end. It was also divided by a river or stream. Could this have been the Styx? Once in the astral plane the reincarnation experiences would happen. These were also highly symbolic, as if this was the best way of conveying a higher teaching. There was also a further experience, the start of which was signalled by Light or a Star, a rising upwards. At this point heavenly visitations were granted, but sometimes these were not remembered by the percipient, so my notes about these happenings are the only record. The benefits received by those who came to me were so striking that I felt I should extend the work. I was being led into the Priesthood of the Goddess for what I was doing was giving people preparation for re-birthing.*

My brother then created a chapel to the Goddess by altering our old Anglican chapel. We began getting groups together for Goddess rituals and I gradually discovered that ritual was important. Until I saw how important it was for my brother, I had not used ritual at all. I had used our library in which to hold sessions and wore ordinary clothes, as did the percipients — I only asked that they remove their shoes. I did not use candles or incense, just closed the curtains and locked the door, as an untimely interruption could jolt the person in trance back into everyday consciousness.

Our first important ritual was the Isis Wedding Rite, used for my niece Melian and her Indian husband, Swadesh Poorun. I learned much from him about the Indian use of symbolism through the ritual use of the elements. My first two books, pub-

*Olivia Robertson's technique is not to be confused with the New Age discipline of Rebirthing.

lished under our own imprint Cesara Publications, were the *Wedding Rite* and *The Call of Isis*. The Rite reached a nationwide audience when it was reviewed on Irish television. Meanwhile, my brother had written *Goddess of Chaldea, Syria and Egypt*, published by Cesara, the first of his source-books on the Goddesses, and we again received wide press attention. All the time I had been a respectable Anglo-Irish novelist. I had never received such attention — a refined review in *The Times Literary Supplement* or *The New York Times*, yes, but not the British Sunday press!

Why was this? We had touched the funny-bone of the establishment. We had added 'ess' to God. Of course the witches were doing the same thing, but the fact that my brother was a clergyman and that people did not particularly associate the Goddess with witches — linking them with cats and spells instead — made us the target of humour, astonishment, speculation. A new humanity will find it hard to understand the total contempt the twentieth century held for women in the priestly role. I remember one joke in *Punch*, pre-1914 that illustrates this attitude. Two ludicrous caricatures of suffragettes are depicted seated in a prison cell. One is saying to the other, 'Don't despair dear. Have faith in God. *She* will look after you.' I was wondering why nobody was at all interested in my socialist, pacifist, or anti-blood sports views, but then it dawned on me that these ideas were all over the place — they were not news. There were all sorts of headlines in the *News of the World*, and the *Sun*, and the *Star*: 'Goddess Rites Shock Rural Eden'. 'I'm No Witch, says Rector', '2000 AD: Women's Rule', 'Clonegal's Castle of Mystery', 'In the Library we Hear Eerie Laughter', 'Eerie Quest for Peace in Castle Dungeon' and my favourite, 'Bizarre Rites of She-God Cult'. I like the term 'She-God', but it was obviously used with the same kind of contempt as one would use the term 'She-Goat'. (Just for the record the feminine name for God is 'Goda'.) I noticed that in these articles all our rites were 'bizarre' and journalists were always on the lookout for 'orgies' and 'nudity'. However we did not permit this entertaining spate of rubbish for no reason — it brought us so many new friends!

The Fellowship of Isis was founded by Lawrence, his wife Pamela, and myself at the Vernal Equinox in 1976. We then produced our Manifesto — which remains the same today — and our local co-operative duplicated it for us. We distributed it far and wide to authors we liked, people who might be interested, and so on, and received an immediate response. At the time we only expected that there would be a few members, say a dozen or fifteen. Curiously enough, however, our increase in numbers has been quietly consistent. There have been no particularly large jumps in the numbers of members except after an excellent *Sunday Times* magazine article, and a British television show, *After Dark*. The publicity did bring new members and pleasant contacts, but our real growth has been as a result of word of mouth and a small notice each month in the esoteric magazine *Prediction*. The grapevine of other occult magazines has also helped increase membership.

Looking back now, I can see how all this must have been planned through the agency of the inner planes. The Fellowship of Isis was launched at the right time in the right place. The Goddess, the feminine manifestation of the supreme Deity, showed Herself in our age in order to heal the terrible wounds inflicted on the earth herself and all her children through unbalanced male aggression and the misuse of technology. During the last two hundred years the Call of Isis came through Apparitions of a heavenly Madonna to thousands of Catholics, but the Lady was also summoning her sons and daughters through individual vocation. To quote our Manifesto: 'Growing numbers of people are re-discovering their love for the Goddess. At first this love may seem to be no more than an inner feeling, but soon it develops and becomes a longing to help the Goddess actively in the manifestation of Her divine plan. Thus, one hears such enquiries as, "How can I be initiated into the Mysteries of the Goddess? How can I experience a closer communion with Her? Where are Her nearest temples and devotees? How can I join the Priesthood of the Goddess?"

We found that we were guided to supply these needs ourselves. One member, Pauline Fields, asked my brother to ordain her as a Priestess of Isis. We both did so, having been inspired to produce our ritual 'Ordination of Priestesses and Priests'. I became the channel for such Goddess-inspired writings, but at these times I still retained consciousness. My method is to let the Goddess know the evening before what I wish to do. Then, the next day, I feel I have been helped during the night while out of my body. I sit, having performed a ritual, and when I feel the inflow of Power, which is like a gentle fall of silver rain through my head, I know that Her influence is coming through. I have no idea what to write until I do so, but it all passes through my own mind and so I would not accept ideas that I do not like. The Goddess and I are in the relation of mother and daughter as I am not denied my individuality. The Divine Mother is Origin, so each of us has her unique originality within ourselves. Equally, without the variety of every creature She would be incomplete. So began our Priesthood, which now consists of 203 priests and priestesses in 17 countries.

Archpriest Michael Okoruwa of Nenin City in Nigeria has the largest congregation and Temple of Isis. He is described in *The Irish Times* as having been inspired to join the Fellowship of Isis by seeing a vision of Isis-Ngame. Ngame is the Triple Moon Goddess of Africa, 'of whom none greater'. Michael is a famous healer and has spoken at length on Nigerian television. He also writes and publishes books on spiritual development. He wrote for *Isian News*: 'Our new Temple of Isis and Ngame has greater accommodation and we have a Guest House. We have 15 rooms of 100 to 150 feet, and an Outer Court, with night watchmen and supervisors. Every week we receive our usual 800 people who come in a continuous stream. Of course our statues of Isis and Ngame, made by Nigerian sculptors, are prominently displayed'. African music is used during the ceremony, including their evocative drumming. He can certainly channel through powerful energies by the laying on of hands and prayers to the Goddesses, using Their Names.

The Isian Priesthood sees the Goddess as Isis of Ten Thousand Names, so they serve Her divine plan through the Name most suited for them. They have found that for their ministry to be effective, they need to work in groups. At first we had just one Centre, or Iseum, that of Rhiannon in Britain, but soon Iseums began to appear all over the world — in the United States, Japan, Ghana, Australia, New Zealand, Finland and Iceland. One of the most treasured of these was founded by the Principle Chief of the Cherokee Nation, Chief Hu Gibbs, Igaehinudoequa, and his wife, Donna Gibbs, Ageyunnega. There are about 10,000 Cherokees, but the Chief only introduces new Fellowship of Isis members after a test of worth has been undertaken. In Germany there are now eight Iseums, in Britain and the United States over fifty each and in Australia seven. Our most exciting discovery, however, was the Ammonite Foundation of Egypt. We now have four Egyptian Priestesses and Priests and an Egyptian Iseum of Auset and Ausar.

To give you an idea of the work an Iseum does, I quote from an account from the Reverend Mrs Ikwo Bassey Okono who, with her husband, also of our Priesthood, founded the Iseum of Queen Isis. Now they also run a Lyceum of the College of Isis. Mrs Ikwo is a trained hospital nurse and writes, 'Recently, out of twelve petitions for healing sent to us, seven have been reported successful, the greatest success being with the patient with epilepsy. We are grateful to the Divine Mother for She has used us for Her divine

work in this Iseum and we thank all our fellow members for sharing the wisdom of Mother Isis with sincere people all over the
world.' From Scotland, the Reverend Swami Prem Sudheer of the
Brighid Iseum and Lyceum reports 'Since my ordination and initiation, during which the Goddess Persephone spoke to me through
Her priestess in the Castle Temple, large changes have happened
in my life. It proved to be a powerful and lasting experience. Persephone has appeared to me several times in meditation and given
more teaching messages. We continue to perform the Fellowship
of Isis Mysteries.'

I was very happy when I realized that communion with the Goddess was happening as a result of our rituals. Like many spontaneous mystics, I had never used rites, nor belonged to an Order.
At first I assumed that our rituals were a trial run for actual inner
experience, but I discovered that actual happenings occurred during our ceremonies. The ceremonies themselves had been inspired
by the Deities. I was also delighted when, in every Ordination
ceremony, our candidates felt spiritual power, either the sensa-
tion of silvery 'rain' in the head or glowing in the heart.

I was then inspired to write rituals of the Mysteries, an enactment of Divine personalized Truths. At first I regarded these as
mythic dramas, but then I found that people became overshadowed
by the Deity they were playing, bringing about communion with
the Deity, changing their lives for good. Because of this I never
brought evil characters into our dramas. Also, I regarded these
as but a temporarily distorted reflection of the Deity's True Selves.
There could not be war in true Heaven and if an Angel 'fell' he
or she would no longer be an Angel. In the same way, you cannot
have a *bad* God or Goddess, for Deity implies only good attributes. So, by creating, or, rather, re-creating the Mysteries of Eleu-
sis, Babylon and Greece, we are identifying with the Deities and
thereby awakening our own Divine Spirit, which is also part of
the God/Goddess.

I received a letter two days ago indicating the effect of an Oracle delivered through myself, veiled, as channel for Hecate. This
new recipient of a Magi degree writes: 'It was such a wonderful
experience, words cannot describe it, and I think no words *should*
be used to describe it. I think it should just be experienced and
treasured. It certainly is a new beginning, perhaps not in the way
I expected, but I accept Her plan for me and the gradual revelation.' In just this spirit, my brother and I founded the College of
Isis, with its 32 working and 33 mystical degrees. We found that
the Iseums that were using our rituals wished to have a struc-

tured degree course of more advanced Isian work. The words 'The College of Isis' came to me and on reading *The Return of She*, by Rider Haggard, I found he described just such a College as having existed and suggested its continuance in Mongolia! I counted our rites and found that we had 32. The 33rd I felt should be kept for spontaneous revelation that could happen to anyone at any time. What, though, was the design of such a structure to be? It had to be a matrix and we chose a spider's web because the universe is made of spiral galaxies. I was particularly inspired by Sirius, the eight-pointed star of Ishtar, so I drew this Star over a four-coiled spiral dragon of Tiamat. The Star represented Time and the coils, space. I counted up the centres where the Star and coils touched and found they numbered 32 — the 33rd began the next octave. In the centre I drew the Ankh or Grael — that was Home, the matrix from which one emerges — moving withershins — and to which one returns on a higher spiral, clockwise, rather like circular hopscotch! Rites could be associated with each

*Star of Ishtar and the Web of the Universe*

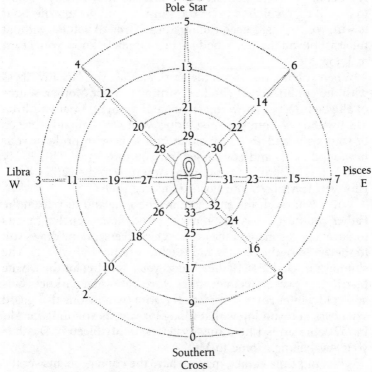

*Tiamat Dragon around the Divine Matrix*

intersection point. The rites concerned the three sacred, basic mysteries of birth, rebirth and marriage, time and space, the Mysteries, the planets and the zodiacal constellations. Our Rainbow network had emerged. We could now start our Magi course. In this our Priestesses invoke the Goddess Nuit of the Milky Way galaxy by saying 'Mother of the Gods, the Great Deep, the Celestial Abyss, Nuit, protect us as we face the Mysteries. Aid us, who dread the Unknown: wrap Thy starry mantle about us, Thou Who archeth the heavens with Thy body that holds the Milky Way as Thy Veil. As Thou art great, pity our littleness, as Thou art mighty, strengthen the weak; as Thou holdest all time and space in Thy darkness, bring our souls into their true fruition of Eternity'.

The Oracle of Nuit is given in reply: 'Fear not the unknown, for I am the Unknown. From me riseth suns and their children the planets and when suns reach their appointed time, I take them in my dark embrace for I am both Birth and Death. And the sun that loses its brightness in my Abyss, returns to greater life in other spheres for I am Mistress of the Spheres, I am the space within each atom — from its heart I give birth to new galaxies. I take to myself that which is to be transformed into greater life. So it is with yourselves! I need each tree, each one of you for without the least of you my starry body is incomplete! I know you. Learn to know Me.

'When you honour Me as the Earth Mother, you face my Abyss with the confidence of children turning to their Mother, source of all good. As you grow in activity and thought, I put you from Me. I withdraw from you, first aiding your steps, then I leave go of your arms and you walk alone. You walk with pride in your newfound skills and conquests and you forget me! This is My will. You walk into the light of day. You turn to the Father. From Him you learn laws and how to enforce them.

'When you reach the end of your schooling and turn from the Father, you turn to Isis. She lures you with strange enchantments to the magical sphere of the moon! Queen Persephone draws you to the world of the Shades and teaches you mysterious arts. The shining Sun Goddess, Hathor, brings you a longing for the Divine Marriage of twin souls in deathless love. Yet, when darkness falls and cold winter comes, you face the grim twin pylons that guard My Abyss and you know that I long for you, as you long for Me. In my azure arms I hold the Mysteries. In My Sleep of Death is your Awakening. Come to Me.'

When our time comes, may we have the courage to answer the Call of the Goddess and accept Rebirth.

# 2
# Priestess and Witch

## Vivianne Crowley

Vivianne Crowley's childhood vision of the Goddess, sustained by many seemingly coincidental encounters and validations, has found its manifestation within one of the oldest religions of all — that of Wicca. For all seekers, the joy of finding one's way to the spiritual Home is an experience to be treasured and in Vivianne's uplifting chapter, the richness and beauty of the priestess' vocation is fully realized. All people have mystical experiences of the unseen worlds and their empowering archetypes, yet few share these visions with others for fear of ridicule. Once it is realized that the otherworld is all about us and that we can each discover the Goddess within our lives, we find freedom to pursue our spiritual vocation. Vivianne's vision is one of joy and wonder, qualities that those who are orphaned of the Goddess need. Both reverence and worship are the indwelling gifts that the Goddess gives us in return.

*Dr Vivianne Crowley is a Witch and a High Priestess of Wicca — the name given to the pagan religion of witchcraft. She was initiated into Wicca at the age of 19 and has for many years run a Wiccan coven. She believes that there are many paths to the one centre that is the goal of all religious, magical and mystical systems, but for many women and men in today's society, the answer to their religious impulse lies in pagan religion, which gives due honour to the Goddess, the Divine feminine.*

*Vivianne Crowley teaches witchcraft and the religion of the Goddess through seminars and workshops in Britain and Europe. She is secretary of the Pagan Federation and has a private practice as a psychologist and healer. She is also the author of* Wicca: the Old Religion in the New Age *(Aquarian Press, 1989), a contributor to* Voices from the Circle *(Aquarian Press, 1990), an anthology of Neo-Pagan thought edited by Prudence Jones and Caitlín Matthews, and numerous psychological works. She lives in London.*

# Priestess and Witch

I was standing naked, bound, and blindfolded before an altar. I felt a hand touch my womb and a voice said, 'I consecrate thee with oil'. The hand then touched my left breast, my right breast, then my womb again, making the symbol of the downward pointing triangle. 'I consecrate thee with wine', the voice said and the same four movements followed. 'I consecrate thee with my lips, Priestess and Witch'.

I had come to the end of a long quest. What did I feel? I cannot describe it except as peace, unutterable peace. I was 19 when I was made a Priestess and now it seems to me to be very young, but then it seemed as if I has waited an age and in a sense I had.

I had been initiated into Wicca, the religion of witchcraft. Many people are surprised to find that witchcraft is a religion, but this is what it is. Witches worship the Elder Gods, the Goddesses and the Gods of our pagan ancestors. Followers in this way call it Wicca, or the Way of the Wise. It is the most ancient wisdom, that is, the knowledge of inner and hidden things. It is the knowledge of the properties of plants and of herbs, of the planets and stars and their effects on the lives of women and men and of magic — those ancient methods of mind control by which we can cause change. It is the power to heal — to cure and to remove pain — and it is the knowledge of people, of the darkness and light within us and the joys and sufferings of humanity as we struggle towards our spiritual destiny.

Unlike the patriarchal monotheisms, Wicca does not teach that there is only one correct version of God and that all other God forms are false. We worship the personification of the female and male principles, the Goddess and the God, recognizing that all forms of the Goddess are aspects of the one Goddess and all Gods are aspects of the one God, and that ultimately these are reconciled in one divine essence.

Those who are initiated into Wicca enter a priesthood and are also initiated as Witches. Sympathetic and natural magic form an integral part of the reglion. Psychic and magical powers — the ability to perceive that which is beyond the sensory realm and the ability to effect change — are seen as latent in all human beings, but traditionally, those who worked to develop these powers were set apart. They were called Shamans or Witches.

For many who are drawn to Wicca, the start of it all seems to be some kind of psychic experience, an experience that leads us to believe that there are other realms of being, other realities. There is often a sense of being 'called' — the true meaning of the word vocation. For me both experiences came when I was very young. 'I have been with thee from the beginning', says the Goddess in the Great Mother Charge that every Witch hears at initiation — 'from the beginning'.

I was six years old. I was lying in bed and a voice was calling me. I could not understand the words, but I knew that I had to follow. I rose out of bed to follow the voice and floated out through the bedroom window (the glass was no barrier). I was flying. I weaved and soared on the air currents in a kind of ecstasy. My body felt free, freer than swimming in the sea.

I flew across the fields that surrounded our farmhouse and down into the woods where I usually played. Everything was light, but it was not like normal daylight — more like a kind of golden radiance. Finally I became tired and returned home. I flew back in through the bedroom window, lay down in my bed and woke up. My mother was calling me. I ran downstairs, shouting, 'Mummy, Mummy, I can fly'. Mummy was not impressed — 'Eat your corn-flakes', was the only reply.

I ate them quickly as I could and ran outside, anxious to try out my new skill. I found a large fallen tree trunk, hauled myself up on top of it and then leapt off, wildly flapping my arms like bird. I landed on the ground with a bump. I obviously hadn't quite got the hang of it. I climbed up the tree trunk and tried again, but always with the same result — bump. Again and again I tried, but it was always the same. After half an hour I had bruised heels and I decided it was time to think things through. I came to two conclusions. First, I could only fly at night. Second, adults didn't seem very receptive to the idea of flying so I would keep this to myself.

A period of my life followed when each night I left my body and flew about the trees and woods around my home. I also experienced a change in my daytime consciousness. When I went out into the woods, it was as though trees and plants were no longer solid. When I gazed at a leaf or the trunk of a tree, it seemed to be made of crystals of light. The trees especially seemed to be alive in a way I had not perceived before. They were individuals, personalities and, if I was quiet and still, I could commune with them, although the language they spoke had no words. I did not associate this with religion or magic, but it seemed very important. Although as a child I could not find the words. I knew that there was another realm behind the more solid world of every-

day reality. The material world seemed like a barrier that I somehow had to break through.

I had already encountered two beings I thought of as fairies.
This happened a couple of years before, when I was four years
old. Again it had been at night, in the world of the lucid dream
and I found myself, I thought, awake. The bedroom had changed.
A dark tunnel had opened up in the bedroom wall in front of
me and small people were emerging from it, surrounding the bed.
The beg began to move. The tiny people were pushing me and
the bed down the tunnel. The tunnel emerged into a room. It had
no windows,but there was a soft light. Two very tall, slender people came forward and peered down at me. They seemed very beautiful. 'The King and Queen of Fairy', I thought.

Gently the woman touched me on the crown of my head and
then on certain centres down my body. Later I discovered that
these centres were the chakras. The woman smiled at me and
seemed somehow to approve. Then something very strange began
to happen — it was as though my mind was expanding, I began
to see pictures of cities, ancient cities, but they looked as if they
were on a speeded up film. The walls rose and stood, then crum-
bled and disapeared to dust. Then the pictures ended. The woman
disappeared and it was a long time before I was to see her again.
The fairy people reappeared and pushed my bed back to the
bedroom.

These childhood experiences profoundly affected my view of
the world. Many children have such experiences, but they are
usually dismissed as childish fantasies. However, to these children the experiences are important and meaningful. They give
a sense of having touched another world, a magical world. To me
these experiences convinced me that the world was not what it
at first seemed. Nature was *alive*, inhabited by entities that now
I would call devas, and behind the everyday world was a magical
world of possibilities.

'Do you think you have a vocation?' The Priest's voice was soft
and gentle in the cool stillness of the confessional. We were surrounded by silence in that strange impersonal intimacy of con-
fessor and penitent. I was 13 and my voice was hesistant — not
with fear or doubt, but with the awful momentousness of the
answer. The thoughts had been in my mind for about two years,
ever since I had gone with the school to a 'Vocations Exhibition'.
This was not the usual type of careers' fair, but an exhibition of
different orders of nuns, monks and priests (the Catholic Church

liked to begin its recruiting drives early). I had picked up literature for different orders and had sat and wondered and eventually it seemed to me that the call had come, but now the question was being articulated by someone else. To answer it meant to bring my own inner resolve out of the world of romantic fantasy and into the world of the real. I took the plunge — 'Yes, I think I have'. 'Pray to God and he will guide you', said the Priest.

I emerged from the confessional and lit a candle, not before the statue of Christ, but before the blue-robed Virgin on her blue-covered altar. She stood serene, her arms outstretched and her eyes raised to heaven. 'Dear Lady', I asked, 'show me what to do'.

A year or so later, my family moved to London. It was a terrible shattering of my quiet life in a country village with just five houses in it. We moved to a land of concrete and the power of the earth was battened down under layers of tarmac. The horizon was shut out by buildings. Used to obtaining energy from trees and the growing things around me, from the sky, the earth and the sun, in London I felt like an uprooted plant. I struggled to root myself, but the concrete barred me.

I went to school at a convent — I had found the address in a Catholic newspaper before we moved (I had long since taken charge of my own education, my fey mother being happy to leave such practical things to me). I was keen to further my resolve to become a nun and this was the first step.

Clutching the piece of paper with the school's address on it, I went a few days after we arrived in London to see the Headmistress, the Mother Superior. She was a tiny woman with that beautiful skin so many nuns have. I thought she was 30, but later I discovered that she was, in fact, in her early fifties. We talked for a while and eventually she said I could come to the school. 'Have you any idea what career you want to follow?', she asked. I wanted to say that I wished to become a nun, but I couldn't — my tongue seemed to stick to the roof of my mouth. Now the question had come, I could not speak. I had come to the convent intending that it should be the first step along a path as everything had seemed to lead me here. When I had first seen the advertisement for the school, it had seemed to leap out of the page at me. Having no idea of the geography of London, I did not know where it was in relation to our new home, but it turned out to be just a mile away. Initially when I spoke to the Mother Superior, she said that the school was full. After a while, though, just as I had known she would, she relented. Now I could not answer her final question. 'I don't know', I said, 'I'm not sure'.

I left the Mother Superior's office feeling very confused. What was it that had prevented me from saying what I had come to say? The religious impulse seemed as strong as ever and somehow I could envisage no life-style in which religion — this struggle to become at one with the divine — did not play a central role. I thought of the nun and her serene smile. She reminded me of the statues of the Virgin in Catholic churches — calm and at peace, but detached from the world, her eyes turned ever upwards to heaven. Then the answer came. I could not be a nun because I could not accept Christianity's view of women.

The early Christian Fathers were misogynist to a horrifying degree and they struggled to disown the Goddess, to banish the female aspect of the divine. This proved more difficult than they expected so they compromised. Fearing sexuality, but unable to suppress people's love for the female aspect of the Deity, the Church authorized the veneration of Mary, the Mother of Christ. Mary, however, was not to be venerated as Goddess or as a human being with failings, but as something in between — the Immaculate Virgin who had conceived 'without sin', that is, without sexuality. The Goddess who had always been worshipped as triple — Virgin, Lover/Mother and Layer-out-at-Death — was now to be venerated as a Virgin Mother. Her sexuality was denied her and thus denied to all women, for this was the Christian ideal of womanhood — ever the mother and never the lover.

My growing body was full of sexual desire and I could not accept that physical love was wrong. It seemed to me potentially the most beautiful expression of love between two human beings, a spiritual act. To follow the full religious path of Christianity, to become a nun, I would have to forsake my sexuality. To experience my sexuality, I would need to become a wife and be debarred from a life of full religious dedication. Whichever way I chose, would necessitate following a path of submission to the male. As a woman I was not to gain wholeness through my own achievements and finding my own destiny. My role was to serve the male, whether that was a male God or a husband. Ultimately it was not only the lack of the Goddess in Christianity that I could not accept, it was the way Christian mysticism denied the world, denied human love and sensory experience. To me the divine was in the world around me: it was in nature, it was in people. To flee this was to flee that which we most sought.

Despite this change of heart, I loved the convent. Every hour there was marked by prayer: the whole school prayed together at morning and afternoon assemblies, we prayed before every lesson and at 12 noon we said the Angelus — 'The angel of the Lord declared unto Mary and she conceived by the Holy Ghost. Hail Mary full of grace the Lord is with thee. . .'

Fed on this diet of prayer, my soul soared. The barriers between the collective unconscious, the world of the archetypes, and my personal unconscious began to dissolve. Poems poured through me, emerging complete into consciousness. Sometimes they came at the rate of two or three a day, but, they were not Christian. First came a poem about the God:

'The Pipes of Pan

In caverns deep the Old Gods sleep,
But the trees still know their Lord
And it's the Pipes of Pan which call the tune
In the twilight in the wood.

The leaves they dance to the Goat God's tune
And they whisper his name to the winds
And the oak tree dreams of a God with horns
And knows not Christ the King'.

As I wrote, my hands had moved across the page as though of its own accord. When I read what I had written, I was shocked. What was happening to my Christianity? What I had written was blasphemous.

Soon after this I was lying in bed in that state between sleeping and waking when visions come. This time it was the Goddess who came to me:

'She came to me in a waking dream
A woman whose eyes were the grey of the sea
And her eyes were mocking as she said to me:
"I shall destroy you, O woman of little faith".'

I seemed to be in the far, far North in a place of pack-ice and cold, grey water. A woman was walking across the water towards me, her feet gliding over the surface of the waves as though they were glass. I was afraid, but something stronger than fear rooted me to the spot. The woman wore a long black coat and her blue-black hair flowed over it so that I could not see where the one ended and the other began. She was neither old nor young — she was beyond time. She looked at me and I rcognized her eyes. They were the eyes of the Queen of Fairy whom I had seen long ago in my childhood. Then the eyes had smiled, but this time they did not.

'I shall destroy you'. The words she spoke were silent. Her lips did not move, but her voice echoed in my head and in my heart, reverberating through my memory. Then the tension passed — I laughed, I was glad. Then she smiled and somehow I knew I had passed a test. I had understood that nothing I needed would ever be destroyed by this woman — I need not fear. In her I could have Perfect Trust. She turned and left. Later I learned to call her 'Hecate' and sometimes by another name, 'Arianrhod'.

It was my *Christianity* that was destroyed. A little while later, I wrote a poem about the crucifixion of Christ. The thunder rolled, the sanctuary of the temple shook and the veil was rended. Christ was dead and there was no resurrection — for me it was the end. I knew that some process was happening inside me, but I could not hasten it. The Goddess had set her mark upon me and She would come for me again. Something else awaited me — but what? I knew it would be difficult, but I was not afraid. A rhyme came into my head:

'I am Fire and I am Water
I am that fair Witch-Queen's daughter'.

The vision of the woman with the sea-grey eyes brought to me a sense of an undying centre that gave me strength. A poem came that affirmed my own sense of selfhood, the Goddess within:

'I am Vivianne
Daughter of the sea
And daughter of the wind
Daughter of the Earth
And daughter of the Moon
Daughter of dawn
And daughter of sunset
Daughter of night
And daughter of the mountains

And I have sung a song of the sea
And I have listened to the sighing of the wind
I have heard the hidden secrets of the Earth
And I have drunk of the tears of the Moon
I have seen the beauty of the dawn
And the sorrow of the sunset
I have lain 'neath the darkest dark of the night
And I have beheld the might of the mountains

> For I am stronger than the sea
> And freer than the wind
> I am deeper than the Earth
> And more changing than the Moon
> I am the hope of the dawn
> And the peace of the sunset
> I am more mysterious than night
> And older than the mountains
> Older than time itself
> For I am she who was
> Who is
> And who will be
> For I am *Vivianne*.'

Later I adapted the poem into a Goddess Charge.

More poems came and other visions. They spoke of the past, and I asked myself, 'Are these memories of reincarnation? I could not decide, but the cities of my childhood dreams returned — this time with names: Babylon, Ninevah, Rome, Ephesus, a pagan past of lost pagan glories.

> 'In Babylon was I
> And yes she rose and fell
> And dust and lizards play
> Where once was a citadel ...'

I dreamed of other places that I had never seen in reality or dream — of the islands of Greece set like jewels in the sparkling sea, of the coastline of Ireland, that farthest edge of the Western World where the waves of the Atlantic Ocean beat hungrily against the rocky shore, and of the deep forests of Germany where the wolves howled — and always there were temples and strong, proud women, warriors and queens. My dreams were pagan dreams. Then the witchcraft came back to me.

Earlier, when I was six or seven, I had discovered my first talisman. It was soon after the flying began, one hot, dusty summer afternoon. I had been playing in the woods and was going home for my tea. I was walking up the hill to the farm when, on the right-hand side of the road, I saw something shining. I picked it up. It was a stone, hot from the sun, shaped like a flattened egg. One side was brown and plain, but on the other were black markings that depicted the face of a goat. 'A goat-headed stone', I stared at it in wonder. Then I secreted it in my pocket and hid it in my room. Every day I would take it out and hold it in my hand. To me it was a thing of power, a thing of magic and if it had power, then I too had power. The idea came into my mind that if I wanted to I could make things happen — magical things. It was a year or so before I experimented, though.

One lunchtime in the school playground I had an idea. That afternoon was our sports afternoon, but the weather was cold and the thought of an afternoon on an exposed playing field was not appealing. I wondered if I could make it rain. I had seen rain-dancing on cowboy and Indian films and it looked easy enough. A lot of people, strange chanting and dancing in a circle seemed to be all that was required.

I gathered together a group of would-be rain-makers and we retired a discreet distance from the teachers and the school build-ings. We began to dance and shout. This went on for about five minutes (children's attention spans are short). Ten minutes later it rained. I repeated the experiment again a few weeks later and it worked again. After this the other children started to call me a Witch. 'Vivianne's a witch! Vivianne's a witch!', they'd say. Some-times they said it with admiration, but sometimes with a fear and underlying hostility that I did not like. I felt confused about my witchery. Was it wrong to 'make things happen'? I found what I thought was the answer.

At the same time as I had been discovering rain-dancing, I had found that I had been baptized a Catholic. This had been the beginning and end of my parents' religious efforts. Having disco-vered this new label, I was anxious to know what it meant, I enquired of the small contingent of Italian girls in the school and they made a suggestion, 'Come along with us to Mass'.

The next Sunday I had gone with them. The Latin fascinated me, as did the incense, the flowers and the music. The sights and the sounds seemed to blend into one harmonious whole. I felt transported in a way that had only previously occurred when I was alone with nature.

I decided to educate myself in this new religion, and joined catechism classes at the church in order to prepare for the Catholic sacraments of first communion and confession, but there was a conflict. The more I found out about Catholicism, the more I dis-covered that magic could play no part in it. For the Church, magic was wrong. I had to make a decision between the two. I made a gesture I later regretted.

I had decided to make myself a personal altar in my bedroom. It was to be an altar to Mary. I assembled all the most beautiful objects in my possession, together with a piece of blue silk and some net curtains that I had bought in a jumble sale. I covered the altar with the silk and draped the curtains down the sides like a veil. I found bluebells in the wood and I placed these on the altar, together with a small silver dish and an ivory box in which I kept my jewellery. To me it looked very beautiful. Then I took out my most precious possession, my talisman, my magical goat-headed stone. Reverentially I placed it at the centre of the altar. Against the delicacy of the silk and net and of the blue, white and silver, the stone looked large and crude. It was out of place. There was no room for the power and magic inherent in natural things in this new religion of incense and pretty statues — witchcraft and Catholicism were incompatible. I took the stone from the altar, went into the woods and threw it into a stream.

I then turned my back on magic — I thought forever, but years later in London, the wheel turned. Not long after I had the vision of the woman with the sea-grey eyes, I came across a book in the local library by the anthropologist Margaret Murray, entitled *The God of the Witches* (Oxford University Press, 1970). From it I discovered that the pagan Gods had not been completely stamped out by Christianity but for centuries their worship had survived in the Witch covens of Europe. Then I saw a television programme.

I had turned on the television by chance. It was a Saturday evening, my parents were out and what I saw transfixed me. Two people were being interviewed — a man and a woman called Alex and Maxine Sanders. They were Witches. They began to describe witchcraft and said that it was a mystery religion they called Wicca. I learned that Wicca was an intitiatory system and that each person who was initiated became not only a Priestess or a Priest, dedicated to the service of others and the Gods, but also a Witch. They spoke of it as the 'Old Religion' and talked of Wicca's worship of the Goddess. Something within me leapt in recognition. The set of beliefs that Alex and Maxine Sanders were describing were the same as my own.

They used the phrase 'Priestess and Witch' and explained that in Wicca there is no division between religion and magic, but rather a joining together of these two elements. Here, in the religion of the Goddess, I found the marriage of the two sides of myself. On the pagan altar my talisman could lie and not look out of place. I knew in a blinding revelation, like that of Paul on the road to Damascus, that I had been following the wrong path.

The great psychiatrist Carl Jung believed that to find resolutions to inner conflicts, we must be true to both sides. Neither side of the psyche is then repressed by the other and a higher and greater synthesis can be found. Jung himself faced the dilemma of whether to study medicine or religion. For him the solution came through the study of psychiatry:

> 'Here alone the two currents of my interest could flow together and in a united stream dig their own bed. Here was the empirical field common to biological and spiritual facts, which I had everywhere sought and nowhere found. Here at last was the place where the collision of nature and spirit became a reality'.

> (Carl A. Jung, *Memories, Dreams and Reflections*, Vintage Books, Random House, 1970.)

In Wicca I saw the end of my own inner conflict, between that part of me which wanted to serve the divine, and that part which sought to be active in the world and make use of those powers that human beings since the dawn of time have called magic.

Now that I had the answer, I was determined to find some Witches and to be initiated by them — but I was only 15. From the television interview, I had learned that Witches did not initiate anyone under the age of 18. I would have to wait.

In the meantime. I began to teach myself the skills that I associated with witchcraft. I learned to read palms and experimented with séances. I learned to read the future in the cards. Initially I read playing cards and then later the tarot, which was more difficult to obtain in those days. I learned about astrology and how to construct a natal chart. I read books on magic, most of which were way beyond my understanding. I began to experiment with ritual.

My eighteenth birthday came and went and then my nineteenth. I knew I would have to do something about finding a coven, but I was happy with my life as it was. I was enjoying my teenage life of flat-sharing and boyfriends and the freedom of leaving home and earning money. There seemed to be no urgency. Then one evening that label which had haunted me as a child reappeared, 'Vivianne's a witch!'

I was sitting on my bed. The evening sun was streaming in through the window and I was reading the tarot, which was spread out in a pool of sunlight across the bed. Suddenly Simon, one of the men who shared the house where I lived, came into my room. He stared at the tarot cards. 'You're a witch aren't you?', he said, 'I know you are'.

Simon's voice had that same underlying hostility that the children in the playground had had many years before. I looked at him startled, not knowing what to say. 'Was I really a witch?' I asked myself, or was it just an elaborate game, a childish fantasy?

I did not have to answer Simon's question because he turned and left the room as abruptly as he had entered without waiting for an answer, but it seemed like a sign. I had to do something. I had to find out if I was really a Witch.

Events began to lead me in a certain direction. A few days later I went into W. H. Smith's to browse through the magazines. It was not the most likely place to find a signpost to one's spiritual home, but, as my eyes wandered over the paperback books, staring at me from the shelves was a book called *What Witches Do* by Stewart Farrar (Coward, McCann & Geohegan, 1971). It was a book about Alex and Maxine and their particular branch of Wicca — Alexandrian Wicca. I bought the book and read it eagerly on the train home. The book gave most of Alex and Maxine's address and it did not take me long to find the rest.

In great trepidation, I went first to a 'Question and Answer' session for people wanting to find out more about Wicca. I didn't know what to expect — strange 'weirdos' with piercing eyes and large dangling pentacles? I sat down among the people and listened to the questions and the answers. There were plenty of dangling pentacles, but no weirdos. The more I heard, the more I felt I had come home.

In order to be initiated into Wicca, one must ask for initiation. I was determined to ask, but for me this was a terrible ordeal as I was painfully shy. How could I bring myself to ask this terrible question — 'terrible' because the implication of refusal seemed so great.

I came back later that week for the coven's psychic development evening. Afterwards I began to talk to Bob, one of the Priests. 'Why have you come?' he asked. His question seemed to echo that of the Mother Superior's five years before, but this time the answer came with no hesitation — 'I want to be initiated'. Bob offered to enquire on my behalf and we all adjourned to the pub. Bob disappeared into a corner to speak to Maxine. A few minutes later he came back with the reply: 'You're already a Witch. You can be initiated the week after next'.

The sense of relief was indescribable. That strange label 'Witch' that had haunted me for so many years had now been confirmed by someone else who was herself a Witch. Now it had been accepted by others. I could accept it myself. I went home from the pub walking on air.

So it was that I came one Friday evening to a Wiccan temple

in London's Notting Hill Gate, an unromantic location for an initiation. The ceremony drew to a close:

'Take heed ye Mighty Ones of the East, that Vivianne has been duly consecrated a Priestess of the Great Goddess'.

The final presentation to the Lords of the Watchtowers, the Lords of the four cardinal directions and it was done. I was sworn forever to the Gods, a Priestess and a Witch.

People often ask if we immediately feel different after initiation. For many the answer is 'yes', for some the change comes more slowly, but for me it was 'yes' *and* 'no'. It was not so much that I changed, but that in the sacred space of the magic circle, I could become myself. I had much to learn, however. I learned how to make the sacred space.

'I conjure thee, O thou Circle of Power . . .'

The sword was heavy in my hands as I began to make the circuit of the temple. I was casting the magic circle within which the rites of Wicca take place, creating a psychic barrier between the everyday world and the magical realm.

'. . . that thou beist a boundary between the world of men and the realms of the Mighty Ones . . .'

I concentrated on the point of the sword, allowing the etheric energy of my body to flow down the blade and out to make the barrier.

'. . . a guardian and a protection which shall preserve and contain the power which we shall raise within thee. Wherefore do I bless and consecrate thee, in the most sacred and powerful names of the Goddess and the God'.

I completed the circuit. The Priest who knelt by the altar took the sword from me and handed me an athame, the ritual knife of witchcraft. I went to the East, the first of the four sacred directions, and began to invoke the elements.

'Ye Mighty Ones of the East, Eurius Lord of Air, I summon, stir and call ye up to guard our circle and witness our rites'.

I went to the South to invoke Fire and then to the West and North for Water and Earth. I stood in the centre of the circle, in the centre

of my own created universe. It was as though my psyche was spread
out around me, mine to access and to use as I willed. I knew as
never before that I was in charge of my own destiny.

Within my own universe, I wrote in my magical diary, I was
God. Once again, I had found my pen racing ahead of my conscious mind. I was shocked at the words I had written. Was this
some monstrous manifestation of the ego? 'No', some other part
of my psyche answered, 'you must learn to be strong'.

My earlier religious experiences had taught me a sense of reverence and worship. What came now was a revelation of power. I
wrote a poem that began:

> 'O Wine of Power, sweet is thy song
> Sweeter far than the grapes of Lebanon . . .'

Demaris Wehr, a Professor of the Psychology of Religion at Boston
University, points out in *Jung and Feminism: Liberating Archetypes*,
(Routledge & Kegan Paul, 1988), that women are undermined by
the low value that society and patriarchal religion place on the
feminine. Woman is unclean, unfit to serve at the sacred altar,
except to clean it and adorn it with flowers. Christian images of
women are of the devoted servant who asks nothing. They deny
us power and authority — 'Behold the handmaiden of the Lord',
says Mary. To break free of this image we must seek the Goddess.
Demaris Wehr says in her book:

> 'Vesting the divine power in the masculine reinforces internalized
> oppression in women . . . If we allow ourselves to change our reli-
> gious language to feminine language . . . We will begin to see the
> degree to which our feelings have been conditioned by the dearth
> of symbols of female authority in our society. To see beyond the
> false claims of androcentric religions and, at the same time, not
> to lose sight of the central importance of religion in human life,
> as well as to find spiritual paths that nourish women, is one of
> our most challenging tasks today'.

Initiation into Wicca confirms our identity as women with both
passive and active qualities, for Wicca is a combination of cup
and sword, of religion and magic, of priestesshood and witchcraft, of love and will, of worship and power.

First I learned the way of the sword, to control the circle of power.
Then I learned the way of the Cup.

> 'I invoke thee and call upon thee
> O Mighty Mother of us all . . .'

I was standing with my back to the altar, my feet were a little apart, my arms outstretched to the heavens to form the symbol of the Star Goddess. The Priest was invoking the Goddess, calling Her to enter the body of her Priestess.

'By seed and root and bud and stem . . .'

My awareness of the people around me faded. I felt my body grow taller. The voice of the Priest was becoming distant. The circle seemed far below.

'By leaf and flower and fruit . . .'

I was becoming the World Tree. My feet were rooted in the Earth, my arms were branches that touched the arch of heaven and around my head swirled the stars. I lost all sense of self — my body was empty, a vacuum waiting to be filled.

'By life and love
I do invoke thee and call upon thee
To descend upon the body of thy servant and Priestess.'

I felt the power — Her power — flow through me and out into the circle. My consciousness was dissolving into unity. There was no longer any 'I' and 'other' — only 'She'. Words came unbidden from a place deep within me:

'I am thy Goddess
High-born full-blooded and lusting free am I
The wind is my voice and my song . . .'

After a while it came to an end. The Priest kissed my feet bringing my consciousness down to Earth once more. I looked at the circle of people around me. I did not need to ask. I could see by their faces that the invocation had worked. Together we had touched that other realm and crossed the boundaries between the self and the infinite.

Within the circle, I had learned to unite with that deep centre within myself and to manifest the Goddess, but this was not enough. The Goddess is not only for the temple, she must be carried out into the world to wherever She is needed. I learned to heal.

'Gently now' said the healer who was instructing me. There was a warmth in my solar plexus — a soft and soothing heat. It rose within me and began to flow down my arms and into my hands. My hands were drawing the energy, wanting it to be there. I looked at them, and my fingers seemed to be surrounded by light. Slowly I moved my hands towards the woman I was healing, taking care to move gently into her auric field. I felt my hands, sensitized by the energy within them, passing through her aura as though penetrating a delicate mist.

I placed my hands on the woman's head and the rhythm of our breathing united as one. A stillness began to pervade the room and to flow through the woman and me. I moved my hands to the woman's neck, the site of a whiplash injury, and the energy flowed from my hands of its own accord, without conscious intervention. The boundaries between myself and other were beginning to dissolve. My mind reached out to the woman to feel her pain. 'Let her be healed' said a voice within me. Was it an entreaty or a command — I did not know. The muscles of the woman's neck, long tense and knotted with pain, began to relax under the heat from my hands. My conscious mind let go. The woman and I united at that deep level of the psyche where we are all at one; where all parts of the Goddess' creation are reunited, at one with each other and at one with Her.

Thirty, maybe forty, minutes later I became aware of myself again and the woman opened her eyes and smiled. I looked at her, wondering if it had worked. As though she had heard my unspoken question, the woman answered, 'The pain has gone'. I then became aware of the healer sitting beside me — I had forgotten her presence. Within me was a deep feeling of peace. I had made an act of magic. The power of healing had flowed through me. Was it my power or Her power? Was I receptor or transmitter? Was it the work of a Priestess or the work of a Witch? Was I the cup or that which flowed from it? Somehow I had been both.

Many woman can identify with the romantic image of the Priestess. She is good, white, pure, holy, but to understand ourselves fully we must also examine the meaning of that other figure of feminine spiritual power — the Witch.

In the tarot, the Witch can be seen in the card of Strength. She stands with her hands upon the Lion, that noblest and most powerful of the animal kingdom. She is in contact with the world of nature and mistress of it. She is the doer — the Woman of Power. She is the Great Mother Goddess Cybele, the Lady of the Beasts. The card of Strength is ruled by Leo. Ruled by the opposite sign of Aquarius is the card of the Star. The Star, too, is an aspect of the Witch. She kneels by a pool of water, naked and unashamed in the natural world, seeking to know and experience the secrets of the elements. She is not yet Mistress of Nature, but Nature's pupil.

The card of the High Priestess is passive. It is ruled by the Moon. Unlike the Witch, her contact is not with the natural world, but with the world of the spirit. The Priestess sits enthroned before the veil of the inner sanctuary of the temple, awaiting those who would seek her knowledge. She will give forth her wisdom, but only if sought, only if asked.

What relevance are the Priestess and the Witch to the problems faced by women seeking to fulfil themselves in society today? Above the ancient temples of initiation were carved the words 'Know Thyself'. To know ourselves we must harness those qualities that lie buried deep in our psyches. Jung describes the feminine as the full Moon, the Grail, the Earth, the pool of still water, matter, the ploughed land, the circle, the cauldron — all that receives and contains, but woman is active as well as passive. She is Witch as well as Priestess.

The qualities of the Witch are those that are frequently denied to women: Word, Power, Meaning and Deed. As women we must recognize these qualities as ours, the qualities of Cybele. We must find the strength of the feminine; the strength of She who is Mistress of the Lion. Demaris Wehr writes:

> 'Sexism consists of limiting beliefs about the "natures" of women and men . . . it is particularly wounding to women because women are the ones who stand outside the definition of the fully human . . . Because this is . . . reinforced constantly . . . in religion, in psychology, in popular culture — women find many difficulties in claiming adult status, responsibility, authority'.

If society is to change so as to integrate the powers, attributes and talents of women in more satisfactory ways, then women must find positive images of power and authority with which they can identify. Religion and magical systems can assist in effecting such change because they operate in the realm of symbols. Demaris Wehr also writes:

> 'Symbols have both psychological and political effects, because they create the inner conditions (deep-seated attitudes and feelings) that lead people to feel comfortable with or to accept social and political arrangements that correspond to the symbol system'.

In integrating into our self-concepts symbols of womanhood that go beyond the limitations which patriarchy has imposed, women can come to a new sense of destiny. In the search for such symbols we come to the pagan image of the woman of power — women such as Maeve, Queen of Connaught, who led her warriors into battle and boasted that she could best 30 men a day — in the battlefield or in her bed. Many of Maeve's activities are those that society has stereotyped as masculine, but hers is a true image of womanhood. It is far removed from that of Mary Queen of Heaven — Maeve's realm and desires are Earthly.

The Goddess has become an integral part of my life and that of many women today, but who and what is She? In part She is that divine centre within us that Jungian psychologists call the self. In part She is the life force, the divine immanent in nature. In part She is something beyond both these things, existing in Herself, beyond the world of matter, the transcendent deity.

Before the Goddess, all are equal. Every woman is a Priestess and every man a Priest. The Goddess is within all equally — not in white rather than black, or in male rather than female or even in human rather than animal or plant — all life is sacred to Her and all is holy. These are beautiful words for a beautiful concept, but what relevance has the Goddess to the problems that face the world?

Many people today have lost a sense of the sacredness of life, of the divine immanent in nature, but we lose this at our peril. If it is not regained then our world will die. Human beings with their skills and their talents have learned to dominate the natural world, to turn its precious resources to their own use. We do not work with nature (as does the woman-Witch in the card of Strength, gently taming the lion, not tying him or changing him, but working with him in harmonious partnership) but are destroying nature. Our environment is being burned and buried by the destructive egotism of human beings, who, thinking only of their own short-term desires, seek to dominate and use nature for their own ends.

The purpose of archetypes such as the Goddess is, as Jung tells us in 'The Psychology of the Child Archetype' *Essays on a Science of Mythology*, (with C. Kerenyi, Bollingen Series XXII, Princeton University Press, 1969).

> '. . . to compensate and correct, in a meaningful manner, the inevitable one-sidedness and extravagances of the conscious mind'.

It is to counteract imbalance — between women and men, between men and their inner feminine, between humankind and the world we inhabit — that the archetype of the Goddess has arisen in the world today. Long-buried in the human psyche, the Goddes has awoken and in dreams, visions, art and literature pursues us. Some ignore her call, but many answer and through religion, magic, art, music, poetry, craft and vision they come to Her. The Goddess lives and all who desire may serve at Her altar.

'Know that each man has it within himself, by virtue of his manhood, to be a Priest and each woman by virtue of her womanhood has it in her to be a Priestess...'

'We in this life have found that to which our own nature is attuned, and that is the Cult of the Great Goddess, the Primordial Mother. This Goddess is symbolized by space and the inmost earth. She is Rhea and Ge and Persephone, but, above all, She is Our Lady Isis, in whom all these are summed, for Isis is both Corn Goddess and Queen of the Dead — who are also the unborn — and the lunar crescent is upon her brow. Under another aspect she is the sea, for life first formed in the sea and in her dynamic aspect she rose from the waves as Aphrodite.

'Know this: the symbols of cult after cult are the worship of the same thing by different names and under different aspects, but our practice is not the austere Egyptian faith, not the radiant Gods of Greece, but the primordial Brythonic Cult that has its roots in Atlantis and which the dark Ionian Kelt shares with the Breton and Basque.

'For this is older than the Gods of the North, and there is more of wisdom in it, for the Gods of the North are mindless, being the formulations of fighting men, but the Great Goddess is older even than the Gods that made the Gods, for men knew the function of the Mother long before they understood the part played by the Father and they adored the Bird of Space that laid the Primordial Egg long before they worshipped the Sun as the Fecundator.'

Dion Fortune, quoted in *The Alexandrian Book of Shadows*

# 3

# The Voice of the Bitch Goddess

## Margaretta D'Arcy

'Ich am of Irelande,
And of the holy lande
Of Irelande.
Goode sire, pray ich thee,
Of sainte charite,
Come and daunce with me
In Irelande.'

In this medieval carol, Eriu, the Goddess of Ireland's Sovereignty, invites her love to dance with her in Ireland. Since the Normans invaded Ireland, the reality has been less pleasant. This act of invasion can be seen as a paradigm of women's inner reality and its rape by patriarchal values: its creative spirit bludgeoned by force of arms. Margaretta D'Arcy here personifies the female reaction to such rape in a tradition that has given us Maeve, warrior-queen of Connacht and Scathach, the Alban warrior-woman to whom even the mighty hero Cuchulainn went for instruction in arms. Who else but a warrior-Goddess could cope with the unrealities of the uneasy peace in which the Western world now finds itself?

Margaretta D'Arcy *is a polemical feminist, born in 1934, Irish with Asiatic strains. In 1980, after her second imprisonment in Armagh Gaol with Republican women (recorded in her book* Tell Them Everything, *Pluto Press, 1981) she decided to end her participation in the authoritarian-totalitarian culture of approval/disapproval based in the Judaeo-Christian ethic and instead share her energies with women in building an alternative culture. She has been spending parts of every year at Yellow Gate, Greenham Common, joining in non-violent direct actions against the military/industrial complex. She works from home in Galway, Ireland where she set up Women's Scearl Radio and Galway Women's Entertainment. She also works with her neighbours' children on video and music. Her 30-year creative partnership with John Arden has produced over 20 works — the latest being the nine-play cycle on early Christianity,* Whose is the Kingdom? *(BBC2, 1988)) and a book of essays, verses and titbits,* Awkward, Corners *(both published by Methuen, 1988). Video-making is an essential part of her narrative and of her present work-in-progress, an epic opera entitled* Opera ag Obair, *where all will be activists and all will be participants, about women and the patriarchy. She is a member of, and financially supported by, Aosdana, the Irish artists' Parliament. She has four sons and a grandson.*

# The Voice of the Bitch Goddess

'*Bitch*: one of the most sacred titles of the goddess, Artemis-Diana, leader of the . . . "hunting dogs". The Bitch-goddess of antiquity was known in all Indo-European cultures, beginning with the Great Bitch Sarama who led the Vedic dogs of death . . . In Christian terms, "son of a bitch" was considered insulting not because it meant a dog, but because it meant a devil — that is, a spiritual son of the pagan Goddess.'

'Early Christians viewed Diana as their major rival, which is why she later became "Queen of Witches".'

Barbara G. Walker, *The Woman's Encyclopedia of Myths and Secrets*
(Harper & Row, 1987)

All bitches refused, in mind and spirit, to conform to the idea that there were limits on what they could be and do.

A contemporary feminist description from *The Bitch Manifesto*, by
Joreen.

The limitless power of women has been the chief obstacle to men's control of the world. To evade it, they have had to 'asset-strip' the Triple goddess and create, from her bitch-voice, an elaborate artefact of moralized good-and-evil, god-and-devil, fall-and-redemption. The other voices of the Goddess, maiden and mother, they were able to colonize. I was brought up into one of those colonies.

I am an Irishwoman, reared as a Catholic. I spent six years of my life in an enclosed Dominican convent of nuns, while being educated for the honour and glory of God (male), but I was taught that it was the Mother of this God whom I should really try and copy. She herself was not a goddess, even though she was born without sin, and when she died she was carried up body and soul to join her son in heaven. Her sole function in heaven was constantly to lobby her son on our behalf. All she asked in return is that we should live our lives in a similar purity and not cause her to blush in heaven by immodest behaviour. We believed in her utterly in these things. If we did not believe we could not be Catholics. Our belief, without understanding, was the test of our obedience. That was what faith was all about.

I had difficulty in coming to terms with her role as supplicant to her Son. I felt that there was something degrading and manipulative about it. On the other hand, in the May processions, when we followed her statue around the gardens, singing 'O Queen of

Heaven' and responding to the litany of 'Star of the Sea, Mirror of Justice, Seat of Wisdom, Tower of David, Tower of Ivory, House of Gold, Morning Star, Ark of the Covenant', my whole being was taken up in the worship of her.

I found recently, however, that I could not remember the exact words of this litany with all its pre-Christian images. I live in an Irish farming village where everyone is a practising Catholic and so I asked the postmistress if she could remember the words. She said, 'No' — she had thrown her old prayer-books out when the post-Vatican II new liturgy came in. I then asked another neighbour, a small farmer, who I knew had a very good memory. She had not thrown her prayer-books out, but she said that since Vatican II all these forms of worship had been abolished and she missed them and felt a lot of other women missed them too. We suddenly realized that all the old titles relating the Virgin Mary to the ancient matriarchal worship have all vanished in Ireland. My neighbour thought it was something to do with accommodating Irish Catholicism to the Protestants of the North.

While the Mother is being removed from the lower, poorer, oppressed sections of society, she is gaining rehabilitation among the intellectual, liberationist elements. I quote from the December 1988 edition of an Italian Catholic journal, *30 Days (in the Church and in the world)*.

> The Dominican, the Witch and the Inquisitor
> A year of silence for a controversial American priest . . . Dominican Father Matthew Fox, who wants to downplay the importance of original sin and emphasize instead the concept of "original blessing". The case also involves a self-proclaimed witch named Starhawk, who is Fox's colleague at a California college.

The chief irony of the story is that Father Fox is a Dominican. His order was expressly founded in the early thirteenth century by Saint Dominic to root out the female-orientated Cathar heresy in the south of France. When I was at school under the Dominicans, we were told nothing about this aspect of their history, except that they established a great reputation for education and truth-seeking and that the greatest saint they had was Saint Thomas Aquinas. He was the 'Angelic Doctor', who 'preferred to be thought a fool rather than to think that a fellow-monk would tell a lie' and who wrote the definitive *Summa Theologica*. If we structured our daily lives and the process of our thought upon the philosophy of this book, heaven would be our reward. Also Saint Thomas was 'favourite son of the Virgin Mary'.

The Cathars in the early thirteenth century had a virtually independent state in Languedoc. Dominic went to preach there and was ignored because the Cathars found the masculine priesthood of Rome unacceptable. The central position of women in the Cathar church was the main doctrinal difference between the Cathars and Rome. In all Christendom this was the only area that had women priests. It was also the area where Mary Magdalene was venerated. Devotion to Mary Magdalene was always a matter of suspicion to the orthodox Catholic hierarchy because of the great importance given her in suppressed gnostic gospels (one of which presented her as the teacher of Jesus, 'The woman who knew all, who would rule above all in the coming Kingdom of Light') and because of her sexual associations, which suggested the cult of the Triple Goddess in pseudo-Christian disguise. It was the 'blessings' of Jesus, however, that the Cathar women emphasized, rather than the message of the Cross.

The Dominicans decided, therefore, that the Cathars had renounced the Cross and were therefore heretics. The Pope proclaimed a crusade against them and hundreds of their villages and towns were burned and the women, children and men executed. In 1233 Pope Gregory IX orderd a General Inquisition and put the Dominicans in charge of it.

Once the Cathar church was destroyed, the fear then arose that the ideas behind it had survived and were being passed on underground among women, that the devil was controlling them in a secret kingdom of witchcraft that flourished even in the midst of the supposed kingdom of Christ.

Two hundred years after the Cathar massacres the Dominicans again moved in to suppress women. This time they did it with a book written by two friars of the order — Heinrich Kraemer and Jakob Sprenger — entitled *Malleus Maleficarum*, or 'The Hammer of the Witches'. In 1484 they sent a copy to Pope Innocent VIII and induced him to publish a papal bull defining and denouncing witchcraft, delegating Kraemer and Sprenger as Inquisitors to deal with witches throughout northern Germany. The bull was included in the preface to the book.

By means of the new invention of the printing press, copies were spread rapidly all across Europe. The book's format was based upon Aquinas' *Summa*, but, where the *Summa* laid down our attitude to God, the *Malleus* prescribed an attitude to women (as witches) that has shaped women's views of themselves to this very day. The extermination of perhaps as many as nine million women over the next two hundred years can be laid directly at Kraemer and Sprenger's door. This book could have served as an example for all future forms of witch-hunt, including, perhaps, the Nazi Holocaust.

The book delineated the devil's secret kingdom in great and apparently unchallengeable detail.

> Divine law commands that witches are not only to be avoided but also they are to be put to death. It would not impose the extreme penalty of this kind if witches did not really and truly make a compact with devils in order to bring about real and true hurts and harms.

The authors' technique was to find out every single bit of misogynist writing from the documents of the Church and to collate them to make a watertight case. Thus at the time an abbot related:

> '. . . certain abandoned women turning aside to follow Satan, being seduced by the illusions and phantasms of demons, believe and openly profess that in the dead of night they ride upon certain beasts with the pagan goddess Diana and a countless horde of women, and that in these silent hours they fly over vast tracks of country and obey her as their mistress, while on other nights they are sullen to pay her homage'.

To Kraemer and Sprenger however, the demons involved were not illusions or phantasms, but authentic reality. It was this apparent authenticity of their examples that so convinced their readers. No proof was ever found, but thousands of confessions were extracted by torture and thousands of incriminations followed. Women were compelled to inform against women, and women were compelled to watch women burn, knowing that if they raised their voices against it, they too would be burned. Over and over again Kraemer and Sprenger insisted that people who refused to believe in witches must be part of the witch-cult themselves and must be punished accordingly.

The traumatic effect of those terrible centuries has been handed down through succeeding generations of women. The damaged psyche is still with us, the self-doubt, the fear of any woman who is different, the fear of ridicule, the fear of being told by men that a woman is different, the fear of women who call for action (the longing to join is there, but then comes the pulling back). Initial courage turns to hurt and this is externalized against those who have inspired it.

The origin of this state of mind has not exactly been forgotten. But has been increasingly exploited as entertainment. The sick, distorted images of Kraemar and Sprenger — pointed hats, black cloaks, broomsticks, women's features hideously transfigured — are bought by mothers at Hallowe'en from multi-national supermarkets, while at the same time the backlash against women's economic and cultural independence is daily displayed. The phenomenon has now reached Ireland, a country where the fears of witchcraft had never taken deep hold because there never was a total acceptance of centralized authority. Is there a connection between it and the removal of the Queen of Heaven? Is there a connection between it and the daily propaganda in Ireland that the nation should give up its neutrality and join some sort of military alliance associated with the European Community? The abolition of the Virgin's titles by the Church, some might think, would be progressive, because these images of maid and mother held women back, but on the contrary. . .

Listen to Dr Connell, Archbishop of Dublin, in a radio interview on Easter Sunday, 1989, uttering as direct a piece of Catholic misogyny as one could imagine: he opposed divorce, opposed abortion, opposed artificial contraception, which, he said, made people unhappy even though they do not realize it, opposed women priests as a natural impossibility and declared his own 'unhappiness' at the current practice of employing young girls to serve at the altar. He also said that the extent of poverty in Ireland is exaggerated. Significantly, only three days earlier statistics had been published indicating that women in Ireland are the lowest-paid and in the lowest grades of job. The majority of Irish women do not work outside the home at all and, if they are married and have children, their only personal income is the state's child benefit.

The mysogyny of the *Malleus* and its influence was carried over into the new Protestant Christendom from the old Catholic dispensation.

Kraemer and Sprenger, even though they were Dominican Inquisitors hunting out not only witchcraft but also reformism and free thought in the Church, were the only orthodox Catholic authors of the Middle Ages to be taken up by the ideologues of the Reformation, starting with Luther (who himself was a witch-hunter) and flourishing within the more extreme Calvinism. In John Knox's Scotland, for example, the witch-hunts were ferocious. Calvinism was particularly hostile to the cult of the Virgin and believed strongly in Saint Paul's theory of the man as having

authority over the woman. This anti-feminist Calvinism was trans-
planted by immigrant Scots of the seventeenth century into the
north of Ireland where it now manifests itself as a form of racism
against Irish Catholic women. The *Irish Independent* of 24 March
1989 quotes a northern Irish loyalist woman as believing that
Catholics worship '. . . a giant phallus streaming with semen'.

To return to my own history, however. It was my mother (she
had broken away from her own patriarchal Judaism to marry an
Irish Catholic of the old IRA, thereby breaking *him* away from
the anti-semitic orthodoxies of his own faith) who fought like
a ferocious bitch to disentangle me and my sisters from the insidi-
ous propaganda of the nuns. She saw her four daughters being
transformed by the all-embracing liturgy and ritual of the Church
that had persecuted her ancestors. Every minute of every hour
of every day had some liturgical claim upon us. The Angelus twice
a day, the repetition of prayers and indulgences, the wearing of
scapulars, the sickly sentimentality of the holy pictures and statues
approved and sold by the Church — all of which we felt we had
to have to save our parents from the damnation of hell.

In the holidays we would spend our time shouting and crying
because our holy pictures and our relics had been taken away
by mother. She even threatened to stop us going to Mass, which
would have meant damnation for *us*! My mother had actually put
us into the convent as a way of protecting us in the event of the
Germans invading Ireland. De Valera had told the Irish-Jewish
Community that he could not undertake not to hand them over
to the Nazis and although my mother was not part of the 'Jewish
Community', — I am sure she sensed the atmosphere — there is
always a great deal of unthinking anti-semitism in Ireland.

My mother's life — and indeed our own — could have been easier
in Ireland had she become a Catholic and taken Irish citizen-
ship, but by doing that she would have had to accept the Catholic-
orientated Constitution (framed by De Valera in consultation with
the Bishops) whereby women's only guaranteed place was 'in the
home' as breeders of children. She would have had to accept the
Catholic teachings on childbirth, whereby the safety of the unbap-
tized child (as opposed to that of the mother) is paramount. She
would have had to accept the Irish law of domicile, whereby her
official home could only be where her husband dwelt. In other
words, she would have given up every individual right as a thinking
woman in order to live a docile lie. She saw the hypocritical docility
and conservatism of the majority of Irish women concealing the
deadly competitive savagery of one woman towards another in

their mutual serfdom. She therefore refused to surrender her sexuality. The voice of her refusal was the voice of that aspect of the Triple Goddess that women find so difficult to accept because men have suppressed and distorted it and waged war against it for so many centuries.

How was the Bitch-Goddess, the Great Hag, concealed from us? How did we become so conditioned that we ever believed she was evil? I would accept a Marxist analysis, that posits that whoever controls the wealth and the means of production and so on controls the gods and changes them to suit the requirements of power. The world no longer worships the Goddess because women own only one per cent of its assets, are paid five per cent of its revenue, and do two-thirds of its work — the majority of that work — not even being given the status of *work*, because it entails the servicing of men and is therefore considered a 'duty', a 'labour of love.'

I would also agree with Mary Daly, who writes in her *Gyn-Ecology* (Beacon Press, 1978), that this state of affairs was achieved by our women's myths being stolen, obliterated and re-issued in a transformed guise, to make a '. . .distorting-lens through which we can see our background.' In the case of the Greeks, for instance, whose mythology has permeated our Christian culture, the myths appear for the first time in the works of Homer and Hesiod and already they are the 're-issued version'. Homer, the princes' bard, perhaps to placate the aristocratic ladies of his audience, did show a sympathy for women's condition (Samuel Butler and Robert Graves actually suggest that this emphasis in the *Odyssey* was due to a *female* Homer). In the writings of Hesiod, the peasant poet, the cruel, petty, revengeful, jealous male gods are revealed in all their sour authority. They demand a sullen submission, like tyrannical landlords from whose power there is no escape, except by blaming those with even less power than oneself — women, the slaves of slaves.

To start with, the new myth-makers eclipsed the mother as creator. Zeus — chief god and habitual rapist — created his own children, the Jewish God created people to serve him and the Christian God created both his son and the mother of his son.

Next, women's judgement and instincts had to be discredited. If she were left alone, the Old Crone (now disguised as the Devil) would incite her to the world's destruction. In the Garden of Eden, Eve, by listening to the serpent, brings about the Fall. In one stroke that myth made women distrustful of themselves and of each other and made men feel not only distrustful of women but also thoroughly superior — right down to the present day.

There had been a transitional stage of the patriarchally-distorted myth, however. Pandora's box of all the evils was opened in dis-obedience to Zeus (who knew however that she was bound to open it and had deceitfully arranged her disobedience as a punish-ment for those mortals who had offended him). Pandora, there-fore, was 'in the service' of a God, not of the Devil. Pandora's story is a classic piece of myth-reversal. Originally her box was a honey-vase, a vessel of death and rebirth from which she (as beneficent Goddess) poured out blessings. In the patriarchal version of the tale, Zeus, in fact, tells her that the box is this vessel of blessings, but that she is not, on any account, to open it. However, he lies, humiliating her — and thus all women — through the terrible consequences of what were good intentions.

Both the Eve and Pandora myths are thus part of the psychological-warfare technique of undermining women, but they do also show, in fact, that men themselves had been psychologi-cally undermined by their inability to cope with the third aspect of the Goddess — death and rebirth, or winter and spring.

I take the Triple Goddess to be an illustration, a personifica-tion, of the threefold cycle of nature — the growth season, the harvest season, and the still season, which is preparation for another growth season. Unexpected natural calamities, such as storms, floods, earthquakes, droughts, and so on, that despite the destruction, lead to changes, discoveries and greater knowledge, were seen as disorderly fragments of the 'still season', out of place and apparently out of control. They were none the less always aspects of the wisdom of the Goddess and contained within her overall being. Also the Goddess' three aspects relate to our human condition, physically and psychically. We should not take without giving. When we die we are replaced by new, young life, which in turn must learn its history from the old life about to die.

So, it was the Old Woman, with her role as midwife, practitioner of healing, teacher of the young and burier of the dead, who both closed and opened the cycle. In order to break the cycle and con-firm their own control over it, the patriarchy had to remove all these functions from the Old Woman (and thereafter from women). It did not happen all at once, but was a gradual pushing-out of women from the social, economic, and cultural spheres.

Each phase of persecution — Augustus Caesar enforcing child-birth as a state duty upon all married women, Saint Paul forbid-ding women to speak, the papacy forbidding the Cathar women to be priests and murdering those who were, the witch-hunters torturing herbalists until they confessed to diabolism and then burning them to death, the legislators forbidding women to own property in their own right — took power and the use of skills away from women, giving them to men and to the exclusively all-male organizations, such as the church, the law, the medical profession and so on — with prime emphasis always being upon the control of women's sexuality and fertility, until men's control was almost complete over the whole functioning of society. Today men have created for themselves their own military, industrial, necrophiliac phallus-world of guns, bombs, tower blocks, prisons, leaking supertankers, nuclear plants. They evoke death, emit death, all with the rationalized arguments that they are, in fact, saving us from a devil (either a political devil or the devil of unsubdued nature) and bringing us into a better world.

'1.8 million dollars a minute is spent on global military expenditures (1987). Military defence bugets in the Third World are about seven times as large as in 1960, but for one person in two the only water available to drink is unsafe and possibly deadly.'

R.L. Sivard, *World Military and Social Expenditures 1987-88.*

I left the all-inclusive security of the Catholic Church because it condemned non-violent protest against the H-bomb, a protest with which I was involved. Priests I went to about it told me it was none of my business, that I should accept the Church's wise authority.

In Ireland we didn't have H-bombs — instead we had the voice of Ireland, the Lady Eriu (or Erinn), the Triple Goddess, calling out that she was still in chains and demanding freedom. This 'Celtic mystical nonsense' enrages her British captors: 'There are no goddesses: why must the so-called Christian Irish confuse everyone by bringing in this image of a warrior-woman calling for blood?' They denied her existence because she denigrates the ideal image of woman 'standing behind her man' that the Western patriarchy has fought so hard to instil for thousands of years. The British ruling class, proud of their tamed Britannia, will never recognize that they are waging war on the Goddess: 'There is no war! The Irish are just malingering backward criminals of low intelligence!'

The poetic tradition in Ireland had never made the Goddess completely subordinate to the God. The great warrior queens, Scatha, Macha and Maeve were rulers of land in their own right.

Even the great male warrior, Cuchullain, owed all his fighting skills to the instruction of Scatha. The British conquest and the economic mistreatment, of Ireland, meant that the voice of the wronged Goddess became more and more strident and ever-hungrier for revenge. From the beginning of the twentieth century her myth spurred the imagination of young people — men and women equally — to take action for national freedom, for the right of the people of Ireland to own Ireland.

I first heard the voice of the Lady Eriu in the mid-1970s when Miriam Daly, an Irish historian from Queen's University, Belfast, stood outside the Dublin General Post Office and denounced the sentence of death imposed by the Irish Government upon Marie and Noel Murray, anarchists. I had never heard a women be so passionate and ferocious. She urged us into action, to march and picket the Dublin jail. It was frightening and disturbing.

Later I was on another picket with Miriam, this time in the north, organized by Women Against Imperialism to support republican women in Armagh Jail. Eleven of us were arrested and three of us were subsequently put into jail ourselves. The function of Women Against Imperialism was to destroy the contemporary myth that women in the national struggle have always stood, and have to stand, behind the men. When the British Army first took the offensive in the north in 1970, it was weaponless women who came out of their houses against them, banging dustbin lids, dancing, driving them back to barracks. In fact, Irish women have always been in the forefront of resistance. The men have simply followed them up and then have taken over. Women had been betrayed in the past and were not going to be betrayed again.

The British military and politicians know this. That is why, when the republican prisoners, male and female, refused to abandon their political status in return for 'criminalization' and shortened sentences, the first mass attack against them was upon the women in Armagh Jail. If the women could be broken, then the men would follow suit. Male warders were sent in to beat up the women and sexually abuse them. Then they locked them up for three days and would not let them use the toilets. The result was the 'no-wash protest' — it was led and held together by young Mairead Farrell. I was in the jail at this time and I, too, smeared my excrement on the cell wall. In the act of doing that, alongside the other women, I was conscious that I was breaking the biggest social taboo of the patriarchy. The waste of my body, instead of being disgusting, was something to be proud of. My body, my bodily functions, my mind, all came together. I truly heard the voice of the Goddess Macha, here in Armagh, her ancient seat, from which she had been dispossessed by Christendom and where she had cursed the men of Ulster, saying that in their hardest hour they would find themselves helpless — they had forced her during childbirth to race against their horses.

While I was in jail, Miriam Daly was assassinated in her home in Belfast. In 1983 Mairead Farrell was assassinated by the SAS in Gibraltar.

Where else should the Great Hags of History meet but outside the RAF and USAF airbase in Berkshire, Britain, 1982, when it was planned to site the Cruise missiles there. Their ultimate function was to obliterate the USSR. Consequences of their function would be to obliterate Europe. To protest against the possibility of this twentiety century extermination, women came from all over the world. They came with their energies and awareness released by the recognition and breaking-open of women's *hers-tories*. As Mary Daly and Jane Caputi put it in their book, *Websters' First New Intergalactic Wickedary of the English Language* (Womens' Press, 1988):

> 'They were the long-lasting ones, survivors of the perpetual witch-craze of patriarchy whose status is determined not merely by chronological age but by Crone-logical considerations: one who . . . has dis-covered depths of Courage, Strength and Wisdom in her Self.'

Their unconscious rallying cry, from the throat of the Gaelic Triple Goddess Ana/Babd/Macha was: 'Where Hags are, will be Spells, Where Women are, will be Spells'.

The world's media applauded but Governments were appalled. They were caught unawares with no laws ready to prevent the women from camping on the common and no laws preventing them from entering the base. They were casting their spells on the British Army, who had never experienced the like. Working-class women in Belfast with dustbins, yes, young republican women smearing their cells with their excrement, yes, but not middle-class British women tying their used sanitary-towels lovingly on the fence, hailing their menstruation as a weapon of strength against war, holding mirrors up, weaving spider-webs. All the ingredients at Greenham Common proclaimed for the first time in the written annals that a matriarchal Goddess-world was extant. Money poured in from all the well-wishers who wanted this new world and women came in their millions, thanks to the well-organized network built-up since the 1960s by the international women's movements.

It was a miracle from the Goddess. Young, old, all religions and none, the marginalized and the well-to-do came — from now on it was going to be different. Women were going to show the world that life was more important than wilful destruction and death. Her sexuality, for the first time, could flourish unhindered by the control of patriarchy. There would be no male hierarchies and every womam would be committed and accountable to herself alone. Greenham is one of the most remarkable episodes in women's history, an open declaration of women's rights and that no man should subdue her and keep her from her destiny.

It was remarkable that at Greenham the military had placed their bases plumb in the middle of the most ancient religious sites in Britain. Here was the battlefield for war to end and life to begin. The actual spot for the missile-silos was the grave site of the last witch killed in Newbury. She who had danced on water and defied the Parliamentary Army, singing against them and throwing their bullets back at them when they tried to shoot her — it was only a steel sword through her temples that finally killed her.

Why does Greenham, after only seven years, seem as stale as an old crust of bread left in the bin? What has happened to those millions of women who found that they had unlimited courage, wisdom and strength to face, weaponless, the greatest armies in the world? There are still women living there, in the same conditions as when it all started, still women facing the army, being arrested, charged, going to jail, but why does it not matter any more, when a women like Sarah Hipperson — working-class, from Glasgow, aged 60, Catholic — is taken away in the middle of the night (26 October 1988) has her breasts pulled about by a police-woman and is told neither what is happening nor where she is going to go. It happens in El Salvador, but at Greenham?

Why does it not matter any more, when iron bars are deliberately thrown at women from an American Cruise convoy vehicle marked *Every Day Torture?* Why does it not matter any more, when Allison is leapt upon and savaged by military guard dogs or Katherine knocked unconscious and handcuffed on the ground or Janet pulled handcuffed from the courtroom dock and put into solitary confinement in the psychiatric wing of a jail because she refused to be examined by a male doctor? I will explain why as simply as I can.

First come Parliament and the military. New laws were hurriedly brought in to criminalize the women at the Peace Camp and to give new powers to the Ministry of Defence police.

Second, there was unlimited money alloted to subsidize these powers. No questions were asked as to how the powers were enforced — such as the fact that 270 women were strip-searched at Greenham over a period of two years.

Third, there was an abuse of due process of law and police procedure in the interests of government policy.

Fourth, there was unlimited money available for two-pronged government propaganda, the first prong was a vicious smear campaign intented to turn public opinion against the women at Greenham. The second prong was a policy of media silence on Greenham, making the women's actions and the official abuses against them invisible.

The patriarchy had finally got its act together and systematically attempted to destroy the Goddess at Greenham in the old way, which was to set women against women as in the days of Kraemer and Sprenger. The patriarchy (of the left as well as of the right) persuaded women journalists who had previously supported Greenham women that Greenham was a non-event and that 'gushing' stories about it were now old news. Their confidence undermined, these media women turned against the Greenham women, attacking them, ridiculing them, undermining *their* confidence and new-found wisdom: '. . . it was all a lovely dream, but we're grown up now, and that is not how you change the real world! The women, we might concede, have had something to do with the INF agreement and getting rid of the Cruise, but now that the leaders of world governments, capitalist and communist, are coming to their senses, leave it to your natural leaders, go home and do useful work'.

The Old Hag, however, still screamed out, with a new louder voice: 'Where's the proof? We don't believe it. We will not give up our non-violent direct action until all the weapons of the world are abolished and all the money spent on them is given to the women of the world. We will not be used as partisans in the men-only club of the superpowers. We give no allegiance to our own military governments or to anyone else's. We are partisans of the world and of the women of the world. Women still do two-thirds of the world's work. They are starving and robbed. Welfare not warfare. Women count, count women's work'.

This was viewed as rabble-rousing extremism, that this was neither the time nor the place for such thought and this Hag's voice was no voice for the feminist network. The feminist network, bribed by the sweetmeats of textbooks, university departments,

women's studies, cultural artefacts and festivals (all laid on to chain
her up and tame her into abstract ritual), turned into vicious
painted birds when they heard the persistence and consistency
of the cry. They huddled back inside the security of the patriarchy to build their reassuring nests.

'Greenham's been betrayed', they wailed. 'It's been taken over
by the "black mafia" who have bewitched the women at Yellow
Gate'. They called themselves Greenham Women Everywhere
because most of them were no longer at Greenham. They had
abandoned the harvest before it had ripened, but kept on returning saying that they really hadn't left, but, in any case, the harvest
was theirs and they had to be the ones to reap it.

The movement was now split into two polarized camps, Greenham Women Everywhere and the women at Yellow Gate who live
outside the main gate of the airbase and refuse to budge.

In practical terms, Yellow Gate women held fast to the uncompromising autonomy of the original intention — women-only and
non-aligned protest. They were helped by another autonomous
women's group, the King's Cross Collective, that did not belong
to the 'network', but consisted of black women, Asian women,
prostitutes, all highly organized, declaring that women can never
reclaim a fair share of the world until Western middle-class women
listen to and work as equals with the huge majority of women
from the rest of the world. It might appear that peace groups,
church groups and Greenham Women Everywhere had been calling for this same thing all the time, but, if one looks closer at
their structures and at their spokespeople, it becomes clear that
they speak all the time *on behalf* of those robbed, thus holding
power on behalf of clients, and thereby breeding the corruption
of paternalism.

These latter feminists stopped all money and goods going to
Yellow Gate, mounted an extraordinary campaign of hatred against
them in the press, and — as part of a festival called something
like 'All Women One World' — carried out a *ritual march* to expel
(unsuccessfully) their Yellow Gate sisters.

In the beginning at Greenham, because women had not felt the
immediate power of the patriarchy they thought it was going to
be easy, but, as time went on, they realized that by consistently
defying the patriarchy and consistently going to jail, they would,
in the end, be altogether excluded by the patriarchy, and becoming permanent criminals and outcasts. History shows, though, that
the Hag, under the patriarchy, *must* be a criminal outcast and that
the object of patriarchy has always been to get women themselves

to cast her out from among their number.

We can sing with Caesarina Kona Makhoere the songs that she sang at Greenham and had earlier sung when she served six years in a South African jail for resisting apartheid.

It does not matter
If you should jail us
For we are free and kept alive by hope,
The struggle's hard
But victory will
Return the lands to our hands.

We shall not give up the fight
We have only started

We can listen to Allison, 18 years old, who lives at Yellow Gate:

Women have screamed:
'NO MORE! WE WILL NOT BE PARTY TO YOUR MALE SYSTEM, WE WILL NOT PLAY YOUR WAR GAMES. WE WILL NOT DIE FOR YOU!'
And the whole world listened, and the whole world changed, and life went on ...'

The Crone calls and we have three choices: one, to despise and ignore it; two, to listen, recognize and misrepresent the call as a mere voice out of the past, fit only for aesthetic enjoyment or academic research; or three, to listen, to recognize and to act.

# 4
# The Testament of Rhiannon
## Caitlín Matthews

One of the prime tasks of the priestess is to distinguish
between inner and outer reality. The danger of one reality
overlapping another is that the priestess may identify with
the archetype in a personal way. The following is an account
of such a superimposition and the problems of possible delu-
sion. My mediation of Rhiannon is best prefaced by R.J.
Stewart's words from his perceptive study *Advanced Magical Arts* (Element Books, 1988):

> 'True mediation is always accompanied by a disturbing echo of
> undeniable deep personal insight; it often indicates areas of weak-
> ness that require inner attention and development of rebalance.
> In this role alone, work such as mediation of advanced forms of
> consciousness or god- and goddess-forms is of immense value to
> us, *though its resulting personal insight is only one of many side-effects
> and not a major aim*'.

I hope I have shown that this statement is true to the core.
Just because one may reverberate to an archetypal note does
not mean that one is unable to make one's own music.
Indeed, that piercing tone becomes the very base chord about
which one's own song is woven

Caitlín Matthews *has been influenced by the Goddess since her early teens when she began her lifelong quest for the Divine Feminine. She has worked widely within the British Mystery Tradition as a shamanka, ritualist, and priestess of Rhiannon: roles that she combines with what has been described as 'spiritual promiscuity'. However, she takes the Goddess where she is to be found. Caitlín is primarily concerned with the practical applications of ancient wisdom from the widest possible field, including the musical, poetic and story-telling traditions. She is the author of 15 books, including a two-volume history of the Western esoteric tradition which was co-written with her husband, John Matthews, her partner in the esoteric and Arthurian fields. Together they have designed* The Arthurian Tarot *(Aquarian Press, 1990), which draws upon the Celtic and otherworldly realms for its inspiration. She has written a two-volume study of* The Mabinogion, *the British mythological cycle as well as two other books on the Goddess:* The Elements of the Goddess *(Element Books, 1989) and* Sophia, Goddess of Wisdom *(Unwin Hyman, 1990). Caitlín has lectured widely in Britain, Europe and America. She has one son and lives in London.*

# The Testament of Rhiannon

Dream Diary, 30 September 1988

Last night I dreamed of Gwawl again . . . His head streamed
with lightning strands of long black hair. His eyes had the pupil-
flooded opacity of the possessed, of the maniac. He wore a livid
yellow jacket, but was otherwise dressed in solid black that was
deeper than shadow.
I was in a car with my lecture-tour team, with my husband and
son. Gwawl erupted into the car at one of the stops, forcing us
to go along with him by no other coercion than that of his own
dark presence, and we all sat, humouring him, wildly racking our
brains as to how to subvert his dangerous plans without infring-
ing our safety. I was especially concerned for my son, for I knew,
from past experience how dangerous Gwawl could be.

There was no conclusion or escape from this dream other than
waking. The ominous brooding intensity of the dream remained
with me throughout the day until the evening when a poem arose
fully-fledged (as poems rarely come) as I started the washing up.
It came with such purgative force that it was more like being violently ill than being creative. Indeed, I had to sit on the threshold
of the kitchen door to write it, sitting 'neither within or without'.
Neverthess, the poem (on page 104) was a healing for me. I was
able to let go of a burden I had been carrying unconsciously for
about seven years.

The dream and the answering poem arose directly from the myth
of Rhiannon, a British Goddess with whom I have been in an intimate and unusual relationship with for many years.

I am not Rhiannon and Rhiannon is not me, yet sometimes she
is superimposed upon my life, making it both more extraordinary as well as creating special responsibilities that seem to plunge
me into the supra-mundane.

My search for Rhiannon began about 22 years ago. This chapter is a record of that search, of my relationship with an archetype that has uncovered areas of my psyche which would have
remained unknown to me otherwise. It is also a search for myself.

My childhood and adolescence very naturally led me into the
field of esoteric knowledge, for my aptitude was for the imaginal
and the sacred. My inner world led me to find and train with
those who could be my authoritative guides. These were hard to
find and the few teachers who were experienced enough have truly
been companions rather than gurus.

Like many young women who approach esoteric work for the

first time, I was full of false impression, enamoured with the exercise of power and overconfident about my own self-control. This time of life was once utilized to the full in primal socieites of our ancestral past. The young adolescent, male or female, was a tremendously powerful channel of mediation: clear, pure, fiercely truthful and steady as a flame. Of course, such traditional mediation was carried out under the supervision of experienced elders who ensured that the maximum potential of the adolescent was used with the least risk. Because it was a revered skill, essential to the life of the tribe, there was a deep tradition underlyng and supporting it.

My childhood had been one of intense joy and misery because I would experience numens, spirits, beings who would throng my play and my story-telling in uncanny and inexplicable ways. It is no fault of my parents that the insights and feelings which would well up in me were neither recognized nor understood, for they were not raised in a tradition of esoteric perception. Nevertheless, I spent a lot of time being very angry and frustrated when I was not imagining or remembering scenes of exciting rituals.

In a society where rites of passage are administered, where the gods and the other world are accepted and loved presences, I might have found balanced training and empathy from my relatives and friends, but in the Fifties and Sixties, there were no such opportunities. I grew up, as many children currently do, wondering if I was mad. I couldn't help feeling exotic and peculiar with the unbidden access I had to inner worlds feeding me with insights and knowledge that came from outside my own mundane experience. The account of what follows might never have happened if I had had adequate guidance and tuition in my youth. I know also that I must be one of many who have encountered experiences for which there is no provision in modern society.

Even within the Western tradition, in which I trained, there are still, sadly, great areas of knowledge virtually unexplored by experienced teachers. My generation has been one that has had to find out for itself and make do. I have made a particular study of the Celtic tradition, trying to find ways of re-animating these mysteries that are appropriate to our time and I must admit that, although I have been given great gifts from the ancestral and otherworldly levels of that tradition, I have had to question and test everything before accepting it.

When I happened upon that neglected work of British mythology *The Mabinogion* (edited and translated by Jeffrey Gantz, Penguin, 1976) in the school library, I little knew what I had

discovered. These curious, magical tales formed my early cosmol-
ogy and mythic furniture, but it was chiefly in the tales of Pwyll,
Prince of Dyfed, and Manawyddan, Son of Llyr, in which the story
of Rhiannon is told, that I discovered the archetype of my
priestessly mediation. A précis of that story follows.

Rhiannon was the daughter of the King of the Underworld. She
had been betrothed to Gwawl, a great warrior of her father's kingdom, but she did not care for him. Her father judged that she
might only ascend to the Earth, if she married there, lay with a
mortal man and bore a child to him — only then could she avoid
her contract with Gwawl.

Rhiannon, therefore, set out for the mound of Arberth, one of
the mighty gates of the Underworld. The kings of Dyfed had a
tradition that whoever stood upon this hill would either see a
great wonder or receive many blows. Pwyll was king at this time
and, as he sat in contemplation upon the mound, he saw a veiled
woman in a golden gown riding along the road on a white horse.

Three times he dispatched a man after her to detain her, but,
although the men used their swiftest horses, none could over-
take her. At length, Pwyll himself mounted up and pursued her.
The woman went at a gentle, even pace, but he couldn't shorten
the distance between them, no matter how fast he rode, and so,
he called out to her to stop.

She unveiled her face and Pwyll was stunned by her beauty. She
told him that she had been seeking him to invite him to come
to her father's house in a year and a day when she would prepare
a feast against his coming.

The year passed and Pwyll rode to the court of the Lord of the
Underworld. Halfway through the celebrations, just before Pwyll
should have taken Rhiannon to his bed as wife, a noble guest
appeared. He wished to beg a favour. Pwyll, in expansive mood,
asked him to demand whatever he wished, if it lay in his power
to grant it. Rhiannon was angry for the noble youth was none
other than Gwawl, her former suitor.

Gwawl asked for the bride Pwyll was about to bed and for the
feast. Pwyll did not know what to say, but Rhiannon advised him,
'Take this bag and keep it well. I shall be given to Gwawl a year
from today, but the feast is not yours to give since I prepared it
and I give it for my guests and household. Come back in a year
and a day and, garbed as a beggar, ask simply for food and drink
to fill the bag. This bag of mine is bottomless. When Gwawl com-
plains, say that it will never be full 'til a man of noble blood presses
down the food in the bag with his own two feet and says, "enough

has been put into this bag". Only by doing this can you win me back'.

A year and a day passed. Pwyll returned to the Underworld in order to attend Rhiannon's wedding feast. There sat Gwawl in his own place between her and her father. Pwyll entered the hall boldly, dressed as a beggar, and made his request as instructed.

Pwyll's request for food was soon granted, but the bag looked as though it would eat up the whole banquet. 'Will it never be full?' asked Gwawl. 'Noble Lord, only if a man of noble birth puts both feet into the bag and declares, "Enough has been put into this bag", only then will it be satisfied.

Gwawl did just this, but no sooner had he entered the bag than Pwyll pulled it over his head and knotted it tightly, calling upon his men to aid him. Each of his men struck the bag one blow (a game that was subsequently called 'Badger in the Bag'). Gwawl begged for mercy, but Pwyll, at Rhiannon's behest, made Gwawl promise to recompense all the beggars and musicians at the feast and never seek revenge for what had been done to him. So it was that Pwyll won Rhiannon and returned with her to Dyfed.

In the third year of their marriage, the people of Dyfed began to complain of Rhiannon, since she was childless. Pwyll counselled patience and, soon enough, Rhiannon gave birth to a boy on May Eve.

Attending her confinement were six women, who were to watch over her, but they fell asleep on that most magical of nights. When they awoke, they found Rhiannon's baby boy was gone. Lest suspicion fall upon them, they killed some puppies and smeared Rhiannon's face and hands with their blood and scattered the bones about her as though she had eaten her own child. Then Rhiannon woke, asking for her son, but the women accused her of unnaturally killing and eating the child. Rhiannon saw that they were concealing something through fear and promised to support them, but they held to their story.

Pwyll's counsellors tried to persuade him to put her away, but he was adamant that she remain his wife. Since Rhiannon could not persuade the women to change their story, she accepted the punishment that the druids and wise men set for her: that she should wait at the mounting block for seven years and tell every stranger her story, offering to carry them into the hall on her own back.

Meanwhile, in the realm of Gwent Is Coed, its king, Teyrnon Twrf Lliant was having difficulties. Every May Eve, his white mare foaled, but every year the colts mysteriously vanished. This year, he resolved to stay up and see what happened.

At the stroke of midnight, the mare foaled and, at the same time, a great arm came through the window and seized it. Teyrnon hacked at it with his sword, severing the clawed hand. From outside came a terrible noise and he rushed out to find out what was happening. He saw nothing, however, and returned to the stable, only to find that a child in rich swaddling clothes lay near the colt. He took the chid to his wife and they decided to pretend that she had been pregnant and had had the boy that very night. They called him Gwri Gwallt Euryn — Gwri of the Golden Hair.

He grew up rapidly. At the age of two he was as big as a six-year-old boy and by the age four he was already bribing the grooms to let him water the horses. Teyrnon's wife thought it was a good idea for the colt that was born the same night as Gwri to be given to the boy to have as his very own.

Teyrnon heard the strange story of Rhiannon's punishment and his heart was moved. The more he looked at Gwri, the more clearly he saw the likeness between the boy and Pwyll, King of Dyfed. He and his wife decided to take the boy home to his parents.

As they reached the court of Arberth, Rhiannon called to them saying, 'Go no further, let me bear each of you into the hall. This is my punishment for killing and eating my own son'. Neither Teyrnon nor Gwri would allow her to do so. Pwyll greeted them and soon Teyrnon's strange story was told. Said Teyrnon to Rhiannon, 'Lady, I restore your son to you', Rhiannon replied, 'If he is truly so, then all my troubles are ended'. 'Rightly do you speak, Queen of Dyfed', said Pwyll's counsellor, Pendaran, 'You have named your son Pryderi' (*Pryder* means anxiety or trouble). 'Should he not be called by his own name?' asked Rhiannon. 'No, it is better that his mother's first words on hearing of his joyous restoration should suffice', said Pwyll.

Time passed and Pryderi grew up. After his father's death, he succeeded to the princedom of Dyfed. He became friends with Manawyddan ap Llyr, the brother of Bran the Blessed. Manawyddan married Rhiannon.

One day, Pryderi, his wife Cigfa and his mother and her husband went up to the mound of Arberth. When they came down, the country had been laid under enchantment and the four of them had to support themselves for several years, during which time they traded in enamelled saddles, shields and shoes, which they were able to do because of Manawyddan's skill.

On their return to Dyfed, they encountered a white boar, which

Pryderi chased into a mysterious castle. Inside the castle was a fountain over which a golden bowl hung. Pryderi took hold of the marvellous bowl but was unable to let go of it again — both his hands and feet were stuck fast. When Manawyddan returned home alone, Rhiannon berated him and she went herself to find him. She also stuck fast to the bowl and then the castle disappeared.

Manawyddan and Cigfa strove to support themselves by sowing crops, but although Manawyddan seeded three fields with wheat, two fields were destroyed by the next day. He kept watch on the third night and caught a pregnant mouse that ran slower than her fellows. He set up a miniature gallows on the Mound of Arberth to hang the creature and was accosted three times by a man who offered to buy the mouse for successively higher sums. Manawyddan then named his price — the freedom of Rhiannon and Pryderi and the removal of the enchantments upon Dyfed.

The stranger turned out to be Llwyd, the cousin of Gwawl, who had abducted Rhiannon and her son in revenge for the blows suffered by Gwawl. When he released Rhiannon and Pryderi he revealed that Rhiannon had had to wear the hay collars of the asses after they had finished their day's work about her own neck, while Pryderi had had to wear the knockers of the gate about his neck. They were restored to the kingdom of Dyfed and Manawyddan made Llwyd swear never to take revenge again before he lets the mouse go. (For commentaries and insights on *The Mabinogion*, see Caitlín Matthews' books *Mabon and the Mysteries of Britain*, (Arkana, 1978) and *Arthur and the Sovereignty of Britain: King and Goddess in the Mabinogion* (Arkana, 1989).

This story of Rhiannon has always struck home to me, resonating strongly with my own personality and make-up. It is a story that I have had to assimilate in terms of my own experience. In order to unfold my tale, it is necessary to probe into painful areas of my life. I do not write this with pride — for I know what I am and how hard it has been to admit even this much — but, rather, that other women may read and see that, even in the most uncompromising of circumstances, the most intractable mythic entanglements do have a resolution.

As I have said, our modern society does not initiate young men and women into the spiritual nature of sexuality, although they both seek and expect this teaching unconsciously. I was no exception. This search for the completion of oneself in another is rooted in an esoteric pattern of the priestess–priest relationship and is possibly experienced in one or many incarnations. The perfect *hieros gamos* was what I sought — a relationship that could be consummated on the physical, psychic and spiritual levels.

When I met F. it was on the rebound from my first lover. F. was Welsh and bore a name that was both his honour and his curse. He was an outcast from paradise, a natural elemental character in whose line ran the blood of Irish tinkers. He was also an alcoholic, as many people of this elemental kind are — it is their mantle from the hard scrutiny of the world. We formed an unlikely pair, bonded only by our common esoteric quest for roots and meaning. It was by no means 'love at first sight' nor incarnational recognition, though this latter may have played a part. I was partially drawn to F. because he believed in the gods — not in a vague, psychoanalytical way, but in actuality.

Together we joined a Gardnerian coven — in those days the most appropriate and almost the only mode of spiritual expression. It was not a great success, from my point of view. I felt that the simply rituals, based on Celtic mythology that I had once performed alone in the woods near my home when I was a teenager, were more valid than anything on offer here. However, I stuck it out for six months or so before backing out with my integrity mostly intact.

Before initiation it is usual to choose a magical name. Rhiannon seemed the most appropriate for me. No one seemed to think this presumptuous, although other Goddess names — those particularly used within that coven — were discountenanced as unsuitable for mortal women. I certain took it with the same reverence with which Spanish mothers name their children Jesus or Mary, but I was also too inexperienced to realize that every name has its responsibility for there is an art in choosing names. I certainly did not take the name with any intention of wallowing in the myth, although some readers may judge this to have been the case. Indeed, much of the unfolding pattern has remained totally hidden from my consciousness and I have only been able to reconstruct it in hindsight.

It was during this period that I had an important dream that confirmed my vocation. The priest and priestess of my coven appeared to me as we were all in the circle at a meeting. They appeared numinously, larger, greater, more powerful and I had no doubt that godly archetypes inhabited their forms. With the ancestral power of primal parents they gave me a silver bracelet. This was shown to me in great detail, including its inscriptions which read:

Regina

P  P  P
R  R  R
O  O  O
S  D  S
P  I  E
E  G  R
R  A  P
   L  I
   I  N
   A  A

FILIAT

This piece of dog-Latin must have come from some crevice of consciousness, since I had never learned the language of scholars. Framed by Queen and Daughter, the inscription reads 'Prosper, Bountiful Prosperpine' (Prosperpine is Latin for Persephone). Persephone, the Greek Queen of the Underworld, fulfilled the same archetype as Rhiannon.

The significance of the dream was immediately obvious to me. Such bracelets are only presented to priestesses who are to start their own circle. There was no question of this happening at the time, so I was puzzled. Before I was able to follow the advice of the bracelet, or indeed be worthy of it, I had first to enter the Underworld. Had I been more percipient and experienced, I might have been warned, for when the archetype manifests in one's dreams it is only a prelude to its appearing more mundanely.

My marriage to F. soon reached a point of ultimate conflict. Due to the worries and stresses of the relationship, my physical condition deteriorated. Hovering on the edge of colitis and with F. increasingly dependent on me, I had to leave drama school just before the end of my training. This period was my own enactment of the renunciation and burden-bearing part of life that in the myth is marked by Rhiannon's decision to become a mortal. To leave what was a most fulfilling existence for an uncertain life with an alcoholic was my own decision, to some extent. At the time I felt that it was my duty to support this weak man and bring him to wholeness.

In order to bring healing, however, one must be whole oneself. I had left the coven because it did not fulfil my spiritual needs, but I now needed the support and nourishment of a spirituality big enough to help me in my appointed task. I attempted to enter the Catholic Church, in which I had been interested for many years, and experienced an immediate feeling of homecoming, although, in fact, F.'s previous marriage was an insuperable impediment to my being accepted at that time.

Strangely I had no sense of incongruity in passing from coven to Church — indeed, for me, the whole the Western Tradition is a seamless garment in which I feel totally at home. I knew then, as, indeed, I still affirm, that spiritual syncretism was my way. Indeed, I am aware that every step of my spiritual path has been a recapitulation of dedication made in other lives, in many faiths. I did not feel obliged to give up any of my former beliefs since my response to the Church was based on mystical not fundamental awareness.

I was certainly very grateful for the spiritual support that was available to me, for I was becoming increasingly more isolated. To my friends, I showed nothing of the anguish I experienced. Indeed, I was such a good actress, that it wasn't until F. and I separated that anyone realized anything was wrong. My physical condition deteriorated, I lost two stone in weight and was totally exhausted most of the time. F.'s dependence on me was vampire-like — he wouldn't allow me to go anywhere other than to work, church or the shops. During this dark time, I still prayed to the Mother to help me, though with decreasing confidence as things worsened.

On one occasion, when F. had disappeared on one of his drinking bouts, I returned to my old drama school where my fellow students were in their final term. It was their end of term show, their great debut, in which I should have shared. Afterwards, I went round to meet them. Their welcome was unconditional. The great embrace of the theatre went round my shoulders, but it only emphasized my misery. Inevitably, they asked me about my new life. Inevitably, I told them what I could not tell anyone else: my own wretched circumstances, the pettiness and occasional violence, the cheating and pilfering from my purse that I endured. Their sympathy was genuine, but I began to feel like a body at a wake. I ran home, crying, full of bitterness. I had begun to tell the story about myself, against myself.

I was truly working out the Rhiannon/Persephone archetype with a vengence. Do we make our own circumstances? Esoteric philosophy says we do, that we are not puny pawns of the gods moved at random over the board. However, I had unconsciously fallen into that most deadly of esoteric traps — a mythic tape-loop. Having assumed Rhiannon as my magical name, I had tuned myself to the wavelength, but instead of tuning myself in to Rhiannon's resourcefulness and patience, I had tuned myself in to the lower octave of the myth and become a victim of it.

Tibetan Buddhism recognizes this condition as being trapped in a karmic chain reaction that is sometimes activated when the individual starts any form of improperly-supervised esoteric training. As Tsultrim Allione puts in in *Women of Wisdom* (Routledge & Kegan Paul, 1984), 'We end up with a whole fantasy world centred around the ego. A story-line develops . . . and one thing leads to another'.

My state of mind was frightening. I had been forbidden to write, sing, make music or meditate by F. who, jealous of every minute of my own recreation, dragged me into the living room to watch *Match of the Day* or some puerile light entertainment programme whenever I sought refuge in the bedroom. I was truly in the Underworld, powerless to get out. Indeed, had it not been for my growing friendship with my second husband, John, I might still have been with F., working out some ghastly karma, with extreme patience until I died of it. All tunnels, though, have light at the end of them and so did mine.

It still saddens me when I think of women trapped in loveless, masochistic relationships because they are financially or emotionally dependent on or depended upon by their men or who have children, which often makes separation impossible.

One night I came home from work and F. was lying in his chair in front of the TV as usual, having given up going to work (I had become the sole earner in the household). He suddenly said to me: 'I think we'll move to Essex and grow cabbages. Then you can have four children and give up work'. This ultimatum, uttered in a tone of Celtic camaraderie, did not have the effect he obviously hoped it would.

Involuntarily, my body bore me to the bedroom and I found myself pulling down the suitcase from the top of the wardrobe in the time-honoured gesture of spouses who leave home. Immediately F. was on his knees, begging me to reconsider. He followed me on his knees all the way to the telephone kiosk at the end of the road, using every artifice, piling on the guilt, wheedling like a beggar and weeping. I did not give in, though, knowing that my very sanity and physical health were at stake, and that I must walk out of this parasitic relationship. I picked up the phone and called John, asking him to meet me. Then shaking off the clinging F. I got into a taxi. I was out of the physical relationship and on my way out of the Underworld, but I wasn't totally out yet.

John and I very romantically ran away together. You will note that I initiated my own abduction, but, like the myth, loitered

by the roadside in true Rhiannon-like fashion. The trauma of separation, the change of environment and the sheer relief of being
able to do normal things again without making excuses was confusing initially. Just as Rhiannon was not considered an acceptable bride for Pwyll because she was of alien stock, so I seemed
to be haunted by the Underworld part of my life. My attempts
to make a new life, a new home and relationship were continually dogged by F. who made such embarrassing scenes at work
that my employers threatened to give him my address in order
to get rid of him! Like Rhiannon faced by her unjust punishment, I accepted that I might have to make another descent into
hell.

Eventually divorce proceedings were instituted, but the pain and
guilt returned in a physical form, that of colitis. Like many people who contract this condition, I was conscientious to the point
of self-sacrifice at work. As my department suffered more and more
cuts and an increasing turn-over of staff, I grew less and less able
to cope at work and kept breaking down. I had become an embar-
rassment to my employers. One morning I came in and found
that I just could not go on. I fled to the staff entrance and sat
down on the threshold, weeping.

Then, a wonderful thing happened. It was 9.30 and through that
door came the usual slow trickle of latecomers. Like the people
who passed by the 'man who fell among thieves', they all point-
edly ignored my presence. Not one stopped to ask why I wept
or sought to comfort me. I could not have articulated my grief
in any case, but it seemed that they were entering the building
upon my back. I suddenly saw — so clear that it hurt my inner
vision — Rhiannon herself. I saw her at the mounting block, stopping all those entering the hall and repeating her supposed crime
to each, offering her back that she might carry them. In the depths
of my misery and pain, she had come to help me. The great glad
tears fell from me and my healing began from that time.

The poetic therapy by which I began to understand my inner
nature and hers began in a long sequence that was written over
the course of the year 1977 entitled *The Search for Rhiannon* (Hunting Raven Press, 1980). The sequence was written nearly always
at twilight while I was travelling by train to visit a special friend
who enabled my escape from the Underworld and patiently
listened to the bizarre and seemingly unconnected metaphors and
images that were thrown up in the book.

The way back from the Underworld has been arduous. It was
not until a few years back that I realized the full implications of

the Rhiannon myth in my life. John's own guiding archetype was related to that of the innocent youth who sees into the heart of things. This archetype was a mirror of the one whose name F. bore. However, John had gone in and delivered me from the Underworld, just as Pwyll had done. I also recalled that F.'s totemic beast had always been the badger. In the myth, Gwawl is captured in the magic bag and has to submit to being the victim of the game 'Badger in the Bag'. I had blindly staggered into the full significance of my recent troubles.

I dare say that I might have reached this point quicker by means of psychoanalysis, but 'there is nothing so well learned as the lesson one beats upon one's own back'. This image seems particularly appropriate since the mound at Arberth, whereon Pwyll sits, has two qualities: one either sees a wonder or else receives blows. This lies at the mythic core of Rhiannon's story and has certainly been borne out in my own life — it is either all or nothing.

John and I have gone on together to write numerous books outlining aspects of the Celto/Arthurian Tradition and, after a more formal esoteric training, we have given tuition in the magical and mythical corollaries of that Tradition. We have worked as magical as well as marital partners. I hope he has forgiven me for having made him run away with me and that he finds the patience to bear my sometimes surprising bouts of speed as I gear into another myth.

I thought the myth had let me go, but I was wrong. In December 1985 we gave a weekend course on the Four Branches of *The Mabinogion*, with particular reference to the releasing of Mabon. This innocent boy, lost from before time began, was stolen from 'between his mother and the wall' when he was three nights old. His myth was that of Pryderi and that of his mother, Modron, was identical to that of Rhiannon.

It was a magical as much as an academic weekend. A ritual to release Mabon from his time-bound imprisonment was enacted by the 60 course-members. Three days later, our son was conceived. As someone later remarked sagely, 'Well, if you work with the archetype, you must expect it to manifest!' The day of conception was the Gaulish goddess Epona's day, 18 December, on which, in the Roman world, all horses, mules and donkeys were released from their burdens and allowed to graze freely: Epona was another counterpart for the archetype of Rhiannon.

If you have been following the mythical overlay, you may be wondering whether I am fearful of a similar fate overcoming my child as befell Rhiannon's. I can say, though, that he is the appeasement of such anxieties, and that, while he may cause me no end of trouble before he grows up, he is a normal little boy, not a superhero. I am determined that no such archetypal overlay will affect him. He will have his own story to work out when the time comes.

Motherhood tenderizes the heart tremendously but also toughens it up. I remember, after Emrys' birth, weeping over the news of wars and disasters, when once I would have stoically ignored the details. I discovered access to marshalled defences within me, a real warrior woman, who would have physically torn apart any person harming a child, but, when the hormones settled down again, I returned to being my normal self. Perhaps motherhood, though, was another point of connection with the mythic overlay?

We kid ourselves that we are whole and sorted out when, in reality, we are wandering around with all sorts of wounds that are in need of healing. Late in 1987, I became increasingly aware that all was not well with me. There I was, teaching, acting as a priestess, guiding others when I actually needed to be on the receiving end of these functions myself. I then felt a terrible hollowness and reluctance to teach others because I felt that I was being a hypocrite.

The root cause of this hollowness was an unacknowledged trauma. In 1979, my first book — to have been a large, illustrated guide to the Goddess — was cancelled by my publisher just prior to printing. This terrible experience was a major blow to my professional pride but, more radically, blocked an important channel of spiritual support. I felt as though I had miscarried. I had, in effect, lost a 'child'. All writers will attest that the 'children' of the pen — books — are their offspring quite as much as children born of the womb.

Up until that point, I had had a deeply fulfilling relationship with the Goddess, particularly with her wisdom aspects. After the book's failure, I encountered a kind of dark night of the soul. It felt like the kind of estrangement that one experiences with a close friend, caused by some insignificant trifle, but that lingers on and on. The experience had rendered me virtually dumb as it seemed that I could neither speak nor write about the Goddess subsequently with any degree of involvement.

I am grateful to V., a fellow priestess, who invited me to a ritual of the Fellowship of Isis at her temple. (For more information on the Fellowship of Isis, write to Clonegal Castle, Enniscorthy, Eire.) During this simply ceremony, in which the energies of Hathor and Jupiter were raised, I experienced a most extraordinary lightening of consciousness (this ritual is in *Urania: Cermonial Magic of the Goddess*, Olivia Robertson, Cesara Publications, available from Clonegal Castle). It was as though all the trauma of my Goddess book had been lifted from my shoulders and I could commune with my Mother again. Another burden rolled off.

My gratitude knew no bounds as I had found my way again in the twisted forest of life. I felt that I had to make a pilgrimage to Ireland and there formally take on the role of Priestess of Rhiannon. Although I had been a member of the Fellowship of Isis for a long while, I had never been to its headquarters. Olivia Robertson received me with considerable warmth and further helped me understand my role by taking me through a regression (not normally a procedure I would welcome). She helped me get to the roots of the Rhiannon archetype and see why and how I had replayed the myth in many other lives apart from this one.

I was ordained by Olivia as Priestess of Rhiannon, fully understanding the forces for which I must now be responsible in my spiritual life and the consequences of priestly mediation. Thankfully, speaking and writing about the Goddess is once again a great joy.

It was not until the dream about Gwawl that starts this chapter that I realized that I had not done the most important thing in healing my life — I had not forgiven F. As any woman will know, the resentments, self-justifications and guilt that surround a relationship's breakdown are far-reaching. Scenes from one's recent life are replayed over and over in a merciless tape-loop before one's inner eyes. I had thought myself beyond the pain of that time, but the dream brought it all back. I had to be rid of it.

At the basis of the problem was the conflict of the embattled archetypes of Rhiannon and Pryderi. Her release from the Underworld of her father's realm was dependent upon her mating with a mortal man, Pryderi being the result of that union — he was the price of her mortality. Pryderi should have been the son of Rhiannon and Gwawl, to whom her father had betrothed her. In the myth it was Gwawl or his agents who stole the child, attempting to subvert him to the Underworld, as he had not been successful in restraining Rhiannon. I needed to affirm my own mortality by accepting the incarnation I was now in, to be responsible for my own mistakes and to make restitution and forgiveness where possible to those I had hurt.

The ritual healing and forgiveness were quite simple. I attuned to Rhiannon, seeing her in her aspect as Bearer of Burdens and Teller of the Tale, standing patiently at the mounting block. Then,

I merged with her, but, this time the next person to enter the hall was F. I accosted him with my story, just as Rhiannon does in the myth, only this time the story was my own and his. I rehearsed the sorry tale again, sparing no particulars, re-living the pain. Then I said, 'Although we have suffered this and this, although that and that happened between us, in the name of Rhiannon I knowingly release you from all bonds. I fully forgive you, through Her mediation. I consciously lay down my burden and I ask your forgiveness'.

I left the mounting block a free woman. I had acknowledged that the fear, credulity and inexperience were my burdens. The endurance, patience and compassion I received in exchange were Hers.

I do not say that anything recorded here makes me any different to other women. I do not feel, or consider myself to be special, or apart in any way. Many other women and men experience Rhiannon in ways similar or different to my own — there are many mediators, many priests and priestesses. Nor have I come to the end of my exploration of Rhiannon as I still await the realization engraved on the bracelet in my dream, not knowing what form that will take, but conscious that the Queen of the Underworld is married to Plutos, whose name means wealth. Like him, Persephone is the Queen of Riches, the ancestral guardian of inner wisdom and creativity. The capacious, bottomless bag that Rhiannon gives to Pwyll, is a token of the depth of fulfilment we can find in our own lives. Indeed, some part of that experience is coming clear as I explore further aspects of the Divine Feminine, especially that of the Goddess of the Land, the Goddess of Sovereignty. Priestess of Rhiannon I may be, but I am not a one-Goddess woman, for she has many faces, many voices.

The art of mediation is about being able to identify with the gods and mediate their qualities, but it is not a spiritual discipline that is really understood in the West, where it is considered to be the province of the saintly mystic. However, one does not identify one's ego with the deity. Rather, everything of oneself is stripped away for the period of mediation, so that one becomes a channel. It is an art that should be taught carefully (see pages 118-21 and 37-39) in my books *The Elements of the Goddess* (Element, 1989) and *The Western Way: The Hermetic Tradition* (Arkana, 1986, with John Matthews) respectively. Similar techniques are taught in Tibetan Buddhism.

I do not feel that I have become Rhiannon — I have seen too

many friends and acquaintances go the way of possession by an archetype. These charming, fey individuals who suddenly announce, 'By the way, I'm no longer to be called Linda Smith but Morgan le Fay' are, I fear, storing up troubles for themselves. It is one thing to take a magical name and use it that way, but it is another to assume that persona in your everyday life. We were put on earth to discover who we really are, not who we were or who we would like to be. The dividing line between interior discovery and wish-fulfilment is very slight. For this reason, I caution students to avoid reincarnational research unless they feel that they really would benefit from such analysis, which, by its very nature, needs a highly objective mind and mature consciousness to balance its findings. The core of our present life's purpose gives all that any woman needs for self-discovery and growth.

An easy form of self-therapy is to make an objective study of your life's problems, listing them by type; for example, fatally attracted to power, continually disappointed in other people, unable to manifest your ideas or other such typical stumbling blocks that have dogged your life. These recurrent patterns alone will tell you what karmic lesson needs to be assimilated right now (see Chapter 10 of *The Arthurian Tarot* by myself and John Matthews, Aquarian Press, 1990 — the Excalibur Spread facilitates access to very general reincarnational information).

Esoteric life is full of glamour — in its original sense. It is easy to become a victim of glamour, enchanted by inner visions, to bloat one's ego on appropriated archetypes and assume their function (an excellent study of glamour in esoteric life is *Glamour: A World Problem* by A.A. Bailey, Lucis Press, 1950). The numerous pathologies of esoteric existence are legion, producing some of the most unpleasantly aspected individuals you are likely to meet. The fact that one might very easily join their number unless one is ruled by common sense and guarded by a sense of humour, is a thought that should be prominent in the minds of all who would mediate the gods. This is not to say that one should avoid esoteric work for fear of the possible dangers because in so doing one might by denying one's essential vocation. I might, for example, have sought exorcism as the cure for all my ills. However, I always instinctively, if blindly, understood, that my peculiar archetypal resonance was not a case of simple incarnational haunting. By descending to the Underworld with Rhiannon, I had experientially shared with an archetype that which would greatly assist others through me. I had needed to more finely attune myself to the archetype, to tune out my own inadequacies by facing them.

It has been a great relief to discover that my peculiar, otherwordly skills do have a purpose and an outlet.

I am aware of how lucky I am to have realized my vocation — one that I can fulfil in many creative ways. I am likewise aware of how many people are still attempting to clarify their vocations, confused by the lack of provision in modern society for such archaisms as priestess, sibyl, prophetess, medium, ritualist, magician. Nor must I forget all those whose attempts to integrate unusual vocations have come to grief, those who have tuned to the lower octave of their indwelling archetype and who are now diagnosed insane.

Gareth Knight in his article 'The Individuality and the Ghost' in *Quadriga*, no. 15, Autumn 1980, has outlined the kind of danger signs we should be on the look-out for if we are to avoid imbalance in our esoteric training. These features often indicate sub-personalities, a kind of incarnational 'ghost' effect that may dog our steps or a mythic tape-loop which we unconsciously play. They include:

- the inability to complete a task or cycle fully
- giving the impression of being spiritually authorative and more inclined to the otherworld than to this
- having a reincarnational history of alternatingly 'spiritual' and violently earthy lives, revealing patterns of imbalance
- being dominated by the mind — being without compassion
- being unable to form balanced relationships due to an urge to be independent and self-sufficient
- showing little interest in a personal family life
- showing intolerance of others' faults and being dogmatically correct in thought and word
- being lonely, always yearning for 'higher things' and never at home in daily life, unable to deal with mundane problems.

Each of us needs healing. We do not have to be dictated to by the story of our inner archetype, for we each have our own, but, in those areas of special vulnerability, our wounded immortal part, lies also a great human responsibility to oneself and those like one. To be free of our mythic track-record or incarnational tape-loop, we need searching self-awareness as well as discriminating resonance with an archetype. The antidote to the symptoms outlined above are unconditional love for all creation, a firm dedication to the fulfilment of one's present incarnation and the warmth and humour of friends and family. These three things will ensure sanity and the development of a lively and useful vocation.

The problems of mediation can be surmounted with sensitivity, patience and a good deal of common sense, and these must serve many of us in lieu of a proper priestessly training. Let us hope that such training will be available for our children — perhaps based on our own hard-won discoveries — and that the ancient wisdom of the groves and temples will be mediated once more in our own fragmented world.

If this experience has taught me nothing else, I now realize that to mediate Rhiannon I cannot afford the luxury of personal indulgence — I either make the power of Rhiannon available to others or shut up shop. The effect of having shared part of my life with her must make me accessible as her mediator or I am a self-deluded fraud.

Rhiannon is my healer, my sister and companion. I am her priestess and mediator and I am no longer afraid to sing with her the words,

> 'I will be the Bearer of Burdens,
> I will be the Singer of the Song,
> I will be the One who waits for you,
> And though the night is long
> My patience is strong'.

From my unpublished song, 'The Song of Rhiannon'.

## The Testament of Rhiannon, The Poem, by Caitlín Matthews

In the silences, the wood-walking girl journeys —
Beyond the silences she goes.
A clutch of feathers — variegated hues of blackness —
In her slender fist.
She has only to describe the sickle of the everlasting branch
With one curved hand,
And the shadows silver,
Doorways are opened in the mist,
Each feather falling into the wind —
A blizzard blackness of snow becomes
A flock of blackbirds, silver singing.

She knows the crossing places,
And the bright openings.
She knows the way of words —

Equally, the shoals of silence.
Hers is the basket of song
And the woodman's bundle.
All the apt kindlings possess her.
The way of the chill bridle
Is known to her.
Along its etched margins, her hoofprints go.

'There was a time when I stood here,
Fated to snare a mortal man
but none would ask:
"What woman rides in the golden gown?
Who is the rider whose pace never hastens,
Yet who cannot be caught?"
Until Pwyll, I was Shadow Queen.
In him, existences began.
Maidened no more, but mothered,
In foal to a gold-helmed child'.
— And if she whinnies in alarm at this telling,
It is because of the grasping, monstrous hand
Thrust through the smoke-hole
That smote the greatest dolour to a mother's heart.

Bereft of him, the son of her making
And mortal twining, she knew her foe.
The yellow and black livery about that hand
Betrayed Gwawl — the Underworld's brightest warrior
And her fate's intended lover.
She wears the grooved earth remembering
The accusations and surmise:
'She ate her own son, the strange slut'.
'Dishonoured her lord's noble bed
With his loin's blood'.
And the judgement of the bridle
Was placed upon her —
That she should go yoked and saddled
From courtyard to hall,
Bearing each new guest upon her back.
Boring them with her audacious,
Unbelieving story, seven years
At the mounting block, relating her trouble.
That path of the chill bridle
Is known to her in every detail,

And its plain track the way for
Every burdened heart thereafter.

The way of the golden chain
Stood wide before her,
Its mirror-doors distorting the mortal realm.
This was no beaten path,
But the slippery road of the glass tower
Downwards to the roots of Annwn.
Her endless descent began with
Unsuspecting ease.
Her second husband, Manawyddan,
Wise in otherworldly ways,
Came home without Pryderi;
And she, returning to the place,
Saw where the bowl hung from the golden chain
And how her son stuck fast to it.
With only rescue in mind
She clutched him and stuck fast herself.
The chain descended and the cauldron gaped.
Black were the towers and parapets grey
With glass. The brightness
Reflected the briliance of Llwyd,
Kin to Gwawl, and his avenger.
'Madam mare and her frisky colt —
Their stable is prepared'.
And the horsecollars descended
About their necks, yoked together.
Seven years the bore the toil,
Bearing the mouldy hay until
The way of restoration was revealed.

The way of the three restorations
Shone the brightest in the wood.
She who had borne so many burdens
Knew that burdens became banners
If carried too long and she sometimes
Shunned this glorious way
When, to free her of immortal shadow,
Pwyll had descended to the Courts of Summer
And, attired as a beggar, had tricked
Gwawl into her magical, capacious bag.
Etched deeper was her liberation from trouble:
When Teyrnon brought her boy —

The gold-helmed Gwri — home again.
Then she was released from the bridle,
Then was the saddle lifted from her sore back,
Then was her trouble over
And lost Gwri was restored in Pryderi.
The third and final restoration
Came from Manawyddan, the craftsman
In shoes, shields and songs.
He tricked Llwyd into releasing her
By stringing the mouse-wife on a gallows.
The shadows were erased,
The burdens lifted, the slavery ended.
Yet her heart was fraught with deeper scars
Than ever joy can ferry over.

The girl between worlds is her naming,
The maiden of Annwn, her title,
The Bearer of Burdens, her nature.
The Queen of Joy's Shadow,
The Black Mother,
Rhiannon,
Despoina,
Epona,
Ech
Ehehehehehehe

And the falling feathers flung into the wind
And the wood-walking girl
Whinnied as her silver singers
Winged through
The bright
And only brilliance
Of the last way.

## Attunement to Rhiannon — Two Exercises

Rhiannon is the patron of story-tellers, prisoners, the needy, the over-anxious and those who suffer injustice. She is the Goddess of Thresholds, helping people make transitions from one state to another. Her empowerment is enduring patience, like the earth's own: percipience, unassuming wisdom, the ability to bear burdens and responsibilities and to transmute them into freedom.

The following set of visualizations are suggested as practical exercises in working with this archetype. Do not hesitate to make your own, based upon your own mediatory goddess.

First, visualize Rhiannon as follows: she is seated sidesaddle upon a white mare, riding from left to right and her long dark hair streams down. She holds keys in her right hand — symbolic of Annwn — while her left is raised, palm outwards in a gesture of blessing. Over the horse's neck is a bag of plenty. Behind her three blackbirds fly. To the left is the mound of Arberth, to the right is a stable/entrance to Annwn. From a nearby tree hangs a silver cauldron from a bough. Sun and moon both shine in the sky. Around her stand the priests and priestesses, story-tellers and bearers of burdens, as well as the enactors of her myth, Arawn, Gwawl, Pwyll, Manawyddan, Llwyd and Pryderi. Now say:

I enter the embrace of Rhiannon
I take shelter under the cloak of tradition
I align myself with the mediators of the tradition

Know that the blessing of Rhiannon is with you, feel the mantle of tradition about you and the companionship of the mediators and bearers of burdens.

A network of light is created between yourself and the emanating brilliance issuing from the Goddess and her enactors and mediators. Their voices may be heard in one's heart, transmitting tradition and wisdom.

Chant her Celtic title, meaning 'Great Queen' — Rigantona — incorporate it into meaningful chants of your own.

The second exercise is the Temple of Rhiannon. This is approached down a flight of steep rock stairs from a room where a golden bowl hangs. Below, there is a square-cut niche over which a curtain is drawn. When the curtain is pulled away, there is a horse-headed women with a child on her lap, or sometimes on her lap are twins. She is quite black, though her robes are brilliant. She is often not visible due to the bright light that shines from behind her, bathing one's face. She is sometimes oracular and will answer questions. At other times she will speak directly to your heart. She also changes from horse-headed to female shape again. Do not be surprised if the Goddess also tells stories that make you laugh or cry — she is, after all, the horse's mouth!

Come to this place when you are in need of counsel, when you are confused or burdened. Brings gifts of incense, candles or flowers and, set these upon your shrine-shelf or altar and visualize it as being within the temple.

Either of these visualizations can be performed anywhere. Just shut your eyes and be there.

# 5

# The Goddess as the Way of the Land

## Helene Hess

The work of a native earth priestess or shamanka is outlined in Helene Hess' re-discovery of the British Goddess of the Land. It has been the recent custom for people from the civilized West to turn to indigenous cultures that still follow a native earth tradition, such as that of the native Americans, in order to make contact with the earth. Helene gives us the confidence to contact the Goddess of the Earth exactly where we are right now, to listen for the voices of the land in the elementals, in the legends and half-remembered lore of our ancestors. The task of the native priestess is to re-discover the treasures that lie 'hidden on our very own doorstep'.

The potent purpose of the Goddess of the Land can be observed on many levels, from the manifestation of certain weather patterns to the political ferment that shapes a country's destiny. Helene Hess provides the ritual framework in which each woman can make individual contact with her native earth and learn the forgotten art of the shamanka.

Helene Hess *lives and works in Wales as a craftswoman, although she has worked professionally as a psychologist. She first came into the Western Magical Tradition 14 years ago when she was studying astrology. Since then she has taught astrology, as well as other related subjects. She has also written a book,* The Zodiac Explorer's Handbook *(Aquarian Press, 1986). Helene's main area of interest is in the Celtic and British Native Traditions. She is a keen student of mythology and folklore, and is concerned with finding links across traditions so that those from different traditions can work together and that the fires of the ancient traditions of her own country may be rekindled.*

# The Goddess as the Way of the Land

My grandmother once told me that the saying, 'May you live in interesting times' was considered by the Chinese as a curse as well as a blessing. To me, 'interesting times' means times of change, times when the hand of the Goddess both destroys and renews as part of her cycle. Outwardly it may appear to be a time where one is under a curse, but inwardly one is dying to a positive rebirth and a new adventure of growth. Presently, too, our world seems to be threatened with extinction through the deeds of our own species and the legacy of our forebears, whether this be through pollution, the wholesale destruction of Nature, or the annihilation of war. We truly seem to be living in interesting times on all levels.

As a child, everything seemed to be so certain, there was so much hope for a bright future, a future that held out the certainty of the wonders of scientific discovery. This hope was reflected in our religious beliefs, beliefs based on the assurance that there was a God in heaven and all was well with the world, as long as we behaved ourselves and looked after our fellow human beings. Then came the revolution of the sixties. No longer was everything so cut and dried. A new influx of religions from the East and a new awareness that other states of consciousness were possible through the common use of hallucinogens started to change everyone's comfortable reality. So many questions began to emerge about the nature of society, the role of women, the reality of war and did God really exist or was it all down to the firing of neurons in the brain and our genetic blueprint?

For some time this also opened up a new world, as they turned to new religious beliefs or looked to the long distant past to re-discover old ones. From all this searching there began to emerge the big question, why was God a man? The ancient mystery schools had certainly acknowledged the feminine as sacred, worshipping the Goddess, even many of the early forms of our present day orthodox religions referred to God in both a masculine and feminine form, but what relevance did this have for us now?

It was against this background that my personal journey in life brought me to the Western Mystery Tradition. I learned that the divine feminine principle held importance. She was Mother of all, giving birth to creation, the source of life and death and the source of Wisdom itself. All this was deeply explored in a number of ways in the formal training within a magical group or school.

My own training came via the cabalistic and Celtic Traditions. There was no question here that the feminine principle was as necessary as the masculine. It was clearly understood that there could be no defined masculine force without the counterbalance of the divine feminine. Even so, the active part of the magical work on the material level seemed to have a predominantly male influence, while the priestess's work was mainly in drawing power into the work from the inner levels.

Much of what is practised in the Celtic Tradition has its basis in applying what is known of magical techniques gleaned from the remnants of the ancient Tradition in literature in the form of myths and legends that have survived down the centuries. The women in these legends are often portrayed as either taking the role of the deceiver who undermines the hero or as shadowy characters who act as catalysts to the hero's exploits. However, looked at closely it becomes more apparent that many of the myths have been overlaid with a more patriarchal outlook over generations of story-telling.

It was after a number of years pondering over what the true nature of the Goddess was as reflected by the feminine archetypes within these myths that I realized that I had been looking too hard, looking with the eyes of the intellect and my formal education. I had forgotten the nature of my own womanhood and the ebb and flow of my own cycle of power. Ironically this awareness did not come through being conscious of my own physical menstruation, but through a struggle to re-recognize my own menstrual cycle after a hysterectomy. I discovered the cycle by watching my moods, feelings and sexual nature and also began to recognize with an inner clarity the ebb and flow of the lunar tides. The lunar phases no longer became something I had to look for in the sky of at an emphemeris for — I really began to feel the magnetic pull and atmosphere of each phase of the moon within my own cycle. It drew me into a mystery that was far beyond thought, touching the depths of my inner being as a woman and a child of the Earth. No longer feeling separate from the Earth, I realized that I was as much a part of her rhythm as a plant or the tides of the sea just as the Earth herself must be a part of the rhythm of the universe itself.

This consciousness of ebb and flow then spread to an awareness of the growth cycle, the weather changes and the changes in the night sky and the sea. All had their rhythm that did not need to be intellectualized, they only had to be felt at deeper levels. We all have this within us and becoming conscious of its nature is like children discovering for the first time that they are seeing a world of colour. To me this is feeling the Goddess herself — Hers are the rhythms of Nature, this movement of energy, this dancing force within the Universe that permeates all, creating ever-changing forms. With this realization, the meaning of Her association with birth, life and death took on a whole meaning. The synchronicity we all experience in some memorable moment or the event that changes our life path is no more and no less than part of Her beautiful dance, which reaches the depths of our being.

The feminine archetypes within those myths and legends then began to emerge from the background. Each female character was another face of the Goddess, sometimes deceptively tricky and sometimes helpful, but without her subtle instigation the hero would not change and grow or seek out his adventures. Similarly, the festivals and celebrations of the annual and lunar tides are found in all traditions, whether it is the annual solar festivals or lunar celebrations of the pagans or the annual Christian cycle. These should urge us on to living within the rhythms that they set, such as the cleansing tide or Lent just before Spring, or the harvest festivals just before the onset of autumn — all can help pace the rhythm of our lives. As wells as finding the Goddess within the Celtic myths, She is also to be found in the myths of all Traditions through the female characters, often in guises of her triple aspect of Virgin, Mother and Crone. These can be acknowledged in depth, as in some of the Eastern Traditins, or lie subtly behind the scenes in some of the more orthodox Western religions. Much has been written on this, but to live what is indicated by it extends much further and can only be conveyed in the experiencing of it.

Sensitizing oneself to the universal pattern of the Goddess brings an awareness of the land and its own unique rhythm. Each locality has its own atmosphere that is sometimes sleeping and sometimes very energized. Developing this sensitivity will put one in touch with the Goddess in Her aspect as the land itself. For some people the concept of the land being associated with the Goddess is confusing and is seen as some sort of primitive idea. However, this is far from true when the idea is looked on in the light of her energy permeating all matter in the tides and cycles worked by her influence. The masculine principle is like a line that is formed into waves by the attraction and polarity of the feminine principle creating shape and form.

The concept of the land as representing the state and aspect of the cycle of the Goddess then becomes not a strange fantasy,

but a living aspect of her energy. Much light has been thrown
on this in recent years in relation to the Celtic Goddesses and
their representatives in myth such as the Celtic Queens carrying
the line of the sovereignty of the land, or the Priestess in ritual
being her representation (see *Arthur and the Sovereignty of Britain* by Caitlín Matthews, Arkana, 1989). This is where the Priestess
comes into her own, in terms of living the path of the Goddess,
by living it through her cycles and learning to mediate her energy
when times are right to do so.

With the ecological balance of the land becoming such an
important issue, it is no accident that there is a growing awareness of the Goddess. Although much healing can come through
working with Her energies, it is also necessary to recognize that
it works in very subtle rather than obvious ways. Here I may be
at issue with some of those who prefer to take a more direct stance
to our demise. However, sometimes it may be important not to
take upon oneself the belief that you should intervene and make
self-chosen and direct changes through magical work. Her cycles
teach us that death and destruction are all part of her cycle and
to cling to establishing a perfect situation within the old order
can be counter-productive — it is inevitable that the fullness of
summer must be followed by winter and the hidden face of the
Moon is still there when her light does not appear to shine because
we may be seeing her dark face, which only veils the light, just
as the hidden dormant seeds are protected by the earth in the
frost-hard ground. The Crone, whose face can be terrifying, as
well as revealing the face of the teacher of ancient wisdom, contains both Mother and Virgin. She gives teachings that may be
valuable from a lost ancestral memory.

What is now happening to Mother Earth as a planetary being
is certainly showing aspects of the face of the Crone. As humans
we can trace much of the damage to our own actions, but in per-
ceiving it in this way we are still separating ourselves from the
fact that we are also an integral part of the planet itself and not
some alien entity in a black box. An awareness of being part of
the fabric of her being however does not mean that we can or
should do nothing on the material level to put things to rights.
We must strive to achieve a new balance and learn from it, much
as our own bodies adapt to the changes that occur within it. In
short, on a magical level, to work as Priestesses devoted to the
Goddess we, as part of Her cycle, need to work towards Her renewal
from Crone to Virgin, transforming Mother Earth. To do this we
need to bring something to birth within ourselves, allowing the

Goddess to imbue us with Her energy so that, through our connection with Her, the alchemy of our change can subtly transform all around us. Once one starts to channel this energy, the
appropriate knowledge comes in so many ways — through realizations from meditation, meeting the appropriate teachers, through
dreams and so on. The trials in life are also Her teachings, for
you can be sure that nothing is unused in what She has taught you.

In the Tradition in which I work, I use the ancient Goddess often
known in Her form as Brighid. She is often referred to as the Goddess of healing, childbirth, of craftspeople, and the eternal flame.
She is also, however, the Goddess of war and is associated with
coming through in the ancient priestess warrior Queens of this
country. In this aspect it should be remembered that Her flame
is not only the eternal flame of ancient wisdom but also the flame
of purification, a much harsher form of healing than that of Her
healing wells. The path is, therefore, not just a gentle one for it
also contains the path of the warrioress, though not in a form
of needless destruction, but in its purifying aspect. A useful visualization to use if you have any doubts about your own intentions
or whether your intended magical work is correct, is to symbolically place it before the image of Her flame. Should it be burned
in any way you will know that your intention needs purifying,
but should it transform into another symbol, then see what it
means. This is a good test should you be intending to use your
ideas to work towards the renewal of land, for the Goddess of
the Land will herself validate or purify your intention.

The acts of the hero within legend indicate the male aspect of
the mystery, and the attraction and trickery of the feminine urge
him along the way. However, little credence is given to the women
who appear in the shadows as the ones who give advice or directions. Often they are old wise women, nuns or mysterious maidens
or even the mothers of the hero. Here there is another level that
is an echo of many legends we still find attached to actual loca-
tions. In the legends the ancient holy and wise women are remembered for their choice of a life, following the ancient way or a life
spent in solitude and prayer. Often there is a feature in the landscape where the legends originated that commemorates some event
in their lives, most frequently a well, spring, cave, place underground or chapel in a wild place. Commonly associated with these
legendary figures is some aspect of caring for something, often
in the form of a healing well or sacred flame. Within the king
myth this caring element is to be found in that part of the myth
that tells of the women who care for the wounded king, who

represents the dying virility of the land.

Legends remain of these women in ancient villages and mysterious parts of the countryside and even today our innate curiosity will urge us to visit such places when staying in the locality and we often will not know quite why we feel this urge. The importance of these legends must have been great for those in the community. Often, even though sometimes the legends preceded the introduction of Christianity by a long way, it would be believed that a visit to or a vigil at a location where they were reported to have lived would have a healing or soothing effect. Over time this builds up into a very powerful thought-form and the character of the legend can be contacted as if it were a guardian or inner representative of the Goddess, especially if the legendary figure has obvious Goddess connections. A typical figure of this kind is Saint Anne who has had many wells attributed to her. As the legenday mother of the Virgin, there are obvious hints that She is the Goddess herself in Her healing and renewing aspects.

In this country, much has been lost of the old traditions and the ancient knowledge and so many are now looking to other cultures, which has heralded a current revival of interest in shamanism. A number of people now regularly come here to teach about the many different aspects of shamanic healing and ceremony. A lot can be learned from what they have to offer on their ancient ways and there are certain aspects that have parallels that fill in certain missing parts in our jigsaw of knowledge. Even so, in the seeking it is very easy to lose sight of the fact that every shaman will start their point of learning from their own culture and evironment. The shamans of our culture were the local healers, the witch or wise woman, the hermit or the local holy men and women. They sought their inspiration from the surroundings, connecting with the God or Goddess of their belief system, as well as learning from knowledge passed down to them through oral tradition.

The lack of an ancient oral tradition, however, does not mean that all is lost. Today we have access to the most amazing fund of knowledge, probably the amount that can be gleaned from the study of the literature is on a par with the amount some of these figures were actually taught. We also have the ability to communicate swiftly with those of like mind who live great distances from us. We do not need to travel these days in order to communicate or be taught a teaching. In my experience, most forms of magical tradition give similar forms of teaching. It is mainly the emphasis on what is taught, or the myths that are used that are different. Similarly, the techniques used may appear to be different, but, again, it is all there, only the emphasis on what tool, method and imagery is used will vary. The temptation is to find a teacher and hand over all responsibility for what should be learned by experience to them, but wisdom only comes with one's own inner practice.

It is not always the case in other cultures that the shaman is taught directly to begin with. I was told first-hand by a Nigerian that his Grandmother became the local healer shaman through a revelatory experience from the local nature spirits. Her knowledge of healing techniques and herbs did not entirely come from knowledge passed down to her, but from her connection with the land and the nature spirit forces in her environment. She had, however, the benefit of living in a culture where this is acceptable and lived her life without the mental setback of a formal education.

Following a tradition of the Goddess today is hard because the lineage of knowledge has been broken, but the connections are still there and a fund of knowledge is existent from those who have gone before. It is only our lack of confidence and the error of an imagined lack of knowledge in our own culture that leads us to believe that our culture does not contain any mystery any more. In doing this we reject the treasures lying hidden on our very own doorstep.

I became aware of the truth of this through practising meditation in my formal magical training. Various incidents in my life had enforced me to spend long periods on my own in the countryside and so I had developed the habit of putting time aside every so often to go outside to do this. One particular place where I lived there was an extraordinarily beautiful mountain waterfall. Gradually I became conscious that there was more to this spot than just its beauty. Often I used to watch the river and learned to observe it so that it became a form of meditation, which helped me to learn about the elements. The sound of the water would quickly get me into the state of deep meditation, its sound sometimes becoming like hundreds of voices to me.

One day, the Sun shone through the trees on to the waterfall forming a column of light. That light, I realized was a glimpse of the being of the waterfall. This was my first very real contact with what would commonly be called a nature spirit. Subsequently I could come and converse in my mind with this being to such an extent that it imparted very comfirmable information to me about my locality and the nature of the elemental beings that inhabited the place.

This was one of many experiences that made me realize that seeking knowledge from books and teachers was not enough. It has also taught me that, although the land is under seige from the ignorant deeds of humans and that the natural places are diminishing, all will not be lost. It was implied that there were energies afoot that would give many warnings to our race, like the Mother warning her child that its behaviour will harm it. The first of these have now started to be evident in the last few years. Also there came up the image of our planet as a beautiful, changing woman with the weather patterns shifting like her moods. No matter how much we attempt to destroy our environment, the natural forces within will lie dormant until it is time for them to come back. This, however, is not entirely a message of hope, for we as a species have the ability to be the instruments of our own extinction with the death and renewal of the Goddess and possibly take upon ourselves the karma of many other species too. The course of natural evolution is set whatever happens, but the path we choose to take is up to us. The Goddess will demand her renewal.

A very effective way to make connections with the land is through finding you own sacred place within it, as I found my place by the waterfall. First, start with your own home by setting aside somewhere to place your own little sanctuary. It need be no bigger than a small side table. You can keep on it anything that you feel is sacred, such as special stones you have found or items that have a magical or sacred meaning to you. If you wish, you can keep a sacred, eternal flame in the form of a nightlight candle. It is also possible to acquire a seven-day candle from your local church supplier. The very ancient Celtic Goddess Brighid — also known as Bridget, Brigantia and her Christanized version Saint Bride or the Welsh Saint Ffraid — used to be symbolized by the eternal flame. In legend her Christanized sanctuary at Kildare in Ireland had a sacred flame tended by nuns within a circular grove. In Wales, this sanctuary is depicted as floating on water, hedged by oak branches containing acorns and empty acorn cups. Use this place for meditation and magical work, building up an atmosphere that is personal to you.

Whenever you are using this space, ask the Goddess to show you where your sacred place is on the land. You will eventually discover where this is, either through some event that will lead you to it or perhaps by stumbling across it. Sometimes it can come to you in a dream or you may find it coming up in your visualizations.

Once you have found the place, thank the Goddess and dedicate it to her. Care for it in whatever way feels appropriate. If there is some special feature within the place, you can be sure that there is some meaning attached to it. Watch it (as I watched the waterfall) and see if it has something to teach you. If you use the place regularly, watch the changes as the seasons and lunar cycles change. You will find that particular months will regularly bring certain predominant colours in the plants and flowers and the growth cycle will change according to the lunar phases. Note how you feel as the changes take place and what your moods and energy levels are. From this you can make a seasonal wheel, adding the information to it as you go along.

Living in what I call the sacred Isles — for Britain is a land sacred to some very ancient Goddesses — I find that practically every area has some form of myth or legend attached to it. If a local legend intrigues you, meditate it in your sacred place. As I mentioned before, many legends of saints hide much older myths and this can also be reflected in the churches named after a particular saint. Legends of a much more recent origin may well also have a hidden meaning, simply because we are linked to the thought-forms of things that may already be there and reflect in later events. However, one warning about this, not everything is benign. Use your sacred space as a protective circle and, if you feel intuitively uncomfortable about a certain legendary archetype or place, leave well alone.

Speaking of the elements, they have much to teach too. However, as beings without our form of consciousness it is best to invoke them in ritual under aegis of the Goddess and the elemental kings. One particularly effective teaching ritual I use is the version that follows here.

## Ritual of the Elements

To prepare you will need to put on a central altar a chalice or glass containing water collected from a local spring or holy well, a clod of earth or a branch (I usually use an oak branch, having asked the tree's permission to take it), a candle and an incense burner containing incense. You will also need matches for lighting the candle and the incense and charcoal blocks to keep the incense burning.

Before performing the ritual, the space you will be using should be cleansed. The traditional way, is to take water and salt, bless them and then sprinkle the salt into the water. Then, taking the salt water around the space clockwise, sprinkle it on the ground, saying as you do so, 'I bless and cleanse this space in the name of . . .' (whatever Goddess you feel appropriate). Finally, in the same way, cleanse the central altar.

The items on the altar represent the elements — the cup, Water, the branch or clod of earth, Earth, the incense, Air, and the candle, Fire. Place these in the directions you feel are right for the elements within the system you work in. Personally I use the most commonly used directions in the British Isles: east for air, south for fire, west for water, and north for earth.

This ritual is best done with five people. Four to stand in the quarters representing the elements and one who is Priestess at the centre who mediates the Goddess of the Land.

First, the guardians of the doorways must be called into each quarter, beginning with the archangelic forces, starting with the east and going round to the north. Raphael represents air, Michael fire, Gabriel water, and Uriel the earth. Visualize them as they are called in turn by those standing in the quarters. When this is done, the same people must then call in the guardians of the land in the same manner. Living in Britain, I use the most commonly used guardians, using Herne in the east, visualized as a large stag with seven tines. Epona in the south, visualized as a white mare running free on rolling hills. Mona as a black cow with a white star upon her forehead standing on an island for the west and Ator the Bear in the north. If your ritual is taking place in another land, the four guardians of that particular country can be used instead of the British ones. In this case it could be that a different allocation of the elements may be given to the quarters and then the archangelic forces can be invoked into the appropriate quarter for their element and the items on the altar may be put in the appropriate directions.

Once the guardians have been called in, the Priestess in the centre lights the candles and puts the incense on the hot charcoal blocks. When she is ready she pronounces: 'The temple is now open and the guardians are at the gates. I now call upon the elemental kings to be present at our working'.

Those at the four quarters then call in their respective Elemental Kings: Piralda for Air, Djin for Fire, Nixa for Water and Ghob for Earth. Each should be visualized as clothed in the colours and qualities of that particular element. The Priestess at the centre then invokes the energy of the Goddess of the Land with the words: 'From the gentle breezes that give the breath of life, from the rushing streams and rivers that cleanse the land and the sea from where all life began. From the warming flame that gives joy and comfort to our lives, from the dark rich Earth that provides nourishment and to which our bodies will return. I call upon Goddess . . .* the heart of the land and mistress of Elements, to bless me with understanding so I may in turn bless and care for the land and all Earth's creatures.'

Each person then in turn says something appropriate to their position in the temple. This should be what immediately comes to mind and notice, too, if any symbols surface as they speak.

The Elemental Kings are then thanked at each quarter and asked to leave. Visualizing them as turning and fading from their quarter, starting with the east and ending in the north, the priestess then snuffs the candle. The temple guardians are then thanked and bade farewell in a similar manner to the Elemental Kings, starting with the Guardians of the Land working from east to north, then likewise with the archangelic guardians. Finally, the priestess declares that the temple is closed, satisfied that all the guardians have left, and bids all to leave in peace.

Now the work really begins. Each person who has taken part goes out on a quest to find something in the environment to represent each one of the elements. At least several hours should be devoted to this if not half a day and each person should go outside on a personal journey. They then observe and watch what is going on around them, notice who they see and meet and what they are doing, also noting the state the elements are in, their various forms and the state of what is living on them. I can guarantee that if this is done in the right spirit there will be some useful and interesting revelations.

Upon returning, they should place the four things they have found to represent the elements on the altar. Once everyone is back, each person should relate their experience and what it has taught them, stating why they have chosen to bring back their items. The items found should then be taken back by their finders and be treated in the future as their elemental gifts. Close with a short meditation and send love and blessing to the elements and the land. This ritual can also be done on one's own and with more or fewer than five people, in which case the various roles have to be adapted according to the numbers present. If you are

*If this is being worked within the Celtic Tradition, use Brighid, otherwise invoke the name of the Goddess that seems appropriate to you.

doing this on your own, when you come back, relate your experience to the Goddess herself.

The various things I have suggested here may seem to be very simple, but they are very effective. Certainly for those who are new to this path it will help you make your first step and hopefully lead you to the next one on the way. The path of the Goddess is very simple in its outer form, but, as the Goddess also represents wisdom itself, from simplicity she brings deep understanding. Blessings in the name of the Goddess.

# 6

# Tested by the Dark/Light Mother of the Other World

## Monica Sjöö

Certain aspects of the Goddess have found a greater acceptance among Her devotees than others. Possibly due to the false and frequently unconscious polarization caused by the idea that 'God = man = good; and that 'Goddess = woman = evil', many people prefer to see the Goddess only in Her positive or benign aspects. The problems of suffering and evil that so beset the world are not absent from the lives of those who follow the Goddess. Monica Sjöö's chapter leaves us in no doubt that the Goddess has other faces, that She is not all sweetness and light.

The way in which Monica Sjöö has coped with bereavement and personal grief while still mediating the Goddess is a testimony to the many gifts of the Mother who gives us creativity in exchange for our sacrifice. The Dark Mother makes us look into the mirror in which our own fears and doubts are reflected — she makes us despair or transform. Only when we can offer Her a heart filled with compassion do we find that the Dark Mother, the *Cailleach*, transforms into the inspirational face of Brighid, She who brings spring to the earth and to every winter-bound spirit.

Monica Sjöö *is Swedish. She has been involved in the women's movement in Britain since its beginnings and is a founder member of the Goddess and feminist arts movements. Her painting* God Giving Birth *(1968) almost caused her to be taken to court for 'obscenity and blasphemy'. She feels this to have been a modern witch-hunt directed against her. Monica Sjöö has for many years exhibited with other women in Britain and in Scandinavia and in 'Woman Magic — Celebrating the Goddess within us'. She has travelled in England and in Europe from 1979 to 1987. Together with American poet Barbara Mor, she wrote* The Great Cosmic Mother — Rediscovering the Religion of the Earth *(Harper & Row, 1987). Monica Sjöö has spent many years travelling to the ancient Neolithic sacred sites that have inspired her paintings and she has also travelled widely giving slide-shows and talks about her art and Goddess cultures. She lived for five years in the Welsh country-side and was involved in pagan groups and with the peace movement. She spent time at Greenham and took part in the walk across Salisbury Plain in 1985. In the last four years, however, because of the tragic deaths of two of her sons, Monica Sjöö has found herself on an otherwordly journey into the inner psychic and Underworld realms. She is still here — or rather, there. She became a grandmother in April 1989.*

# Tested by the Dark/Light Mother of the Other World

It is not easy to write of my experiences of Her, the Crone, Hag, Dark Lunar Mother of Winter, death, and rebirth. She who has taken back to Herself two of my precious sons in the last four years. Now approaching my fifftieth birthday, on New Year's Eve 1988, I am becoming like Her, who is, paradoxically, also white — as white as the silver hairs and the white bleached bones.

The Patriarchs fear the Dark Mother the most, they fear Her lunar-menstrual powers as well as the post-menopausal woman's clairvoyance and Otherworld powers. They refuse to be recycled by the life-in-death Goddess and seek bodily immortality from a 'father God' who never created them nor gave them birth. They have forgotten that the Universe is born, not made or manufactured, in a process of becoming. The Birthing Woman is also Thought Woman or the Cosmic Spider who weaves our beings and destinies. She creates the great webs of luminous fibres that vibrate spirit into matter in the beginning and return us back into Her spirit realms at the end. The great Mother is *not* an 'archetype' created by the human mind. If anything, we are thought-forms emanating from Her dreams.

Paradoxically, in a world where the patriarchs blame the Mother for the existence of death and physical mortality they have themselves set the stage for the worst possible deaths and the possible annihilation of all nature. These would be sterile deaths, that is, without hope of transformation and rebirth from Her magical womb. Patriarchal societies are anti-evolutionary, static, and anti-spirit and are based in alienation, separation and loss. Barrenness is a patriarchal condition and the wasteland is the man-created desert in which the blood-waters from Ceradwen's magical and menstrual cauldron have dried out — the sacred wells forgotten and left untended, the oceans dying, the rivers and serpentine underground waters polluted.

In the mysteries of Demeter and Persephone in ancient Greece, dark Persephone dwelt voluntarily in the Underworld as the Queen of the Dead for six months of the year and then returned to Her grieving mother Demeter as Kore, the Maiden of spring, bringing with Her rebirth, new life, light and joy to all nature. It was Demeter's grief at Her daughter's absence that caused the death of nature in the winter months. In patriarchies, where daughters are turned against and separated from their mothers, Persephone never returns as Kore and Demeter's grief blights the Earth.

In the Celtic world, Brigid/Bride returns from Her mother Cailleach's mountain fastness at Imbolc (which means 'Ewe's milk') in the early springtime — She is the Serpent that emerges from the mound. When She dips Her finger in the waters of wells and rivers, they start to warm. She is the white milk cow, the Milky Way, the white sea foam and the white mare of Shamanistic otherworld journeys. She is White Buffalo woman of the Lakolas who taught the people the sacred pipe ceremony. She is the 'White Lady' often seen ghost-like, by the sacred wells and trees. She is the electromagnetic serpent-power of the life-creating waters and She is also Kundalini, the cosmic generative sexual fire. She is the sacred flame within the mother's womb, as well as of the hearths, temples, kilns and ovens, She is Solar fire. She is mind, clairvoyant powers and inspired poetic utterance. She is the radiant Moon in the dark night. Hers is the white astral light of the spirit realms.

Cailleach, who is Her own mother, Crone-self, is a northern Kali and is as black as the fertile black soil and as blue as the Underground waters. She is the enormous old woman of the mountain ranges, of the Scottish highlands and islands who raised the stone circles, cromlechs and mounds according to legend. She is the ancient chthonic Mother of Earth, stones and the underground winter realms of the lunar Neolithic cultures.

These last three years I have lived through a winter grief and darkness of mind. My young son Leif, only 15 years old, was run down and killed by a car in front of my eyes, on a busy road in the Basque country in the south of France, in August 1985. My oldest son, Sean, just 28 years old, died from Non-Hodgkins Lymphoma, a cancer of the lymph system, in July 1987. I have experienced a great deal of fear, uncertainties and doubts these last years. I have feared the Mother Goddess, strange as this may sound, and even my own work. I have not been able to understand the sequence of events that led up to my young son's tragic death.

Leify, my son, how vividly I so often see your body on the road behind that car, bleeding your life-blood away. You so young, so eager to grow up, becoming so handsome, taken back by the Great Mother. You were/are black, white, and red of mixed Afro-American and Nordic heritage, with auburn curly hair — the very sacred colours of the Goddess. I know that you live on within Her sacred realms because you have often visited me in lucid dreams — oh, how I long for those dreams now.

I know that even before my young son died, I had felt an increasing despair at what is happening in this world. I had lost much of my hope and optimism from the earlier days of the women's movement when I believed in the inevitability of women rising up and the Goddess re-emerging within us. I had also felt that I was going into the Dark, ageing aspect of myself. When we buried my son's ashes, in the centre of the medicine wheel in the Tipi village in the Black Mountains in South Wales, I had screamed, 'Dark Mother, I who am seeking you. Why have you taken my young son? Why, oh, why?' I also whispered, 'I hope you know what you are doing'.

I had not been able to understand why I had seen the awesome face of Wyrd, the Ancient One, on the rock wall of the cave underneath Cerrig Cennan castle near Llandeilo in Dyfed. We had gone there — six women — to celebrate Imbolc in the early spring of 1985. Down inside the rock there is also a holy well and we were sitting by it, meditating and singing, when suddenly I turned my head and 'saw' in the candlelight the hooded white ancient face of the Crone. Heavy black crevices in the rock created an impression of eyes, nose and mouth. I remember my feeling of utter astonishment and awe, a sense of chill running up my spine and my hair standing on end. The woman sitting next to me also 'saw' Her face and we both did a drawing of Her, but when we went up closer, the face was simply not there.

Thinking back on this after my son's death later that summer, it felt ominous that I should have seen the face of the Dark Mother/Crone on the very festival day/night of the Bride, the Maiden daugther. However, I should have understood, as I do now, that all of the Lunar Goddess' Quarterday Festivals of the cosmic and seasonal year are also the times when we encounter the magical ancestors and undertake shamanistic journeys into the otherworld realms. From the Spirits of the Blessed Dead we receive powers of prophecy, clairvoyance and healing. Also, Brigid and Cailleach are, of course, one and the same.

On the Samhain and Winter Solstice of 1988 I had a powerful dream in which I looked out through a window and saw the White Lady standing against a tree and strangely, She was myself. Almost like a reversal of seeing the face of the Crone in the cave at Imbolc, or is it?

In Sweden we celebrate the Festival of the Queen of Light, of Lucia, on 13 December. 'Luce' means 'light' in Latin. Lucifer, the Moon Goddess Diana's brother, was the 'light bringer'. The Lucia is always a tall girl or woman with long blonde hair, wearing a long white gown, carrying a crown of lit candles and evergreens

in her hair. She appears in the darkest hours of the morning bringing Her Light. Z. Budapest, the Hungarian/American Dianic Witch,
says in her *The Holy Book of Women's Mysteries* (parts 1 and 2,
Susan B. Anthony Coven 1, Oakland, California, 1979 and 1980)
that her coven celebrates the birth of the Sun Goddess Lucina
on the Winter Solstice, 21 December. In Zsuzsanna's description
of the ritual, the 'witches' wear evergreen crowns with lit white
candles. The Sun Goddess disperses the Darkness and the women
are purified and consecrated. I assume that Z. Budapest brought
this tradition from Hungary where she had been taught the craft
by her artist mother, Masika Szilagyi, whose beautiful sculptures
illustrate Z's books.

Before I had the dream of the White Lady, I had been travelling
in America giving slide shows and talks about my art, ancient
women cultures, the Goddess and the sacred sites in the Celtic
world that have inspired my paintings. I had stayed with Z.
Budapest while I was in San Francisco and had given a slide show
to her Women's Spirituality Forum in September. While in San
Francisco I heard Marija Gimbutas giving her slide-illustrated talk
about the Goddess of Old Europe. Marija is the brilliant Lithua-
nian/American archeologist — a wise Crone herself — who wrote
*Goddesses and Gods of Old Europe — 7000–3500 BC* (Thames &
Hudson, 1976). She said, among many other things, that white
(the white of white hair, ashes and bleached bones) was in fact
the colour of death to the ancient pre-Indo-European peoples,
and that many peoples — such as the Africans — cover themselves in ashes while mourning. She showed us slides of the
Cycladic statuettes of the starkly abstract Goddess carved in white
marble found in the tombs with the dead. It was as if I had never
really understood this before and it came in some ways as a revelation to me. Thank you Marija — another missing piece found.

Red is the colour of rebirth and of menstrual energy. In the past,
the dead were covered with red ochre and the womb-like underground chambers where the priestesses or shamans of the Goddess on Malta entered the incubatory dream-states to communicate
with the spirits were also stained with this blood-like colour.
Barbara Mor and I have written much about this in our book *The
Great Cosmic Mother: Rediscovering the Religion of the Earth* (Harper
& Row, 1987).

Peter Redgrove has explored the radiant and clairvoyant darkness in his book *The Black Goddess and the Sixth Sense* (Blooms-
bury, 1987). Some exciting books exploring religions of the African
Goddess are Judith Gleason's *Oya in Praise of the Goddess* (Shamb-

hala, 1987). Luisah Teish's *Jambalaya: The Natural Woman's Book of Personal Charms and Practical Rituals* (Harper & Row, 1985).

Judith Gleason appears to be white American but has been devoted to Oya and has lived for long periods of time in Africa as well as having followed the trails of the Goddess to Brazil, the West Indies and to America itself. Oya is mighty powerful — She is the River Niger, tornadoes, strong winds, fire, lightning and buffalo.

Luisah Teish speaks with the voice of the Voodoo Priestess of the Goddess Oshun. She is a black woman and grew up in poverty in New Orleans. She talks of relating to spirits as friends, as members of the family and is herself a fine medium.

The child grows in the dark womb; the seed germinates in the black fertile soil during the winter months. It is in the dark night that we can see the stars of Cosmos. All ancient words for mind and mental visionary activity come from words for Moon, the greater Mind. Life was created in alternating darkness and light: without dreams and the night-time we cannot live. The combined electro-geomagnetic energies of Earth and Moon stimulate the pineal gland, our third eye centre of vision into dreamtime and the spirit world. It is in lucid dreams that we communicate with our beloved dead ones. The Neolithic peoples celebrated their Goddess in the light of the full Moon — or in the dark of the Moon for more secret mysteries — in the stone circles and by the sacred wells. Light is born from womb of darkness. The human child travels through the dark birth-passage out into the light and the newly dead travel through the dark tunnel into the light of the astral world. Women shamans guarded the passage between these realms both ways.

The ancient Neolithic Irish would witness the death and rebirth of the Sun child, from the earth and stone womb of the Mother at New Grange, at the dawn of the winter solstice each year.

Patriarchies, on the other hand, are founded in matricide and the denial of the lunar dreamtime consciousness (now called the 'unconscious') that links us with the greater mind of Earth and Cosmos. With divisive patriarchal religious thinking, one has the absurd and obscene spectacle of male solar light gods attempting to slay and conquer their own Mother and Creatrix, now called monstrous Leviathan or Dragon of Night and Darkness. Without our night-time third eye awareness we become, however, dangerous aliens on this planet whose Mother heart and Lunar mind we are no longer able to be in tune with.

I somehow feel that my young son's death is part of a larger tragedy, a reflection of a general illness and/or an omen of things to come. When he died, it was as if time froze and absolutely nothing made sense any more. I was, and still am, in a state of shock.

I spent 30 hours by my son's brain-dead body, his heart still beating until the life-support machine was switched off an infinity later and, during that Time between Times I experienced flying out with him on great white wings into a great white light and a loving presence. My son communicated by telepathy to me and I received from him the blissful and to me at the time incomprehensible, message. 'The only thing that matters is love the only thing that matters'. I could not understand how this could come to me in the state I was in of utter panic, horror and despair, alone as I was with only a friend and my son's 'dead' body in a foreign hospital.

It is true though that at times, during those 30 hours, as I rested my head against his in a half waking, half sleeping state, I felt his great peace and he was able to reach out to me to calm and comfort me. As he lay dying in the road, I had seen with my own eyes how my son's face had changed to utter beauty and peace only minutes after he had been crying out in pain, trying to lift his wounded head, blood in his mouth, unseeing eyes. If I had not seen that I would not be alive now.

At that time I knew nothing of the many accounts of near-death and out-of-body experiences that are talked of everywhere now. It has struck me how similar they are to what I experienced there at my son's bedside. For a very long time I felt a great confusion, not being able to somehow reconcile these experiences with my former understandings, but I found that meditation and healing were helpful, indeed, essential to my surviving with my sanity intact. I found that only Spiritualism and Tibetan Buddhism seem to have any working knowledge of after death states.

I have already written in 'Journey into Darkness' (an article published in the anthology *Glancing Fires: An Investigation into Women's Creativity*, edited by Leslie Saunders, The Women's Press, 1986, the full version having appeared as 'Journeying through the Underworld: the Darkness in my Mind', *Arachne* — the matriarchy journal — in 1986) about my fears concerning my work over many years with the women's and Goddess movements. I felt that, ultimately, my own work and exhibitions had harmed my son. I, who had for so many years written and talked of the living dead in the Mother's magical other world, now felt that all this had been just so many words, that I had understood nothing and had no right to speak, write or paint any more. I am now doing some work again.

Unfortunately, I had been involved in a women's Full Moon celebration in the house we had visited in the Basque country the very night before my son was killed. This does not help matters for me now. The celebration had sparked off hostilities against me and my son in some of the women who had felt uneasy about such magical work. I had also not been aware that there were quarrels and difficulties among the British women who had rented the large house for a holiday, nor had I known that my son would not be welcome because of his age, size and gender. There were other boys present but they were younger. It seems that my son became the focus for the already bad feelings going around. An argument the morning after the Full Moon ritual left my son upset and therefore more vulnerable and accident-prone. The fact is that this connection became firmly embedded in my mind and I have felt fear at the thought of being in a women's gathering doing any spiritual work. This fear goes against the grain of anything I have ever believed in, but I have had to stay with it for now.

Something else that is eerie and ominous is the fact that I had gone with a friend the day before my son's death to one of the famous Palaeolithic caves in the Basque Pyrenées where there are bone carvings of humans and animals and rock drawings of the corpulant and massive Mother. There, deep inside the mountain, were huge domed halls of glittering and icy, magical stalactites that could be played like organs. I now wonder what spirits dwell there and what revenge they take on intruders who disturb their peace just out of curiosity? This has also led me to think of all the tombs, dwellings of the ancient dead and resting places of the sacred ancestors that have been desecrated, dug up, broken into, their bones and belongings being removed to the museums and to the homes of rich, white Western collectors. Even worse, uranium being taken from the sacred ancestral lands of native Australians and Americans, nuclear waste being dumped on ancient and holy Hopi lands. In the world view of the ancients' time, space, the physical world and the supernatural realms are continuous and interconnected parts of the Universe. Humans and spirits interconnect at all levels and we ignore this at our peril.

Luisah Teish says in *Jambalaya* that the 'Place of Light' — the realm of Yemaya Olokun, the place where the surviving creative intelligence of the known ancestors meets the greatest of the forces of Nature, the womb of the single cell — is at the bottom of the sea. There She holds in Her hand the Great Serpent, Damballah Hwedo, who represents all the known ancestors. Through Olokun and Damballah we are given access to the knowledge and ex-

perience of all the people who have lived before. Our spirit ancestors communicate with us through signs, omens, dreams and during trance states. The living dead continue creating in the spirit
world because the essential energy of existence continues beyond
physical life.

I consider that my first initiation into the Goddess happened
during the natural home birth of my son Toivo, in Bristol, now
27 years ago, even though at that time I didn't consciously know
of Her. He was born in the night-time, during high tides of geomag-
netic energies and, during the birth, I had seen with my inner
eyes great masses of deep darkness alternating with blinding light
— contrasting and empowering each other.

The Birthing Woman is the original shaman. She brings the
ancestral spirit being into this realm while risking her life doing
so. No wonder that the most ancient temples were the sacred birth
places and that the priestesses of the Mother were also midwives,
healers, astrologers and guides to the souls of the dying. Women
bridge the borderline realms between life and death and in the
past have therefore always been the oracles, sibyls, mediums and
wise women.

Native American writer and poet Paula Gunn Allen says in *The
Sacred Hoop: Recovering the Feminine in American Indian Traditions* (Beacon Press, 1986) that the power of original creation thinking is connected to the power of mothering. Motherhood is ritually
powerful and of great spiritual and occult competence because
bearing, like bleeding, is a transformative magical act. It is the
power of ritual magic, the power of thought or mind, that gives
rise to biological organisms as well as to social organizations, cultures and transformations of all kinds. She says that her people
— the Keres Lagunas — associate the essential nature of feminin-
ity with the creative power of thought. The thoughts of Grandmother Spider result in the physical manifestations of all
phenomena, that Her power of dreaming is great and therefore
She gives life to the people. White is the colour of Shipapu —
the place of emergence and of return — that is the Underworld
where the ancestors live and the dead return.

Here the Great Corn Mother lives in Her various guises and
aspects and the rivers of life come together. Shipapu has been
described as a labyrinth and as a vaginal birth passage. Glaston-
bury Tor is such a place of emergence and return. Paula Gunn
Allen points out that women-centred and Mother ritual-based cultures value peacefulness, harmony, co-operation, health and
general prosperity.

In 1968, which happened to be the year of the major lunar stand-still that occurs only every 19 years. I worked on my painting 'God Giving Birth'. This sacred painting came out of both my religious belief and my experience of birth. To my surprise it caused me to be the victim of something of a witch-hunt. The painting was nearly censored many times and in 1973, during our first large feminist arts exhibition at Swiss Cottage library in London, I was threatened with being taken to court for 'obscenity and blasphemy'.

The deity in 'God Giving Birth' is not a white woman, nor is She sexually pleasing or accommodating to men, but is as powerful and impersonal as the Universe itself. I didn't know then that it has been argued that the human race originates from a few African women and the Goddess is indeed black. I didn't know of the Black Madonnas of Europe, images that are most magically powerful and mysterious, and most likely pre-Christian. The Catholic cult of the Virgin stems from the ship of Isis, the Egyptian Black Moon Goddess. I hadn't seen either the innumerable images and sculptures of Goddesses giving birth from cultures worldwide.

During a number of years before the birth of the new women's movement and before feminist and Goddess artists came together, I felt a great isolation. What kept me going and gave me confidence to do my work — living as I did then in poverty, with no formal art school training and having at that time two small children — later they were three — was the memory of my wonderful and dreamy artist mother and having a sense of being used as a medium by ancient women. Painting became to me a shamanistic journey into other realities where past, present and future coexist and bringing back with me visions from ancient women cultures as well as those of a possible future.

I kept coming across images from pre-classical Greece of powerful and dignified women who were clearly bisexual by nature. Institutionalized heterosexuality is yet another perversion created by patriarchal societies and exists to drain women of our spiritual, psychic, emotional and sexual energies to feed the egos of men. I am not saying that loving and joyful relationships cannot exist between women and men, but the patriarchal family institution relies on diminishing women, draining our lifeblood away.

I also found the image of the Theban Sphinx with its woman's head, lion's body and vulture's wings — especially haunting. Only recently have I learned that She was the Theban Moon Goddess, Dark guardian of the dead, of Second sight and of prophecy. I felt that I was called by the ancient Mother to do Her work. I have

been told that there is a strange, almost Moonlit quality in my
paintings. Visually I have also been very influenced by growing
up in the north of Sweden where the light reflecting off the snow
can be blindingly white and the presence of Skadi, the Snow
Queen, is always strong. I grew up on the sagas of trolls and giants,
the nature spirits of the North.

The second initiation into the Goddess, which changed my life
and work, took place early in February, 1978, at Avebury/Silbury.
I had gone there that day with a lover and we had taken some
magic mushrooms. The ancients used mind expanding substances
to gain vision into other realities as do present-day tribal peoples. This is what I wrote at the time:

'Five days after Imbolc we arrived on a beautiful late winter day
at Avebury village, which is built within the stone circle — the
largest in Northern Europe. Amazing, rough, squat, colossal stones
seeming like human bodies and gigantic heads. Here, one feels,
is *the* centre of the Mother Goddess. What would it be like living
in this village, being part of Her living body? The earth around
the stone circle is shaped and moulded in ridges and ditches. Many
of the stones are mutilated, like half a head chopped off — painful to see. Many are missing and ugly-looking triangular shaped
stones have been positioned to mark where they fell and once
stood. They look like the gravestones they really are. During the
Burning Times/Witch-hunts, the stones were also tortured, split
apart and buried. The Church feared their power as they feared
the power of women. There still remains a great power, beauty
and mystery in this place and these stones.

'We followed the earth-works around the entire circle and then
slowly followed the remains of West Kennet stone avenue as it
winds its way across the fields. I now long to arrive at Silbury
mound, the great pregnant earth womb. We have seen Her in the
distance on the road from Bristol and from the village.

'I clutch a stone in my hand for safety as we plod across the
ploughed and muddy fields, having always to cross barbed-wire
fences. By now, gripped by panic, unable to either remain this
side of or to cross over the ugly, now seemingly *so* offensive fences,
wanting to find comfort and refuge with the breast/eye/womb-
belly rising out of the landscape so naked and vulnerable yet so
powerful, we scramble through what seems like marshland and
wilderness. I feel as if transported thousands of years back in time.

'We come closer to the womb and discover that on the road
by Her side there is parked a square, bright red lorry with the
name "Peter Lord" written on its side. "Lord", oh no, is there

nowhere, not even in the Mother's presence, when one is allowed to forget about patriarchy's deadly god?

'Nearer the mound we discover notices saying "The monument is closed due to erosion". Silbury, surrounded by water at this time of year, is everywhere enclosed by treble layers of barbed-wire fencing. Feeling stunned, the earth appears to move and flicker. Some swans are frozen motionless as they swim in the waters of the moat and I feel trapped in eternity. Some teenagers scramble past us up Silbury and we follow them, hoping that they will not talk to us, we who are of another time. I feel fear at treading on my Mother's belly, the grass matted like hair and uncared for. A man shouts from the road, "Get down from there". We sit down on the side of the mound furthest from the road, the teenagers disappearing out of sight and hearing.

'I am overtaken by a sudden unexpected and enormous grief. The Mother, the entire mound, cries through me, I feel Her pain in my own womb. I am at one with Her, grieving for our lost women cultures, for the pollution and death of Her nature all around us. What have they done to you, Mother, what they done? Man shouts from the road. I feel overwheming fear — I am a hunted female animal, I've got to flee, get down from Her womb and away from the road, away. The road appears to stand for everything alien and evil — cars, men with patriarchal authority, oppression. Shots are heard regularly in the distance, coming from Salisbury Plain, which is Ministry of Defence land and used as a firing range. Aeroplanes are overhead — evil, evil danger.

'We almost run, slide down, walk slowly with great effort, tracing our way back around the moat and into the fields from where we had come. We feel a sense of victory because we have been able to avoid the road — we are safe, we are still within Her Nature. I look at the mound — it's so exposed and vulnerable, like veins of a breast streaking the sides — again there are tears and grief.

'I now understand what Mother Earth means — something so enormous and powerful. My body is like Hers — gentle and violent, powerful and vulnerable, dynamic and peaceful, matter and other world spirit.

'Slowly we follow the river Kennet, feeling myself to be floating along with Her, flowing with the wonderful water formations, dancing along with her serpentine rhythms. Suddenly I come to a sharp halt at the sight of the pollution of the waters and the rubbish accumulated here — anger, anger. More barbed-wire fences. We follow the direction leading to West Kennet Long barrow and walk up the muddy track. We see the huge stones covering the entrance.

*West Kennet long barrow — abode of the Dark Mother.*

We walk around them and suddenly we see the stark blackness from the entrance into the dark — this time underground — womb. Fear being swallowed up by the so intense darkness, but I overcome the fear and enter. It's a totally other world in there, one of mystery, power, peace. Sounds are amplified in here and the stone chambers appear for a timeless moment to breathe and beat like a great heart. I feel like gyrating, feel like a spiral, then I have a great urge to sleep on the floor in the innermost uterus chamber. There is a great stillness in Her living darkness. Feeling infinitely 'higher' within this tomb-womb-temple than when re-entering the daylight world outside. This is not just a grave, it is the place of journeys into the spirit realms to connect with the ancestors. I feel strange and powerful vibrations. Here there are no feelings of sorrow or vulnerability — this is the abode of Cailleach, the gigantic Crone Grandmother. It seems that we are welcome.

'We walk down the muddy track and have a feeling of great tiredness — just want to sleep. We retrace our way back to Avebury village and around the stones, then we drive off. We had been there in all seven hours'.

For several weeks afterwards I kept seeing living and breathing forms in the landscape, I experienced Earth's body, and from then on, I started to seek out and make pilgrimages to the sacred Neolithic places in the Celtic world. The stones, skies, sea and wells appeared now in my paintings in a way that they had never done before, especially after we moved to a cottage in Welsh Pembrokeshire in 1980. We lived there for five years until Leif's death. Many powerful Neolithic sites in the area near Fishguard, where we were based, and Saint Non's Well at Saint David's became to me the place of birth, while the bleeding yew in Nevern graveyard is the place of death and rebirth. On the slopes of the Preselau mountains above Nevern, stands the Gateway-Cromlech Pentre Ifan, formerly known to the Druids as 'The Womb of Cerridwen'.

I was powerfully drawn to the magical, menstruating Yew Tree Mother in the darkness of the graveyard. I had also experienced the dark Cailleach on the summer solstice in the Callanish stone circle on the Isle of Lewis on the Outer Hebrides. I had been there with some other women, watching the Sun go down and rise again for the solstice of 1982. That night was the dark of the Moon and we decided to return to the stone circle. As we sat among the stones, singing and calling, it was as if we were overtaken by an ancient power and we started to keen wildly from deep within our bellies, sounding like the Banshee Herself. The next day we made the long track up the Silver Maiden/Sleeping Beauty mountain and had an extraordinary experience of power.

The stone circles on Lewis were raised according to lunar settings and risings above Her ridges. I saw the Silver Maiden again there, watching the full Moon rise above Her in September 1987, the year of another major lunar standstill. She is the primordial mountain Mother, older than anything on Earth.

Never would I have dreamed that I would so tangibly experience in my own life and being the grief and pain I has sensed at Silbury and that I had felt to be Hers, but then I have never felt that anything was just personal, either in my life as it has unfolded or in my paintings. As above so below, or, from macro to microcosm as the ancients believed. It also seems uncannily prophetic that I should have so emphasized in my writing on the Silbury experience, the dangers and evil of the road and of cars considering the way my young son died.

I had not been aware that the Greenham Common US Cruise missile base and other bases were close by Silbury. Since 1982 I have taken part in some actions and gatherings at the women's peace camp at Greenham Common. I feel that it is no coincidence that the women there have always sung, 'You can't kill the spirit, She is like a mountain, old and strong, She goes on and on and on'. This is indeed the Silbury Mother Herself calling Her daughters to rise up at last.

Once, on my way to Greenham on the autumn equinox in 1984 to take part in the ten-day gathering there, I had a strange and wonderful dream when parked with a friend in her van at the foot of Silbury. I dreamed that we were in the dark night by Silbury mound waiting for something when we suddenly saw an immense, luminous and pulsating 'cloud-being' radiating light and resting along the base of the mound. I felt very blessed to have seen this (whatever it was) and I woke up feeling exhilarated.

It was on Silbury on Beltane night, 1985 that I met Musawa (the American woman who I and Leify visited on her farm near the Pyrenées in the South of France the summer he was killed). I had gone to Silbury to meet up with other women — there were perhaps a hundred of us — to walk across Salisbury Plain firing range to reclaim that sacred land. We celebrated Beltane on Silbury and we were heading for Stonehenge at the end. The walk had been initiated by Greenham women and a few Americans, like Starhawk and Musawa, took part. Starhawk is the well-known author, peace activist and witch, Musawa produces the most beautiful *We Moon* diaries. I had known that this walk would somehow change my life, but not that it would utterly change it through the death of my young son.

I had felt warning bells in my head about going to Stonehenge, which I associated with gruesome patriarchal sites and human sacrifices. It is a place well-beloved by Druids and male gurus of

*Leif's ashes buried in the medicine wheel in the Tipi village in Wales.*

all shades. As it was, we found ourselves within the stones, singing and drumming, during the full Moon lunar eclipse on 4 May. That experience was a very powerful one and the whole walk had been totally amazing — we had felt like an invincible and unstoppable army of women. However, I had also felt a little uncomfortable about meeting Musawa, but, to my cost, I ignored this warning and, when she came back with me to Wales after the walk, I had the idea of visiting her that summer in the South of France with Leif. It had seemed like a wonderful idea — an escape from the wet and cold Welsh summer.

Looking back, it seems to me that the Mother at Silbury had brought me and Musawa together. Leif was killed on the Full Moon in August. That morning we had eaten corn on the cob, gathered from a field the day before (I am still unable to eat corn), and Silbury is the northern Corn-Mother, the people gathering on Her womb at Lammas in August to offer Her their first fruits and to watch the pregnant mound give birth to the harvest child. When the news reached Bristol of my son's death (I had managed to phone my other sons — oh, how I wished that they could have been there with me by Leif's side — from the hospital in Bayonne), some beloved friends, who had been like second mothers to my son, immediately went to Silbury where women had gathered for the now yearly women's festival held at the time of the August full Moon. There they danced, naked, singing, drumming, crying on our Mother's belly, communicating with Leify's spirit and sending me healing in my greatest hour of need. The Basque country where my son was killed is known for its ancient Craft Traditions.

In August 1986, the 21-year-old daughter of my good friend Beverly Skinner jumped off the Bristol Suspension Bridge and died on impact — every bone in her body shattered. Beverly is a Goddess artist like myself and together with Anne Berg, we have exhibited in 'Woman Magic — Celebrating the Goddess Within Us' that travelled through Britain, Germany and Scandinavia between 1979 and 1987. Talented, beautiful and disturbed, Sheba had lost any sense of reality. She died on 13 August, the festival of Hecate, dark Moon Mother of the ancient Greeks. The night before she died, I had written a poem called 'This dreaded month of August'. I went with Beverly to identify her daughter's body — two sorrowing mothers by yet another beloved child's cold body; it was too much. I then stayed with Beverly for the next two weeks while she raged and grieved and nearly went crazy. It felt as if we were somehow both being punished for doing our Mother's work in paintings and writings and I wrote this at the time:

'Your cold bodies, Sheba and Leif,
our children gone — one girl and one boy —
so innocent and vulnerable in death.
   Are you some strange fruits,
   offerings of our bodies,
   to the Mother of harvest?
   in the dreaded month of August?
Have we gone wrong,
we artists and mothers of the 'Woman Magic' exhibition,
'Celebrating the Goddess Within Us'?
   Is it dangerous to confront'
   the patriarchal entities, alive in the beyond
   in this destructive age of mega-deaths?
   Are we punished?
Or, are our children blessed and protected
to be the chosen ones,
to be taken back to you
in their youth, innocence and beauty?
   I wish we knew, our Mother,
   great spirit of the Universe,
I wish we knew, I wish . . .'

Is there a struggle in other realms? What patriarchal entities hateful, revengeful and life-denying — have been summoned up or created by collective human thought-forms over several millenia? They have been fed, like the vultures or vampires they are, on blood and fire sacrifices and the hearts of women. Was this the intention, on an occult level, of the witch burnings that for hundreds of years robbed Europe of its most magical and powerful women and of its gay males? At the risk of seeming mad, I have now to ask these questions. This is one more reason why it is of such importance that women rise up and that we all visualize the Goddess strongly and powerfully before it is all too late.

My co-writer Barbara Mor has experienced nothing but gruelling poverty — living homeless in the streets of Tucson, Arizona and not being able to feed or look after her children — ever since the American version of our book *The Great Cosmic Mother* was published by Harper & Row in the summer of 1987. There seems to have been rather too many so called 'coincidences' or disastrous happenings around our exhibitions and the book over the years.

Astrologer writer Demetra George's theory, as propounded in *Mysteries of the Dark Moon* (1987) and *Asteroid Goddess* (ACS Publications, 1986), offers another way of looking at these things. Her theory is that, during the last 5,000 years (the Kali Yuga), the Goddess magnetically withdrew into the recessive dark Moon phase of Her cycle and that she has been sleeping deep dreams, like those of Persephone, in the Underworld. There She distilled Her wisdom into a new seed, renewed Herself and transformed Her being for a rebirth and a new cycle of unfoldment that will start to happen now. Demetra says that the Goddess was *not* disempowered, but needed to withdraw to mutate and transform Herself. Men, however, were especially disturbed by this and felt abandoned by the Mother so they started to fear death and wanted to banish Her forever, which is why patriarchal rule has vilified and demonized the Crone.

There has been a disturbance of the natural balances of energy through such actions as the atomic experiments and the reshaping of the DNA structure, the results of manipulative wrong thinking. Nuclear scientists have been the 'fathers of death', holding the fate of all of Nature in their hands. They have disturbed the dance, there is a rent in the veil — as there is in the ozone layer — of Mother Earth. The etheric web of our sacred sphere has been torn at places like the Black Mesa in America and sites sacred to the rainbow serpent in Australia. Dhyani Ywahoo, the native American Buddhist woman teacher, says that the form of thought generated by human beings has been of such a discordant nature that the elements cannot respond to the Mother's will and that her lifeblood cannot move. Machines are eating the Earth and all the high-density electric cables drain the Earth of her energies. All the sickness is coming to the surface now. Her recommendation is that we pray every day and visualize, weave and create pillars of light around the Earth to keep the elemental beings of fear and destruction out. As she says, however, prayer doesn't mean a thing if it doesn't grow corn, so feed the hungry and get rid of oppression and injustice in the world.

I have come to fear the month of August and cannot but help noticing just how many ominous historical events have happened in this month, including the dropping of the atomic bombs on Hiroshima and Nagasaki in 1945 and to Australian aboriginal women this is the time of year for mourning and grief. Perhaps, however, the Silbury Mother honoured my son and Beverly's daughter by taking them back to Her at this time. She is the Greater Mother who gave us life and creates our destinies so how can we presume to know better than Her? Is Leif the eternal sacred youth, gone in his full vigour and beauty, son of Matrona or Rhiannon, White Horse Goddess of Wales that I have imaged in several of my paintings. Is he a form of Lugh, the Celtic God who died

*Vision of my young son as the Green Man.*

a sacrificial death in August. Lammas was Lughnasad to the Celts and both Lugh and Rhiannon are ancient other world beings.

In the summer of 1988, during the journey in America that became like a pilgrimage to me, I found myself giving a slide show and talk on the full Moon on 27 August, at a West Coast moat of Earth mysteries. It was held in the Valley of the Moon by the Sonoma mountains in California. A friend, in the half waking half sleeping state, had a vision there of my young son looking beautiful and blissful, a radiant full Moon suspended between lunar horns, growing from his head of red curly hair. She 'heard' from him and he said, 'I am the lover of the Goddess now'. She recognized him the next day from my paintings.

On that journey I also spent ten days in the north of Oregon with Musawa on the farm where she now lives. We had a difficult time together, trying to understand what happened in the south of France and in what ways our joint Capricornian energies, or karmic paths, had contributed to my son's 'accidental' death. Why had Leify always seemed larger than life to me, why I was not able to envisage his future or who he would be, why did he himself say several times that he didn't think he have a chance to grow up — why, oh why? Why had I repeated my mother's pattern of living with a man who couldn't tolerate having a child? I was fully prepared not to come back alive from America.

I have re-visited Silbury and Avebury several times in the last few years. The first time was on 23 January 1986, when my son would have been 16 years old. I went there with three women friends and we were on Silbury in the late evening at the hour of his birth. I had brought with me a knife in case I felt the need to end my life there as a sacrifice to the Mother who had taken my son, but, instead, I asked Her for help and guidance, and I thanked Her for the gift of his short life. I felt strongly that She had drawn us there that day and in the early morning hours, I received a lucid dream of my son. I saw him flying out into dark space, looking like 'a beautiful red flame' — these are the words that came though to me. So many times in visions and meditations have I seen Leify in my mind's eye — red Afro hair flowing, African drum slung on his shoulder (the drum that his ashes were buried in and that he played the summer of his death) beautiful and nude, riding a wild white horse — a true son of Rhiannon in summerland. Another time, I lay on Silbury and wanted to scream and cry and curse, but instead felt a great love welling up through my being, from my womb upwards, and I felt that She grieved with me and all mothers on this Earth. However, and this is true also, as Barbara Walker says in her book *The Crone-woman of Age, Wisdom and Power* (Harper & Row, 1985) that Kali, as death-dealing hideous Crone, poses the true test of faith. It is She who appears in the fairy-tales as the hideously ugly Hag who the true hero has to kiss or marry and only when he has proven his humility and real understanding by seeing beyond appearances does She reveal Her radiantly beautiful maiden self. In the same way, She tests you again and again until you retreat into madness and death *or* re-emerge to tell the tale with a greater understanding and knowledge. She is the Tibetan Dakini who drinks your blood from your skull-cap and dances on your bones, but She is also the beauty of the green Earth. Like Inanna, I felt at times that I have been demolished and hung up like a rag on the meat-hook in Queen Ereshkigel's halls in the dark Underworld.

I left everything of my former life behind in Wales and went to live with Sean, my other son, in Bristol where he was receiving chemotherapy treatment at a local hospital and attending the Cancer Help Centre. We existed together in a strange twilight zone — both of us living between the worlds, he in his illness and I in my grief. I had wanted to die and fly away into the great light to join Leify, but had found that it was not possible to do so — I had to remain here to be with my ill son and there was more to learn, even more sorrow and pain and grief to live through.

The first three months back in Bristol we lived in a council-sponsored bed and breakfast accommodation because we were homeless. At that time I was so numbed by feelings of shame and worthlessness, just wanting to disappear down a dark hole or sit naked in a cave, that any humiliation seemed fitting. I was mortified at the thought of meeting any one of my innumerable friends in Bristol, a city I'd lived in for many years before moving to Wales.

Sean and I shared one room between us, which suited us fine, as did the total anonymity of the situation because we didn't have to speak to anyone. We walked the streets like two shadows — when Sean had the strength to walk — and it was a great effort for both of us to achieve the simplest task. We spent many months going back and forth to hospitals and for long periods Sean had to stay in having chemotherapy and blood transfusions. Chemotherapy breaks down the body's immune system as with AIDS and I now know what it is like to live with someone to whom the slightest infection can be lethal. This experience left me with a low regard for conventional doctors, who I consider to be body technicians rather than healers. We also had to suffer the incredible arrogance of consultants.

In the summer of 1986, my son seemed to be getting stronger and we were hoping that he might actually recover and get well again. Sean was convinced that he was a wounded healer, a Shaman who had nearly died and had returned to life to be able to heal and help others.

Through the Bristol Cancer Help Centre, we had got involved in the holistic health movement. My son had been a lifelong vegetarian and was always interested in alternatives. We joined meditation and healing circles, we read widely on out of body and near-death experiences, we went to spiritualist churches and felt relief at finding people there who take seriously the possibility of communication with the spirit realms. Most mediums are women. Sean read up on conventional and alternative medicine, on science and physics — we looked at everything in an attempt to try to understand what was happening to us.

To some degree we also got involved in what can broadly be described as the New Age movement — 'White Lighters' as they are called in California where so much of it originates — but I felt increasingly alienated by its elitist and patriarchal attitudes. It appears to be based in class priviledge, money, a white skin and American manhood. With this follows a 'blame the victims' attitude, which is very ugly and cynical. I have written an as yet unpublished analysis of the movement called *Earth; The Violated Mother — New Age Thinking and the Millennium* (Women's Press, 1991).

Sean made the fatal mistake of getting involved with two irresponsible Rebirthers who practise near Bristol. Sean thought that they would be able to help him get at childhood traumas that he was convinced had caused his illness. We didn't realize at the time that the Rebirthing movement had developed a somewhat unhealthy philosophy of life that included blaming the ill and

*Carrying my son's ashes in my arms.*

dying for sinning against 'God the Father' and a theory of physical Immortalism. The poor, the ill and oppressed are told that they themselves are responsible for their suffering and poverty and that they create their own reality.

Practising 'Prosperity consciousness', the Rebirthers conned my son out of a considerable amount of money for expensive sessions that culminated in a 10-day long 'Intensive' for £400 — money my son could ill afford.

Sean had become increasingly depressed, exhausted and ill as the 'sessions' progressed and he returned from the Intensive very, very ill. It was discovered that he had a growth the size of a football in his lung that was pressing on his heart and that he had pneumonia from sitting in hot bath tubs used by Rebirthers. If he had followed the Rebirthers' advice to ignore any symptoms of illness, he would have died then and there. As it was, he had now relapsed to a far worse cancerous condition and he developed epileptic fits over the New Year of 1986/7 as a result of some cancerous patches developing on his brain. Our lives turned into times of utter fear, terror and dread. This is a poem I wrote at the time:

Suicide
    is a luxury for me
        who has to stay here
            watching over my son
                who is dying a thousand
                    deaths
                    daily
                    nightly
despair and a sense of defeat
gripping at my heart, at our hearts.

                In my dreams
                I am with you my son
                already lost.
                I awake to a grey dawn
                of memories.

        Who am I?
            Why, oh why?
                Tears, grief and loss.

                Leif, my beautiful young son
                with me in forgotten dreams
                    Where are you,
                        oh, who are you now?

Sean, my eldest son, ill and in fear
     from cancer
          living in a shared twilight world,
               him and me,
                    crucified together.

Every day,
     days and days go by.
     How long, oh how long?
          Cancer eating us both away.
          Perhaps we will live
          or perhaps we will not...

There was even a week or so when I was afraid of my son. I thought
he was losing his mind and was afraid of what he might do —
I was afraid for him, afraid for me — and I couldn't leave him
for a minute. Many nights I slept in your room, Sean, reading aloud
*The Once and Future King* by candle-light, trying to calm and comfort you, massaging your back every night and your bald head.
Once I lay on top of you, trying to hold you, while you had a
fit, feeling your shakings and tremors in my own body, fearing
that you would stop breathing.

Sean was in great discomfort and pain much of this time because
of the many treatments he was having at once. He was very weak,
too, and had to walk on crutches. He felt a great temptation to
just let go, to join Leify, but we always hoped and hoped, in spite
of it all, that he would live.

My tall and golden boy, looking like a Saxon king, almost trans-
parent and shining in your emaciated beauty, you who had once
been such a large and well-built man — those last months before
you died.

I had asked you not to leave me when you were sitting up in
your bed so thin, so pale, dreams in your eyes, but I also said
that I didn't want to use emotional blackmail and that if you had
to go, my sweetheart, you had to go.

You were then torn between different realities, having strange
visions and dreams. You had with wonder seen a newborn foetus
in the clouds the last time you were able to go out for a walk
with your brother. When you relapsed a third time, though, there
was no more hope, the cancer moving to your liver and brain.
You just made it to your twenty-eighth birthday, my love. Just after
the summer solstice and on the full Moon of 10 July 1987, you
stopped breathing, in a morphine-drugged dream, surrounded in
the hospital room by close friends, your brother and me. (Both
of my sons died on the full Moon!)

*Bride — White Maiden — with tree and well.*

You had told me that you didn't fear death — you feared only terrible and terminal pain, so your wish for a quick passing was fulfilled. I wished you a journey to happier realms and had visions of beautiful and dramatic, radiant landscapes — like the ones you used to paint and draw — in my mind's eye as I held my hand on your bald head.

Again I was mother, mourner, priestess as I had to witness your tall and thin body 'laid out' as in a crib, cold, so cold. Later I carried your ashes through Leigh Woods where we also held a wake for you with all our friends singing, drumming, dancing and celebrating your being.

For the second time in three years have I carried a son's ashes, Mother. How many times do you have to test me, how much do you think I can take of the unbearable and unthinkable — how much?

I had always felt such a richness in the presence of my three sons, but now I feel a barrenness overtaking me. It feels as if the future has also been cut off, too, as these sons of mine will now

never have children of their own. I have truly been cut to the bone
and hung up as a carcass on the hook in dreaded Queen Ereshkigel's Underworld.

However, during my pilgrimage in America, I was given signs
of hope of a possible future. One important meeting was with
Luisah Teish, the Voodoo Priestess. I felt that my mixed race son,
Leif, had somehow brought us together and it was Sean who spoke
through her when she entered a trance state after having
introduced me to the ancestors and shrines of the Goddess Oshun.

Sean advised me that I can go no further in identifying with
the Crone than by entering death myself, that I must now be
renewed and transformed into the maiden self, and he told me
what to do. As I am writing this it is January and approaching
Imbolc or Bride's day of February 1989, time of the re-emergence
of the maiden.

I wrote myself long ago in *The Great Cosmic Mother* book, that
in the mysteries of the dark Moon there is a fine balance between
madness and death, ecstacy and illumination. Life will tell what
it will be, not just for me but for all of us living as we all do on
the edge of a precipice of universal destruction.

# 7
# The Path of the Solar Priestess

## Sunflower

The visionary world of the priestess, the abode of her inspiration, is focalized most visibly in her shrine. Sunflower's lapidary journey to the Goddess unfolds through the medium of her many shrines, which are the two-way mirror of commucation between the priestess and her Mistress. Sunflower's breadth of vision encompasses the full scope of the Divine Feminine with a loving heart and reverent glory.

Most women are drawn naturally to the moon as the metaphor of their Goddessly service, but the path of the solar priestess reveals a rewarding avenue of exploration for those who need to balance their unconscious yearnings with their manifest priesthood. The breath of Sekhmet and the joyous ululation of Hathor are the prime antidotes to sorrow and despair.

Sunflower *was born in 1958 and grew up in Birmingham. Although not from a religious background, she had a devoutly Christian phase in child-hood, followed by a sharp U-turn into atheism! When she moved to London to study, she encountered the Goddess through women from the Matriarchy Research and Reclaim Network. She felt she had recovered her direction in life, for, although her experience of feminism had helped her define herself as a woman, only through re-connecting with her spirituality could she enrich and deepen this. Since 1981, she has been involved in various ritual magic and pagan groups. She is committed to the revival of the Women's Mystery Tradition and she works as a priestess both within this and in the Fellow-ship of Isis. She is currently exploring the subject of female magical polarity. On a mundane level, she has worked in museums as a restorer for the last ten years.*

# The Path of the Solar Priestess

'I shall never forget her who is the Giver of Happiness,
She it is, O Mother, who, in the form of the Moon,
Creates the World full of sounds and meaning,
and again, by her power in the form of the Sun,
She it is who maintains the world,
And she again, it is who, in the form of Fire,
Destroys the whole universe at the end of the age.'

Hymn to Kali

'She is radiant like the rising sun,
Her beauty lights up the world,
She wears sun and moon as her jewels,
Her eyes are like fish and lotus and darting deer,
Her face is fragrant like chambaka,
Her hair like incense,
She has capacities, she is active,
She is aware, she is fearless, she is free.'

Chandralekha Skills Centre, Madras

I first came across the concept of the divine feminine as the Goddess of the palaeolithic and neolithic period, celebrated throughout the old world as the mother. The dead were buried for rebirth in chambers shaped like her body, heaped over with mounds swelling like pregnant bellies. Encountering the great mother who sheltered the dead in her womb heralded my own personal release from the anxiety of death and also the fear of darkness, which I had had since I was a child.

Like everyone else I knew, I had been brought up in a society terrified of death and old age where people were trying to travel a steep ascent to various success-orientated goals. It was empowering to discover that I was part of another pattern, one that had much more meaning for me as a woman. The cyclical nature of paganism curves the unfaltering line of patriarchal time into a seasonal spirit of growth and decay, marked by the eight festivals of the solar and agricultural year and the waxing and waning of the lunar cycle.

Paganism is not afraid of death, but accepts it as a fact of life. Each individual has a space both at the still centre of the wheel of the year, which to me is personified by the Goddess, sitting like a spider at the centre of her web of creation, and a lifetime journey around it — the wheel keeps turning regardless.

## Shrine of Earth

On 2 February 1985 — Candlemas — at West Kennet, Long-barrow, Avebury, I set up an earth shrine in one of the chambers using an existing stone slab and other members of my group set up elemental altars in the other chambers. On one side of the altar I place a dog skull, on the other a pot of spring bulbs just coming into flower. I cover the skull with a black veil and the flowers with a green one. In the centre I place a Goddess image a friend has made me for my twenty-fifth birthday. In front of it I place dried corn and poppies and unlit candles for each member of the group. I light the triple-branched candlestick containing red, white and black candles and leave the following instructions:

> Remove the black veil to your left and say:
> 'This is the Place of Death.
> See the face of Death behind the veil
> I am the Dark Mother, who awaits you here
> in this stony tomb'
>
> Remove the green veil to your right and say:
> 'This is the chamber of Rebirth.
> Behold, the Great Mother the Life-Giver,
> It is I who await you here
> in this my gentle womb.
>   'See the corn cut with my scythe
> See the corn grown from my body
> Birth and Death are both my mysteries
> Both are part of my Spiral Dance'.
>
>   Then take a white candle and light it when you are ready.
>   Meditate on the mysteries of death and life. Put aside the things you wish to leave behind, surrender them up to the Goddess that they might be transformed. See and accept your own mortality.
>   The candle is a symbol of your living spirit, the eternal flame that cannot be extinguished. The lighting of this symbolizes a new phase, a self-initiation, and you now enter of your free will, in this sacred place.

People may think of the traditional figure of the priest or priestess as a public person, out there in front of the crowds conducting ceremonies. If you choose to work alone or have not joined a group, this path is equally valid as the personal contact with the deity is, after all, what matters, not who is there to see you.

One of the techniques I have used to focus my mind on a deity, is to make it the centre ('focus' literally translates as centre) of my home. Part of the path of Hestia and Hertha, Goddess of hearth and home, to me is the making and dedicating of shrines, to welcome the Goddess in. If I am teaching a group, I also like to set up altars to consecrate the room. Shrines are an important act of magical intent as you are creating a space for the deity to live with you. On inner levels you enter the force field of the deity, so you become linked and not separate. If you want to break this link it will be easy to do so by neglect or disinterest, but while it exists it is binding.

A shrine is a place hallowed by memory and special associations, but, unlike a ritual, it is always there to refresh you and may change from day to day, season to season.

Instead of describing rituals I have been involved in, which, being experiential, are difficult to communicate in a really meaningful way, I want instead to make clear concepts that have been important to me by letting my shrines speak for me.

Having 'set the scene', I shall describe in detail one particular piece of magical work carried out in preparation for my ordination as priestess and talk about the meaning this vocation has for me and others.

## The Yoni Shrine

This was the first shrine I made, in 1982. 'Yoni' is the Indian word for vulva and images of the sacred yoni of the Goddess were set up over the doors of Hindu temples and worn smooth by touching for luck and longevity. I have collected and placed on a red altar cloth (to denote the red lochial and menstrual blood) yoni-shaped stones, cowrie shells and geodes split open, to reveal their secret, inner crystal chambers. A tiny bronze sheela-na-gig peers out from one and at the back of the shrine there is an etching of another from Kilpeck in Hertfordshire, done by an artist friend. (A sheela-na-gig is a sculpture of a woman displaying her vulva, the first of these dating from at least the medieval period and possibly much earlier*.) The shrine also contains copies of very ancient images of the Goddess. One is headless so I have placed a snail shell on her shoulders. She carries an ear of corn, child-like, in her lap and a hazelnut from a Samhain celebration. Pinned

*The largest collection of sheela-na-gigs may be seen by appointment in the reserve collection of the National Museum of Ireland.

up around the shrine are copies of Monica Sjöö's visionary paintings and other yonic imagery of the landscape such as wells, caves
and flowers. There is also a photograph of me sweeping out the
entrance to the Cretan cave of Eilithyiea, Goddess of childbirth.

## Shrine to the Goddess of a Thousand Names

On this north-facing shrine, I have grouped 20 or so small Goddess statuettes from all over the world. Some of these I have bought
or made, others friends have kindly brought back from their travels
and given to me. The little Mexican birth-giving Goddess, carved
from a vegetable gourd, is placed at the front now as I write, but
I move them around with the seasons.

Behind the shrine, this diversity is brought into unity by the
symbol of the Kali Yantra (a 'yantra' is a type of mandala used
for meditational purposes). The form of the yantra is always the
downward-pointing triangle — the yoni of the Goddess. Its cen-
tremost point is the 'bindu', the stillness at the heart of creation
and, perhaps, the all-seeing eye of the womb? I like to meditate
in front of this image.

The other focus of the shrine is a statuette of the sphinx of Nax-
ienes from the Delphi museum. She gazes ahead, smiling serenely
as the seasons change around her. I place seasonal flowers, fruits,
baskets of eggs and other gifts on the shrine at different times
of the year and try to keep candles, lamps and incense burning
before it to keep its heart alive.

Unlike the formidable deities of monotheism, the Goddess shim-
mers in her many aspects and wears a different face and raiment
for each season, each part of her fascination and glory. Getting
to know Her is like becoming acquainted with someone very complex over a long period of time. When you explore her multi-
faceted personality it is like a journey into a labyrinth — you must
follow many paths. You appear to pass the same place many times,
catching a glimpse of mysterious female figures, each an echo of
the ones you saw before. The symbols and aspects of the Goddess layer over each other and repeat, like the meandering path
of the maze or the harmonics of a chord.

This mysterious woman then, is darkness and light, youth and
age, sun, moon, stars, earth and underworld; She is volcano and
mountain, sea, river and well, thunder and lightning; She may
appear in bird or animal form or as 'Mistress of the Wild Beasts';
She may come to you as the Goddess of Love and the Sacred Prostitute; as wisdom She is spirit. Above all, She is the 'Great Cosmic

Mother of All', the Universal Creatix and you, as her priestess, are a reflection of all of those things.

> 'She whom we have called Goddess for human comprehension.
> She is the source, never to be grasped at mystery.
> Terrible cauldron, womb,
> Spinning out of Her the unimaginably small
> and the immeasurably vast,
> Galaxies, worlds, flaming suns.
> and our Earth, fertile with her beneficence'.

> Elsa Gidlow, from *A Creed for Free Women (and such men as feel happy with it)*

## Shrine to the Dark and Light Aspects

On the left of the shrine is a copy of the statue of 'Our Lady of Dublin'. A miracle-working Black Virgin, she spent part of her career painted white, her hollowed back serving as a pig trough! On the right is a white porcelain statuette of Kuan-Yin, Chinese Goddess of compassion. Between them is a card depicting Prajnamaramita, the Tibetan Mother of Wisdom, symbolizing the wisdom that comes from honouring both dark and light. In front of Kuan-Yin is a small statuette of black Isis offering her breast. In front of Our Lady is a tiny white figure of Kuan-Yin, bought in Soho. Behind each figure is half of a Night and Day shell, one side of which is brown and the other white. Before the figures, on an embroidered panel, is a bowl of rose petals. The shrine contains a basket, holding sacred objects associated with the Women's Mystery Tradition.

Near the shrine, on flanking walls, are two life-size wall paintings, done by artist friends, depicting Isis and Nephthys, the light and dark sister-Goddesses of Ancient Egypt.

> 'Who dares misery love
> And hug the form of death
> Dance in destruction's dance,
> To him the Mother comes'.

> Vivekananda

In the nine years I have spent working within the Women's Mystery Tradition and in mixed magical groups, it has been the experience of the Dark Goddess that has been the most empower-

ing and valuable for me. She represents the hidden self, all that
is discarded, shunned or undervalued by society. This denial of
the dark is perpetuated by us as women, by conditioning and
socialization, until it becomes a source, not of renewal, but of fear
and self-hatred.

The Dark Goddess is the aspect of the Great Goddess we first
encounter when we turn inwards. As she is recognized and
embraced as our sister-self, the long-delayed meeting may be both
joyful and painful. In encountering her, we have taken the first
step towards priestesshood, for it is not possible to go far on this
path without honouring the dark.

When we experience the terrifying aspect of the Goddess at her
darkest and bloodiest, only then have we faced ourselves. As we
look into the black mirror of her face, we see ourselves reflected.
When we embrace her terrifying form, we see she wears a smile.
If we continue only to walk in the light, our shadow-selves will
follow until we turn to face into the darkness. Like Ishtar, the
Babylonian Queen of Heaven, we begin our long and painful descent into the underworld, where we must submit ourselves to the
rule of our Dark Sister, who reigns there as Queen, before we are
permitted to return.

## Dream Diary

'I dream that my younger sister, who is pale and blond, is very
angry with me. She has cut out my face from a family group photograph because, she says, "I am the dark sister." In fact, I had at
one time felt myself to be the black sheep of the family. I turn
into a dark-skinned woman with straggling black hair and do a
Kali-like dance in front of her, saying gleefully, "Oh, I am the dark
sister, am I?"'

When we recognize the dignity and beauty of this Goddess within
ourselves we see, like Pandora, that she is accompanied by the
figure of Hope not Despair. The opportunity to change ourselves
only comes because we have dared to face the contents of the box.

## Black Goddess

Many aspects of the Dark Goddess have helped me on my journey to seeing myself as a priestess and understanding the essence
of my womanhood. I have met the mysterious Black Virgins of
Christianity, whose titles like Notre Dame de sous Terre, Notre

Dame des Mortes, belie their chthonic origins. Hecate, Queen of Witcheries, who stands at the crossroads, where the three worlds meet and offers you her key to the underworld, Ereshkigal, Queen of the Underworld who demands that you stand naked and ego-less before Her before you regain your crown of stars.

I have encountered Kali, the Mad Mother of India, whose dance is one of ecstatic transformation. Garlanded with skulls, wearing Her apron of severed hands, She dances the creation preservation and dissolution of all things. Kali, Her red tongue lolling out like a beast, Her dishevelled hair like snakes, who endlessly gives birth then devours Her children. The Morrigan, the Celtic Crow Goddess, who presides over the devastation of the battlefield, is a blood-sister of Kali, who may be seen sitting on corpses in the cemetery.

These Goddesses teach us many things about the nature of fear. They are both destroyers and creators as they give us opportuni-ties to actively release and transform our energy. They also allow us to experience death and to mourn personal losses and unreal-ized dreams. I would like to share with you a piece of work dedi-cated to the red, menstrual aspect of the Dark Goddess. This, to me, was an important part of my path to priesthood. It concerns the solar warrior-goddess of Fire and Healing, Sekhmet.

When I first became involved in magic, I realized how neglected the solar Goddesses have been, although there was ample evi-dence for them. Lunar qualities of clairvoyance, intuition, emo-tions and psychism have been traditionally designated as female and used by many magical — particularly Wiccan — groups. This watery real of dreams and visions was captured beautifully in the evocative poetry of Dion Fortune in *The Sea Priestess* (Aquarian Press, 1989).

> 'Our Lady is also the Moon called of some
> Selene, of others Luna, but by the wise Levannah . . .
> She is ruler of the tides of flux and reflux
> The waters of the great sea answer unto Her
> Likewise the tides of inner seas and
> She ruleth the Nature of Woman'.

However, it was to the fiery radiance and lust for life of the solar Goddess, that I found myself being drawn. I discovered, not only the Moon Gods, but Sun Goddesses of Japan, Egypt and Eastern Europe to cite just a few. The Celts personified the Sun as female — 'Grian' — as did the Germans, calling her 'Frau Sonne'. The source for the word Sun, 'Sunna', is, in fact, feminine. The Celtic

Goddess Brighde, is a fire and solar goddess and Saint Bridget rush crosses, still hung up to protect Irish homes, are very ancient Sun symbols. Brighde and later Saint Bridget* was worshipped in a sacred enclosure at Kildare in Ireland as the living flame. This fire was tended — like that of the vestal virgins in Rome — by priestesses. The true shrine of Hestia, Roman goddess of the hearth and home, was the fiery centre of the earth. In the Eleusinian mysteries of the Goddess in Greece, the initiates experience a great burst of light in the darkness, the transmission of the Gnosis.

Why is is that women are guardians of the sacred flame of the Gnosis, the moment of revelation, of illumination? Is it because we only find this by turning inwards, to the despised earth, the Mother-Self and revealing the hidden Sun within?

## Sun Goddess

In 1984, I came across nine Sekhmet statues in the British Museum. Other statues of Sekhmet can be found in the Bristol Museum, the Burrell Collection in Glasgow and The Louvre in Paris. Sekhmet, worshipped by the Ancient Egyptians as 'Lady of Flame', personified the scorching, destructive power of the Sun, yet she carries with her the ankh symbol of eternal life. The life-sized statues in the British Museum are from a group of over 600, set up by the Pharaoh Amenhotep III in the precincts of the temple of the Goddess Mut at Karnak, near Luxor. Mut was one of the great Egyptian Mother Goddesses who sometimes manifested in Leonine form. Her temple was surrounded by a horseshoe-shaped lake, approached by an avenue of sphinxes.

The statues are of two types: enthroned or standing. They are carved from a hard, black stone, a type of granite, which is an igneous rock formed by fire deep in the Earth's crust. Goddesses, Cybele and Artemis among them, have at times, been worshipped in the form of a black stone. To me, the choice of black stone for the 600 Sekhmet statues represents a dense concentration of power. One particular statue became the focus of a daily devotion when I worked in the area and I have found that other women have also found this statue to be 'alive'. When I visited Bristol Museum last year, I found two Sekhmet statues opposite each other. Standing between them, I felt one to be alive, or magnetized,

*See Sula Sinead Grian's excellent monographs, *Brighde and The Sun Goddess* (Brighde's Fire, 1985 and 1986 respectively).

whereas the other felt quite dead. A closer look showed that the latter waş in fact a copy.

Towards the end of 1986, I did a Tarot reading to gain guidance both on my vocation as priestess within the Fellowship of Isis and aspects of my personal life. The card 'Strength' had a significant place in the reading. Sekhmet, whose name means the Powerful One, is, for me, identified with this card. The Strength card is illustrated in many packs with a woman bending over a lion, holding open its jaws and thus symbolizing the triumph over fear, bringing strength. In the Thoth pack, designed by Lady Frieda Harris for Aleister Crowley, the card is entitled 'Lust' and depicts Babalon, the Great Whore of the Old Testament, riding a lion-like beast of the Apocalypse. Babalon, the Scarlet Woman, is the great Asiatic Love Goddess Ishtar who, as the Sacred Prostitute, bestows her gifts of free sexuality to all who do not turn away from her. The spread also included the Moon, Ace of Cups, Princess of Wands and the Princess of Cups.

This reading was one of the factors that prompted me to apply to be ordained within the Fellowship of Isis as priestess of Sekhmet. I was ordained by Olivia and Lawrence Durdin-Robertson at the Foundation Centre of the Fellowship of Isis, the following year, in 1987.

One of the key legends about Sekhmet describes how her lust for blood almost brings about the destruction of all life. She is stopped by the trickery of her father, the great solar God, Ra, who spreads the earth with a mash of beer and red ochre (an iron-based pigment). Sekhmet gorges herself on what she thinks is the blood of her victims and becomes too intoxicated to complete her task. To celebrate this near escape, orgiastic drinking festivals were held in her honour.

In some versions the action takes place in the deserts of Nubia where Sekhmet has gone to rage in isolation. Although when she is alone in the desert she is a ferocious lioness, she returns as the placid Cat Goddess 'Bast', who has lunar assocations.

It has been suggested by some Egyptian scholars, that this myth is a metaphor for the period of unapproachability, or menstrual taboo. In one text the Goddess is brought back by Thoth, the lunar God of magic and wisdom, who plunges her into the sacred lake to cool down her rage. These lunar associations seem to underline the interpretation of the story as the cycle of red and white, or menstruation and ovulation.

The pre-menstrual phase can be a time when feelings, especially aggressive, angry ones, involute into depression because we as women are not allowed to become the raging lioness, the wild beast that is part of us. We are frightened to 'turn others to stone', as it were, like the Gorgon sisters of the Greek myths, if we show our true face. Sexually, a woman is most free to be herself at this time. Without the fear of pregnancy, she may explore the limits of her physical desire. She may, if she wishes, turn into a wild beast for the night (as in Neil Jordan's film of Angela Carter's story *The Company of Wolves*, where Little Red Riding Hood, discovering her sexuality, turns into a wolf and runs off with her wolf-lover).

Alternatively, she may, in her own home, the seclusion of the menstrual hut, psychically feed off her own womb energies and give birth to the magical child of menstrual possibilities, which is hers alone. She may see visions and dream dreams with the hidden eye of the womb, which is open at this time.

The myths of Sekhmet, Kali and the work of the Tantric sects who valued the Red Goddess have been valuable to me in reclaiming the power in 'She who bleeds yet does not die'. This is because before I knew about them, most months, I would experience feelings of unexpressed rage, violence and the familiar raw physical pain of cramps and migraine. This would alternate with inertia-like states of black depression and sometimes paranoia. This 'other me' was an unwelcome stranger — she was afraid both of herself and others, she did not even seem to inhabit the same body or at least body and mind were so unsynchronized that I was not sure who I really was and I often felt like I was watching life go on around me as if it were a film or television programme.

### Dream Diary

> 'A gigantic force is approaching the city, it is like a whirlwind or tornado, people are scattering in terror. As it comes nearer I see it is a giant red woman whose body is covered in weeping sores. Although I see no way to escape, my feeling is of deep empathy and compassion for her. She is angry and so alone.'

At the onset of menstruation I would surface, although with a tendency to anaemia — I would be completely exhausted and drained by the experience. From ovulation onwards, I would experience the same battle. The situation was exacerbated by my job, which was sedentary and cut off from other people, and my emotionally intense but claustrophobic relationship in which I was sometimes the victim of violence. In retrospect, my inability to change either of these situations, was part of the pattern of fear and blocked energy — after all, freedom is always a scary concept!

However, there were also other sensations that I experienced during these dark pre-menstrual phases, particularly in the couple of days just before the onset of my period. At these times I had erratic bursts of creative energy, when I would obsessively re-organize and re-arrange things and make creative mental breakthroughs. I would feel 'high' and euphoric and could experience visions and hallucinate very easily.

These energies held the key to the whole syndrome, for what was bubbling just under the surface had the potential to be deeply transformative. By exploring them, by working with myth and archetype, I have freed myself to a large extent from the repression, depression and the pain. As I tap into and work with my own Shakti force (the Indian definition of dynamic feminine energy) that is trying to come through at this time, I can liberate and creatively use the energies for empowering and positive ends I have also tried to channel this energy by developing outer physical skills, by becoming the Warrior Goddess in karate, and weight-lifting. Martial arts are a good definition of form and force working together.

The dark and bloody Goddesses of transformation are always healers. They direct us to those forbidden inner territories where our blocked energies have been locked up and bolted down for years. The tension experienced in the pre-menstrual phase is the battle between the free spirit of our potential and the tranquillized persona of passivity we are expected to present to the world.

One of Sekhmet's titles is Lady of Life, for she is also a Healing Goddess, invoked to ward off illness and pestilence. There is documentary evidence that her priests were physicians, possessing a detailed knowledge of the workings of the heart and that they were actually surgeons. Surgery is a form of medicine that seems bloody and destructive but its end is healing.

One of the symbols of Sekhmet is the arrow, which she shares with other martial warrior Goddesses like Amaterasu of Japan, Durga of India, Diana of Rome and others. Arrows are not only the deadly armouries of the huntress, the rays of the sun that may scorch or encourage growth, but are also the weapons of Eros, the God of Love. The weapons of Sekhmet are 'the arrows with which she pierces the heart'. The heart — seen by the ancient Egyptians as the seat of the soul, the true character of the individual — may be touched by the arrows of Sekhmet. This touch for me was the healing love brought about by baring my heart to Her and performing my own 'open heart surgery'.

In the last few days I have found out some astrological details that may explain why I was drawn to this archetype. In my natal chart, Chiron, the planet of the Wounded Healer, is in conjunction with my Mars, the red planet of War, both of which are in the constellation of Sagittarius, the fiery archer.

## Enflaming the Heart

Before my ordination as priestess, Vivienne Vernon-Jones, Priestess-Hierophant of the Fellowship of Isis group I was in, suggested that I carried out a Liber Astarte. This is a lengthy devotional work to one particular deity, inspired by Aleister Crowley's *Magic in Theory and Practice* (Dover Books, 1976). Crowley writes of 'enflaming the heart' with love for the deity, which seemed very appropriate for Sekhmet. He felt that it was important to interact with the deity on every level. With a lioness deity this involved not only reading her myths but visiting zoos or safari parks, in quest of her!

I began my Liber Astarte by making a shrine. I set it up by an east-facing wall, at the only point in my flat where the sun shines directly in. I looked for the most beautiful red, gold and black fabrics I could find to decorate the shrine. I had been given some old Egyptian appliqué panels that I hung at the back of the shrine. The centre of the shrine was taken up by a statuette of Sekhmet I had made with a small figure of the Cat Goddess, at her feet. Behind this I placed an enlarged photograph of the statue from the museum. During any magical work, I kept a small lamp burning in front of this image. Other depictions of lioness Goddesses were pinned up around the shrine.

Each night for three months I would recite prayers at the shrine and attune with Sekhmet. Following this, I would visualize a journey to a temple of Sekhmet in ancient Egypt. It is not important whether you take this literally or not, but it certainly flowed with clarity and ease from my unconscious and affected me deeply at the time.

The visualization fell into three phases, each continuing for one month of the devotional period. The first part involved travelling by boat to the temple. After mooring the boat, I would trudge over the hot sand towards the temple and lay my offerings at the feet of one of the many statues outside. During the first month, the gateway to the temple was always barred, so I explored the domain of the outer buildings.

The second phase was marked by my admission to the temple by the guardian of the gate. The gate opened into a cool and fragrant courtyard garden with a square pool at its centre planted with lotus flowers and inhabited by fish and aquatic birds. Around the courtyard were rooms set aside for healing. Sometimes I would go and sleep in these rooms and on these nights I would take particular note of my dreams.

Towards the middle of the second month, I became aware of a large inner courtyard beyond the pleasant gardens. I was nervous of entering, but eventually I did. After the light and airiness of the courtyard, the room was dark and sombre in atmosphere. As soon as my feet sank noiselessly into the soft sand of the interior, I could smell the pungent odour of animals, accompanied by the distinctive smell of blood. As my eyes grew accustomed to the light, I could make out a hall lined with pillars and shapes of several large beasts lying just ahead of me — they were lionesses. One was gnawing at a flesh-covered bone, its jaws covered in blood. They seemed unconcerned about my presence as I tiptoed around them. Behind the pillars of the hall were more rooms, some of them used as living quarters. They were sparsely furnished with a few personal items scattered around — boxes of cosmetics, jewellery, linen robes folded across a chair. These were the rooms of the three lioness priestesses. Sometimes I would catch sight of them, walking across the hall, the animals following them with a lazy, self-assured stride. I came to wonder which were the lionesses and which the priestesses. I never seemed to see all six at the same time and often, they seemed to blur into each other in the dim light of the hall. A face of a lion would become superimposed on that of a priestess or vice versa.

The teachings I received during this phase were felt rather than articulated — no one spoke to me directly. The teachings concerned experiencing the animal body of the lioness, powerful but gentle. I imagined a chasing game, felling and sinking my teeth into the neck of a gazelle, or feeding and playing with my cubs. The most ancient God-forms are half-animal or half-bird. If you wish to integrate the primal animal side yourself you must be prepared to become the animal.

Life among lions tends to revolve around the female kinship of the extended family. The females are the stable group, passing on territory in the female line and running the home range. Males tend to stay only for a season or two before moving on and have the role of consort rather than king.

At the far end of the pylon hall was a doorway framed by two stone sphinxes. The sphinx is a composite animal with the body of a lion, tail of a snake, wings of an eagle and a human face, the

Greek sphinx being female. The sphinx is a metaphor for the integration of underworld, as symbolized by the snake with earth the lion and with air the eagle, whose wings of transcending spirit fly as shaman-like to the realms of the Gods. The sphinxes ask a question before I am allowed to cross the threshold. There is no right or wrong answer, but it has to come from a heart with a pure intention. At this point, I had to leave my proud lion-heart behind and enter simply as a worshipper.

Behind this third gateway, I found myself at the edge of a large fire-pit, fed from an unknown source far below. There was no path around the pit but only one that led directly across it. At the far side, I could make out the silhouette of a square building, half-hidden by smoke.

If I had been frightened by the lionesses, I was certainly daunted by the route that lay ahead. There seemed little choice but to walk forwards into the flames — in fact, I felt an urgent imperative to do just that.

For the first three weeks of the third month, I traced my steps from the moored boat, to the temple, past the sphinx guardians, who 'examined my heart' and stood in the fires of Sekhmet. Each time I stood in the blinding light, heat and noise of the fires, it was like being in the alembic of an alchemist, the repetition building on itself, calcining and purifying. The alembic of the fiery temple was both my womb and heart, I was able to surrender to the flames of my fear, painful memories, lack of trust and low self-esteem and experience the phoenix-like rebirth of a revitalized spirit.

On one occasion I saw a luminous golden figure of a woman standing on the bridge. She was a person of great strength and beauty and, as she stood in the fires, she seemed to generate her own light. I see her as the high priestess of Sekhmet, who had manifested herself to me, almost out of light, to inspire and bless my path.

During the last week of the devotions I felt prepared to complete the journey across the bridge and enter the inner sanctum. At the doorway to the building on the far side of the bridge, I invoked the Goddess with the prayer I recited at the shrine each night:

'Hail to thee, Sekhmet-Bast-Ra, we invoke thee Lady Great of Magic,
Thou who art the Mighty One, who utters the Words of Power,
In the Boat of Millions of Years!
O Exalted Sekhmet, Thou art the Great Cat,

The Avenger of the Gods, the Judge of Words!
The Queen of Sovereign Powers, and Guardian of this Temple.
'Save us from terror, save us from the burning heat of the desert sun!
Save us from being devoured by our own unconscious.
Light in us the spark of Your healing Flame!
That we may not perish in Your Fire but be transformed.
Praise and Homage to Thee, O Sekhmet, hear us and appear!'

Sunflower, with a tip of the hat to E. A. St George

At last I was in the awesome presence of my Goddess. She sat enthroned some distance from me, much larger than I had expected. A mighty black lioness, a fire-spitting cobra raised to strike upon her brow. Flames and lightning rolled off her with a crackling sound and were reflected in the volcanic glass floor of the temple, Her black silhouette towering above me, contrasting with the red-golden aura of light creating a nimbus around her. The room was filled with a great rumbling sound, which, earthquake-like, I could feel under my feet. Hot, fiery winds scorched my face and I felt that She could have crushed me like desert sand under Her great claws, yet what I could hear was the purring tones of a great cat.

For the first few visits to Her inner sanctum it was enough just to bathe in this magnificent presence. On the last night, though, I asked her permission to become Her priestess. I felt her reply was that, although I had gained much inner knowledge of Her, I had now to serve Her in the outer world as a healer. I felt that, after the long and arduous journey, She had lovingly swatted me with a great velvety paw! As it happened, though, opportunities did come my way in the next year to do healing both for individuals and for groups. I mediated healing solar energies, visualized as golden light streaming from my hands or the ankh I would hold over my heart.

During group rituals, and also for solo work, I would assume the form of Sekhmet by wearing a lioness mask that I had adapted by adding a cobra and sun disc. The mask was painted black and gold with red ochre around the jaws, a tasselled shawl attached to the back as a mane. I also made a red and gold robe (traditionally this should have been red linen because of Sekhmet's title, Lady of Red Linen, to denote the blood soaked garments of her victims).

I also used incenses to signify the martial and beneficent aspects of Sekhmet and a composite based on dragon's blood, frankin-

cense and benzoin for work of integration. I used the 'Mars' and
'Venus' sections from Holst's *Planets* Suite, along with ancient
Egyptian trumpet music. I even managed to find a lioness roar-
ing from a special sound effects record!

A word of warning! When worshipping Sekhmet, take care to
guard flames — I tend to burn everything I cook, although whether
this is divine intervention or domestic incompetence is a matter
of interpretation!

When working the healing ritual of Sekhmet in mixed groups,
I work opposite a priest mediating the energies of the God Ptah.
Although Sekhmet was our independent deity in her earliest forms,
she is later paired with the craftsman Ptah. He is the 'form' that
shapes the Shakti energy of Sekhmet — 'La Force'. This is a good
polarity for a priestess to work with as form will hold and shape
the energy, leaving her protected and free to mediate the force.
I have also, however, worked healing rituals as a solar priestess
opposite an earth priestess (of course magical work is not gender
specific; it would be naïve to think that this is so).

Some people may think that I have been foolish in advocating
working with a Goddess who has associations with war and destruction, yet, the solar force Sekhmet represents, is neither good
nor bad — like all magic it may be directed at will. If directed
by 'Love under Will' — Aleister Crowley's magical dictum — only
positive change can be effected. We must love with focused intent
and direct our wills with compassion.

The child of Sekhmet and Ptah is Nefertum, the Beautiful One,
who wears the lotus crown. The lotus — its roots growing in mud,
the flower floating in the water, its petals opening out to the rays
of the sun — symbolizes the balance of the elements. The Magical Child of Form and Force is therefore a child of beauty and
harmony not of destruction. Sekhmet may occasionally be invoked
in her martial aspect, however, but in the spirit of just wrath, such
as where the innocent suffer or great injustice has been done.

As I worked with Sekhmet, I began to see the pre-menstrual
phase as a blessing in disguise rather than a curse. If we cannot,
or do not choose to, have children, we need to see each month
as in some way bearing fruit. Each month we conceive, incubate
and release energy through menstruation, which we can compare
to a Magical Child, as Penelope Shuttle pointed out so percep-
tively when we discussed this subject together at Peter Redgrove's
talk on the 'Black Goddess and the Sixth Sense' at the Society.
By doing so we are healing the ovulation/menstruation split.

Sekhmet is both a Mother Goddess, fiercely protective of her cubs and a Goddess of feminine sexuality, for she wears the cobra insignia of the Goddess Kundalini on her brow. By actively working with the chakra centres of the body, we are able to link the upper and lower centres, through the heart that is open and free.

The period of devotional work complete, I felt healed in body and spirit by the sacred blood and fire of Sekhmet. I had invoked her daily as the 'Lady Great of Magic'. All magic is transformation: by inflaming my heart with Love for Her, I had discovered my own capacity for Love.

## Blessing of Sekhmet

'Do not fear me, ye who have come from afar to seek my wisdom,
For I am also the Goddess of Healing.
From the fires of destruction, new life is born.
The hardest of battles is that which you wage against yourself.
   It is I who will give you the strength to fight these battles;
Not so you might vanquish the enemy, but that you might struggle
To break through the battle-lines of the warring fragments
Of yourself, that they may at last be re-united!

'Through Me, see your inner anger released, burning like dry reeds,
Turning to black, fertile ash, to scatter on the lands
Of your inner self.
Now you have won your trial by fire,
You have earned the gift of inner light, may you always grow with it!
Come now, kindle a spark from My Healing Flame,
Let it grow within you.
It is the fire of your spirit,
Which gives you eternal strength'.

Sunflower

## Lady of Joy

As I drew nearer to the gentle aspect of Sekhmet, I was able to make contact with her sister-Goddess, Hathor, one of whose titles is 'Mistress of the Mansion of Sekhmet'. Hathor is, like Sekhmet, an animal deity of ancient origin. She is depicted as a cow or as a woman wearing the lunar horns of a cow surmounted with a solar disc. As the Great Cow of Heaven, she gives birth to the sun each day through her body. As the nurturing mother of the pharaoh, she confers rulership through her divine blood and milk. She is also the golden Goddess of sensual love, joy and abundance and is to the Egyptians rather like Aphrodite was to the Greeks. In stellar aspect, she is sometimes shown in a boat wearing a star between her horns.

In some versions of the legend of the drunkenness of Sekhmet, it is Hathor who turns into Sekhmet. This metamorphosis can be seen again in terms of the lunar cycle: Hathor is the white, or golden, ovulatory pole and Sekhmet the red menstrual one.

Every year at the festival of the 'Beautiful Sailing of Hathor', her image was taken by a ceremonial barge called 'The Mistress of Love' from the Mother temple at Denderah to visit the temple of Horus the Elder at Edfu. The first stopping place was the temple of Mut (where the statues of Sekhmet were found) so that Hathor could meet Her Sister and pay homage to Her. This happy festival was full of music, dance, free sexuality and shouts of 'Joy forever, joy forever!'

'I am Hathor, Celestial Cow of Heaven, I created Myself,
All is contained in Me.
My body, dusted with stars, arches over you,
Reach up and I will nourish you with My udder!

I give birth to the sun each day and, in the evening,
I await you in the mountains of the West,
To hold you in My arms and bring you back to life!

Look deep within My mirror, to find within you,
My gifts of beauty and love.
I am the turquoise of the summer sky, the coppery blaze of sunset staining the fields blood-red.
Remember Me on the longest days, as I turn My face to you,
I am the Shining Mother, the Mother of all!'

Sunflower

In mid 1988 I experienced a strong contact with Hathor, in a guided visualization following a Fellowship of Isis ritual to Hathor. We were prompted to ask the Goddess a question and mine was, 'What is the nature of love?' Silently the Goddess poured over me the love of a mother, sister, friend and lover. It was the ecstasy of all loves conjoined, both spiritual and physical, the agape and the eros. The feelings of euphoric happiness stayed with me for days. Perhaps because of the work I had done with Sekhmet in previous years, I was now freely receptive to love. When I had learned not to fear the lioness in myself, I was able to draw closer to the gentle cow. With the lioness on my right and the cow on my left, I had fit companions for the path ahead.

## Pre-menstrual vision

The sphinx, guarding the inner mysteries of the Goddess, sits ahead of me again, on her lion's haunches. This time her breasts are heavy with milk, Her wings are outstretched for flight and beyond her stands the figure of Wisdom, Sophia, who stands half-veiled in the shadows, waiting for me. I move towards her.

Reawakening each aspect of the Goddess as her priestess, invoking Her many names down the silence of the centuries, is like breathing sunlight on a tightly curled rose — as each petal unfurls it becomes more complete, more alive in its beauty and so, too, does our knowledge of ourselves as women. I see the symbol of the rose in its totality, as the outer experience of the Goddess in her many aspects and mythologies. Each Goddess, like an individual petal, may be savoured in turn.

The journey into the heart of the rose, which radiates love and holds the source of wisdom within it, is the initiation into the inner mysteries of the Goddess. The path runs downwards and inwards, through the yonic gateway of the Feminine Mysteries. No one may tell us what we find here, it is the mystery each woman uncovers for herself. This interior space is for us alone, the source of wisdom and renewal. This path is freely available and many women have passed this way before — they are The Sisterhood. When you set foot on this journey, you are already counted among their number and will be supported and blessed by them, as I have been.

## The Sacred Spring of Aquae Sulis, Bath

'We stand before the overflow to the healing spring of the Goddess Sul-Minerva at Bath. The blood-red waters pour out from the dark passageway into the earth. Wisps of steam from the hot waters form a veil across the entrance. The sound of water pouring out of the spring is deafening. I feel a deep pull in me, a resonance and empathy with the Goddess of fiery wisdom who still bleeds here to heal. Tears are running down my face. I turn to the woman beside me as if to ask her if she understands why we have come here. She nods wordlessly — it feels the same for her. We hold each other in comfort in the semi-darkness. We still refrain from defining that moment. It hangs numinous and full of emotion, in the eye of memory.'

Researching and celebrating the many aspects of the Goddess as Her priestess, through rituals, shrine-making, poetry and by visiting her sacred sites, is like the creation of a richly embroidered wall-hanging. After days spent working with total concentration on one symbol, I glance up and the breath catches in my throat at the beauty and immensity of the entire work, only to have my eye caught again by some other detail. At these times, boundaries between the universal and the specific, the deity and the wor-shipper are transcended by the love that encompasses both.

I have been fortunate in working with fellow priestesses and priests whose dedication and extensive knowledge have inspired me and kept me going. I would like to take this chance to thank the Grove of the Compassionate Mountain, my companion priestesses in the Women's Mystery Tradition and the Fellowship of Isis, particularly Olivia Robertson and Vivienne Vernon-Jones. I would also like to thank various people who I have trained in the magical lodges I have worked in over the last seven years. Above all I am indebted to the priestesses who have worked with me as magical partners for their valuable insights and loving support.

What, though, does this business of being a priestess actually mean to me? Primarily, it is making a statement about your beliefs. The Goddess does need us at this time and we need Her, we have to name ourselves even if we are never officially recognized. By reviving the ancient title of priestess, we make links with the ancient past and carry the tradition together into the future.

Some may see the act of calling yourself priest or priestess as hierarchical and egocentric. Often it is the very opposite, however. It is a private and personal gesture to the deity of your heart. Others may think the entire idea is a waste of time, yet, in acknowledg-ing the vocational nature of our lives, we are re-affirming the sacred nature of all life. In this time of crisis, both in ecological terms and with the rise of fundamentalism and materialist values, we need more people to demand a place for the free spirit in a secu-lar world. I feel linked to many people I will never meet from different cultural and religious backgrounds because we share these same values.

Many of us may work for our beliefs in different ways — as sha-man, teachers, healers or in green politics. If we can be seen to offer our skills to the community, then we bring credit to the voca-tion. Each personal contribution we make is in an act of devo-tion to Her and '. . .she rises, we will rise with Her', lovely words from Asphodel. Inner work is not redundant in a time of crisis, it is the well-spring from which we are able to live our dreams and draw our refreshment. The temple of the human imagination must be restored and re-built and its hearth fire kept burning.

The inner growth that results from the touch of the Goddess gives gifts of dignity and compassion and we learn the wisdom we need to live through these often chaotic and troubled times. As there are no rules, except a reverence for life, we must make responsible choices, guided as much by the mysteries of the stars as by the rocks beneath the surface of the water.

The path of the Goddess is not an ascetic, pious one, but is creation-centred and life-affirming. We do not wish to have power over others or to subjugate ourselves before an all-powerful, mother figure. The Goddess is the universe, the star-spangled body of Nuit, 'Our Lady of the Stars', yet She is in each grain of sand and we are each a valued part of Her creation.

As the millennium draws to a close, many of us feel acutely how vulnerable Gaia, the earth, is at this time. She who eternally gives birth and takes the dead back into herself, endures a long and painful labour. We, like anxious midwives, listen to the faint heart-beat in the womb, experiencing her pain, fearing that the child will be still-born.

### Oracle of the Black Virgin.

'I am Marah, the bitter one, salt tears run down My cheeks.
My eyes are clouded and stare ahead, unseeing.
For you have shorn My long, fragrant hair, My forests,
and robbed the crystal jewels from My dark crown.
My life-giving underground streams are dying,
the life-blood coursing through My veins.
You have rent the starry veil of My Mysteries
and poisoned My children who live in the seas and on the earth.

Will you live to regret your foolishness?
You deny Me, you destroy Me,
You hid My blackness and paint Me white.
Hear Me, hear Me My sisters!
And those of you that have not cut the cord,
And are still linked to Me.
For I am the Black Mother, the first and the last,
I am Mater Dolorosa and I weep for you all,
I have not forgotten you.'

Sunflower

With each new turn of the seasons and at dawn, when the rays of the sun first creep over the land, we are reminded that the child will live, that we do still have a chance to give birth to the new aeon together. The anguished cries of the mourners of the sorrowful mysteries give way to the sound of bells, plucked harp strings, a myriad of lilting voices and shouts of 'Joy forever, Joy forever.'

'See through My veil of salt and water
To My self-renewing centre, ruby-red and living.
I am the pearl in the oyster, many coloured,
The Gate of Joy to the Garden of Earthly Delights,
The rich, succulent fruit and pulse of ecstasy.
I am the Snake and the Tree, the carbon that is diamond.
I am all possibility, I am Love and Change.

Come to Me, if you dare and you will learn My Wisdom.
Draw nearer to the crevass and I will,
Snake-like, lick your ears and awaken you,
Whispering the Secrets of Women.'

Sunflower

# 8
# The Search for the Beloved

## Vivienne Vernon-Jones

To some extent we all look outside ourselves for completion. That this is a false pursuit is something that every
priestess and sibyl eventually discovers. Psyche is initially
led astray by her sisters who persuade her that the Beloved
is really a monster. There are many such voices in our own
world, telling us that our cherished ideals are worthless, siren
voices that are ever tempting us into betrayal of those ideals
and a complete loss of confidence in ourselves. But confidence is beauty.

The problems of direction and commitment are dealt with
honestly in Vivienne Vernon-Jones' chapter. Under esoteric
law you are responsible for your own actions. No one can
sort out your mess except you. This takes both responsibility and insight and it is part of the healing journey to the
roots of the self.

Vivienne Vernon-Jones *has been a student of the Mysteries since her early twenties. She has gained experience of a wide variety of magical systems and has also trained as a psychotherapist, specializing in psychosynthesis. She is the founder and facilitator of an active lyceum of the Fellowship of Isis and works in collaboration with a number of other individuals and groups, describing herself as a 'freelance' priestess. Her active concern for the environment has been reflected in both her personal and group work and, for the last few years, she had worked full-time for an environmental charity. She continues to live a semi-mythic life, somewhere in the vicinity of the Forest of Broceliande.*

# The Search for the Beloved

'Look upon the darkness. See the space is as the great darkness the jaws of Seb, the crocodile of Amenti, The Underworld, the hell of Ereshkigal. The ground gives way under you and you feel yourself falling into forgetfulness. You forget your name, your place and your speech. You forget everything except those you love. You are lost in long avenues of darkness ever falling into greater oblivion. Each tunnel leads to another one through twists and turns so that you may never find the way of return. At last you find the end because you surrender in faith. For, though you know not of the Deities, for you know no Names, yet you love, though you know not whom you love. And you find yourself struggling to escape from the pit — and suddenly you are released by the love of the Great Mother . . .'

'Space Magic', *Urania*, Olivia Roberston, Cesara Publications.

I spoke these words like one dazed, not really believing what I was reading. Surely, I had glanced through the ritual beforehand yet didn't recall this passage. My voice faltered and began to break with emotion as I struggled to keep the meditation flowing, yet, upon hearing the strangled sob of my sister-priestess, the pain that was so close to the surface broke through and I cried. It was something that had never happened before in any ritual in which I'd held office. Yet, on this day some weeks before finishing this chapter, it felt totally appropriate to give ritual voice to the agony I felt as one exiled in the Underworld — knowing I loved though not whom I loved. Trusting that the Goddess' love might one day free me.

Some years ago, I was inspired by Richard Bach's *Bridge Across Forever* (Pan Books, 1985). It recounted his haunting by a love who '. . . lives just around a corner in time' and the actualization of that quest eventually creates for both of them the bridge of the title. Certainly I knew that feeling, for my own life and dreams for some years have been likewise 'haunted' and I have had a sense that somewhere, out there, is someone with whom I am meant to share this lifetime — not to make up for a feeling of being 'half a person', but to fulfil an agreement made before incarnation based on a commitment to a shared purpose.

For this to be truly realized in the world has involved a quest. What follows is the story of that quest, which has served, over the years, to deepen my relationship with the Goddess and confirm my vocation as priestess.

In 1973, with no experience of magic, I was literally thrown in at the deep end when I became involved with a man with occult leanings. D. was a Thelemite, the magical system developed by Aleister Crowley early in the twentienth century. When we met, D. was looking for a 'scarlet woman', a priestess in Crowley's terms and I happened to fit the bill, being latently psychic and malleable. However, once I had made a commitment to the magical path, I took to it like the proverbial 'duck to water'. I found that I was more drawn to the work of Dion Fortune and to those trained within the magical order she had founded than to Crowley.

At the time there was little available on the subject of the Goddess. However, Dion Fortune's novels were in print and through these I gained valuable pointers on the mysteries of Isis and the function of the priestess as a channel for the Goddess. No matter how dated or sentimental these novels may seem now, they provided initial role models through which I also realized my need to be a magician in my own right, not just the passive helpmate of my partner (part of Crowley's legacy is an attitude, which still prevails in some of his followers, in which a priestess is viewed primarily as a magical weapon or talisman of the male magician).

In order to focus my attention, I obtained from a museum a reproduction statue of an Egyptian Goddess and lovingly created a shrine. Before this, I performed small devotional rituals and meditated. After some weeks, in a series of vivid dreams, I found myself within an inner Egyptian temple. I incorporated the images of the dream temple in my meditations and soon found that the work gained its own impetus. That early contact has formed the groundwork for all subsequent work I have done with the Egyptian mysteries.

I became aware of a growing desire to return to my birthplace, Britain. As D. also felt drawn to this country, we came to London in the spring of 1976. D. began to feel disillusioned with magic and immersed himself in psychological studies. He became increasingly contemptuous of anyone involved with the esoteric. As I was busy connecting to a variety of people and groups who were following the 'Western Mystery Tradition', our paths began to diverge more and more. We separated when he met someone eager to be his helpmate in his new field and divorced early in 1980.

In December 1980 I had a dream that marked the formal beginning of the quest I was to undertake. It was preceeded by an out-of-body experience that clearly marked the end of one cycle and the beginning of another. I then dreamed of being in a far northern land with a man with whom I shared a close, almost twin-like bond. His body was trapped within a block of galacial ice. I attempted to free him even though I had only a small knife. I managed to loosen the block and, with the spring, the sun's rays broke up the ice. This section fell into the sea and was carried south. I ran through a network of tunnels and was challenged by a warrior wielding a sword. I somehow won through and, gaining the sword, emerged near the sea. Here, in time, I knew that the ice with its prisoner would arrive. I waited and, looking about, was stunned into a lucid dream state by the sheer vitality and beauty of the world about me. I woke before the ice-floe arrived.

Early in 1982 I made my first visit to the Foundation Centre of the Fellowship of Isis at Clonegal Castle in County Wexford, Ireland. I had joined the Fellowship of Isis four years earlier and had been moderately active. In the autumn of 1981, I was proposed as a candidate for ordination as a priestess within the Fellowship.

It was suggested that I be ordained as Priestess of Babalon. According to Kenneth Grant, an expounder of Crowley's work, Babalon is a title of the Scarlet Woman and '. . . means, literally, the Gateway of the Sun' (Frederick Muller, *Nightside of Eden*, Kenneth Grant, 1977). Babalon, the Scarlet Woman, the archetypal Whore, can be equated with the fallen Sophia Achamoth, who wanders the world in sorrow and confusion. I'd not particularly wanted to continue an association with this particular archetype or with Crowley's magical system, but it was thought advisable by the Foundation Centre for there to be an active centre dedicated to this principle. I trusted to Olivia Robertson's judgement and, in anticipation of the ordination, co-founded with a male friend, a sister-centre of the Fellowship and began to hold bi-weekly meetings to do regular meditation and ritual work.

The ordination ceremony was a semi-public affair, as many of the Foundation Centre's rituals are. While I had been functioning as a priestess for some years through my own efforts and the awakening of far memory, this was somewhat unchannelled. In this age-old ritual the established priestess, herself a 'garment of Isis', mediates the Goddess and with her hands, consecrates the candidate. As the energy passes through the priestess, a tangible flow of energy from the Goddess is experienced by the initiate, which carries with it a sense of a seed being planted, of something infinitely precious being given.

The dedication of service by the newly ordained priestess confers on her the authority to function as an oracle and to mediate the Goddess for others. It is an initiation that carries with it the responsibility to be both gateway and guardian of the mysteries of the Goddess.

Along the way, a priestess may find a healing of her own sorrows and will be likely to attain a degree of personal power, but this is the 'icing on the cake'. There is no doubt that wearing exotic clothing and jewellery can convey a strong visual image, but unless this is backed up by an inner quality and connection, it only invites projection. Certainly there are many ways in which one can function as a voice of the Goddess, yet inevitably it is the integrity the woman who brings herself to that experience that is the hallmark of the true priestess.

However, another ritual held a few days before my ordination as a prelude to it had a powerful transformative effect on me that has carried down through the years. The day it took place, I woke from a dream with the realization that somewhere 'out there' was a man who was my true mate. This filled me again with a sense of longing and a need to find him. My dream diary entry that morning noted the similarity to the dream I had had in 1980 about the man I freed from a block of ice.

That afternoon, Olivia and Lawrence Durdin-Robertson conducted my companion and I through the Rite of Rebirth as a formal initiation into the Fellowship. In the course of the ritual one witnesses and participates in the descent of the Goddess Ishtar/Inanna through the seven gates of the Underworld to find her consort Tammuz/Dammuzi. In the process she faces death in the form of her dark sister, the Goddess Allat/Ereshkigal. The rite again stated a theme of searching and that reunion was only possible when the Dark Goddess had been truly faced.

I did not, until quite recently, realize how deeply affected I had been by my participation in this initial rite. The resonances set up have only in 1989 — a full seven years since it happened — come to a satisfactory resolution with the working through of the Underworld initiation.

A quest always involves a journey and it is this, not the goal, that initiates and transforms the seeker. Many of the mythic stories and the lives of the 'Great Goddesses' that have relevance for the women's mysteries are of journeys into the depths. From a strict biological basis, this is no surprise as this function is held within the core of our bodies — to truly know ourselves we must travel within.

Another friend, who likewise ventured into the depths of the Underworld and, against all odds, emerged with her life increasingly intact, has often said that on her tombstone she might have engraved the epitaph 'Choose your archetypes with care'. While I believe this to be not only true but also a lesson of primary importance to any who embark on this path, there is also a sense in which one is given very little choice in the matter and begs the question 'Who does the choosing?' It may be that we enter into an unspoken inner contract to literally play out another phase of the eternal drama that the Gods, Goddesses, men and women of myth and legend may experience through our living and add new threads to the collective story of humanity and the earth. So as to *who* has chosen, I assume that, in a fundamental way, I have. Perhaps not my conscious mind but my self has. Even when it appears that others have projected such an identification, there is usually 'a hook' inwardly that accepts it. There is no doubt that the working out of these patterns can be extremely painful, yet, unltimately, they can be transformative.

When I left Ireland after my initiation, I felt that these dreams and feelings were indicating a specific significant other. I was schooled in the disciplines of transpersonal psychology and so realized that the dreams could well be indicating the need to seek a more complete relationship with my animus, the 'Beloved of the soul', which is a metaphor for Divine Union. The dividing line between such elements is often a fluid one. Jean Houston writes in *The Search for the Beloved* (Jeremy P. Tarcher, 1987; Crucible, 1990) that 'a deep human relationship that increases the beingness of the other will often lead to the Divine Beloved. And you cannnot love the Beloved of the soul without increasing your capacity for loving another human being'. Thus, I considered the two quests interlinked. However, since my separation from D. I had drifted through a variety of relationships feeling increasingly unhappy about my patterns of relating. I had realized that I'd always had difficulties in coping with intimacy and mature emotions. I knew that I needed to change if I was serious about attracting a relationship based on shared spiritual values.

By the summer of 1983, a year after Clonegal, it seemed that my search wasn't going anywhere. I was actively seeking a partner and not trusting either to the Goddess or to destiny. I found it all too easy to fall into a pattern of desiring only the unattainable. In some respects the avoidance patterns that underpinned my apparent willingness to be involved led to my sending out confused signals to others! My inner quest to enter into a more complete relationship with the Divine Beloved was being conducted just as sloppily.

This inherent difficulty with commitment often led me to feel unable to fulfil my position as priestess and co-founder of the Centre properly. It continued to function, but there were difficulties. I felt inadequate because I had no partner — magical or otherwise. An example that illustrates my state of mind at this time was an occasion when N., the other founder, had a vivacious but unstable young witch as a girlfriend. At a major gathering, I stepped down so that she might officiate as his priestess. However, she turned up blind drunk, they had quarrelled, and a scene ensued, but I did not assert my position, with the result that the ceremony was a shambles.

Life, as it inevitably does, provided me with an opportunity to change. L. literally arrived on my doorstep in June 1983 and was the catalyst that helped to change my pattern of avoidance, both in respect to personal relationships and to the Work. I discovered that I was capable of loving — deeply and passionately.

Some months into the relationship, L. experienced a deep spiritual crisis. His reaction was to slip into a netherworld of drug abuse. I had believed, after my experiences in Ireland, that, like Inanna, I would walk into the very depths of the Underworld to find and liberate my beloved, and, here, with L., I had the opportunity to prove this. Eventually, acting as a guide, I led him through his particular Underworld experience. Shortly afterwards, his stay in London came to an end as he was offered a post-graduate position in the north. We tried to conduct the relationship at a distance. Our time as lovers was past and yet I found it almost impossible to let go. I so wanted him to be 'the One'.

Inevitably L. ended things clumsily, which left me feeling betrayed and abandoned. I had always feared that if I let down my defences with someone and they had stopped loving me that I would die. This was the underlying fear behind my evasiveness, which L. had confronted. Yet now my worst fear had come true and, although I didn't die, something inside was broken and I slid into a deep depression.

Feeling that work might be the best remedy for my sense of loss, I became more active in the mysteries. Deeply distraught over L., I was trying hard to be philosophical about it. A couple of months later, in May 1985, I attended a weekend on the works of the writer C. S. Lewis. A number of factors had a profound effect on me during that weekend and one of these was a discussion on two of Lewis' books: *Till We Have Faces*, retelling of the myth of Psyche and Eros, and *The Great Divorce*, which examines the nature of love.

The myth of Psyche (the name means 'soul' in Greek) tells how her mother offended the Goddess Aphrodite by claiming that her daughter's beauty surpassed that of the Goddess. Aphrodite is angered and orders her son Eros to punish Psyche. Shortly afterwards an oracle of Apollo conveys to Psyche's father that, under threat of terrible calamities, she is to be taken to the summit of a mountain where she will be the prey of a monster. As Psyche awaits the fulfilment of the oracle, she is gently lifted in the arms of the winds and carried to a magnificent palace. In the darkness she is joined by a mysterious being who explains that he was the husband for whom she was destined. He disappears before dawn and extracts a promise that she never attempts to see his face.

She is happy for a time, but when she visits her home and tells of the palace and her husband, her sisters sow the seeds of suspicion in her heart that he is actually a monster. Therefore one night, in spite of her promise, she lights a lamp and looks upon his face and so discovers that he is Eros, the God of Love. A drop of wax from the lamp burns his shoulder, he wakens and flies away — the taboo being broken, he cannot remain with her. The palace vanishes and Psyche, knowing herself to be totally alone, enters a dark night of the soul.

As time passes and she entreats the Gods for aid, Aphrodite unwillingly sets Psyche tasks so that she might win Eros back. These are each impossible, but she completes them with mysterious assistance. Through the working out of these, Psyche gains the maturation of her soul. Her final task is to journey to the Underworld and return with a casket containing some of the beauty of the Queen of Hades, Persephone. She is cautioned not to open the casket as she returns to the upper world. However, she does open it with the result that she falls into a death-like sleep. Eros intervenes at this point and flies her to Olympus where Zeus confers immortaility upon her and she and Eros are wed.

While I felt so inspired by Lewis' writings on unconditional love and Psyche's story, I realized the degree to which my own loving, even with L., had been full of expectations and conditions. I doubt that more than a vague sense of 'if only I was like Psyche' passed through my mind, yet, on some deep level of my being, that day, a commitment was made — a turning point to enable me to, likewise, redeem my situation.

Training in the mysteries can take many forms and this particular path of a profound identification with one of the great stories, charting the journey of the soul, has been a way of initiation into the mysteries from ancient times. So, for more than four years this particular mythic cycle imposed itself intensely on my life.

Paradoxically, it was not until I had reached point in working through the myth where Psyche falls into the death-sleep that I woke to an awareness of the cycle. Even then, I did not realize the extent to which I had been identifying with her story — that only dawned during the process of writing this chapter. Certainly, this identification was unconscious and, anyway, if I'd been aware and walked through it with a script, it is unlikely that I could have done it with as much depth.

My ensuing 'dark night' lasted for 15 months from June 1985 as I passed through a period of intense psychological trauma. I had been in a minor car accident on route to the aforementioned weekend. While no one appeared to be hurt, I had hit my head on the car window frame, sustaining mild shock and concussion. I was so intent on getting to the weekend event that I did not seek medical attention or rest.

This was a physical trigger, but other factors combined, including the depression and the amount of inner work I was doing. I began to have a series of intense mystical experiences, both waking and sleeping, and lost a sense of boundaries between the two states. I was terrified that I was going crazy. This fear intensified as I found myself becoming increasingly confused as to my own name and I was having trouble recognizing even close friends. My parents were called and my mother's medical experience came to the fore and she recognized the symptons of delayed shock and concussion. I was admitted to hospital near their home in the Midlands. For over a week I lay in delirium, heavily sedated while my parents took turns sitting with me.

While I slept, I journeyed through various hell-like realms searching for my identity and true name. I was unable to complete the experience and eventually came round to find myself in another hellish situation — hospitalized and heavily drugged. The powerful chemicals completely block higher brain functions and so I experienced a foggy, zombie-like consciousness. Over and over it was stressed that the only way I might be allowed home was by returning to 'normal'. Their view of what constituted normal was, as might be imagined, not supportive of my coming to any kind of terms with the mystical nature of the experience.

My concentration span was severely impaired by the drugs, but I struggled through my much-loved books of imaginative literature that served to stimulate those higher functions. At night my dreams continued but with such an impaired waking consciousness that I made little sense of what was trying to happen.

The attitudes of the established medical profession was not all that surprising, but I was unprepared for the reactions I received from certain friends and peers in the mysteries when I returned six weeks later to London. Even in supposed enlightened circles a 'nervous breakdown' can elicit great fear. Their advice that I should leave the mysteries permanently or for, at least, a period of seven years, initially increased my sense of humiliation.

In the midst of this time I met with Judith, the woman who was my tutor in the Psychosynthesis training programme. In desperation I asked, 'Why me?' Considering the years of meditation and transpersonal therapy I had done, how had such a 'breakdown' happened? Was I indeed now unfit for the mysteries as some had said? Judith suggested that this experience, as devastating as it seemed to myself and others, may have been a result of those years of inner work and not a pathology. It was one of those statements that, while shocking me at the time, in retrospect has made tremendous sense. My experience is not unique and, having spoken with others who have come through similar transpersonal crises, I have found that, while each journey has its own flavour, there are common threads throughout. Images such as Merlin's periodic madness, the three-fold death and the hanging of Odin upon the World Tree are not metaphors. The journey to become a priestess/shamanka, priest/shaman (even of the urban variety) remains a gruelling task, not something capable of being conferred by a few weekend workshops or sweat lodges. The glibness with which such terms are used can be infuriating, especially if they are so pre-packaged. Last year I got talking with a young man who was involved in the American Indian tradition. I shared a little of my own experience and he said afterwards quite sincerely, 'Gosh, do you know there's people who'd pay thousands of pounds to go through that!'

While the 'New Age' contains so much 'instant enlightenment' thinking, there is also a popularized view of magic and the mysteries that has made it seem very safe and acceptable, presenting a rather twee and cosy 'magic is easy and fun' image that not only threatens to rob it of its power, but can be misleading. There was an aspect of the period of abandonment that I went through that was harsher than perhaps necessary. Although I had a great deal of support from some quarters, the inability of those in a position of responsibility in the prominent School, with which I was then associated, to deal creatively and effectively with such a 'spiritual emergency' does not bode well for others who might not have the resources I had. Whatever the justification, sticking your head in the sand until the unpleasantness goes away can never be a noble stance.

Although my intention was only to focus in detail on Psyche's Journey to the Underworld during this past year, it does occur to me that the previous years did have a certain flavour to them that broadly correspond to Psyche's traditional tasks without stretching the point too far.

Psyche's first task was to sort a huge pile of seeds, which she does with the help of ants. Jean Houston in *The Search For the Beloved*, states that this comes from Psyche's ability to 'instinctively order'. My corresponding task came in the form of a new job that involved working many hours overtime in a 'last-ditch' effort to save a company by recreating years of accounts from sketchy records. This called into play my ability to bring order out of chaos as well as to help strengthen my left-brain function, so traumatized by the summer's experiences. Indeed, it was very like trying to sort out a pile of seeds!

Near the completion of this phase I had 'the dream' — one that has haunted me since, that perhaps, in essence, my search for my partner was now futile one. In it I walked by the sea with Jai, a women friend. She seemed to have knowledge of the whereabouts of my love. I was searching for him and was aware that we had agreed to meet at a certain time and place, but I had been distracted along the way, picking flowers in a distant meadow, and thus had missed this meeting.

I waded into the water, searching, but Jai called me back to the land with the revelation that my partner had, in despair, convinced himself that I was a figment of his imagination and left. As she said this, I knew where he might be now and ran to a large house. I found his room, though he was no longer there. The only thing in the room was a refrigerator standing with its door open.

This image linked right back to the dream of 1980. My love was now free from the ice, but I was not there to meet him. I took this dream-message to heart, accepting that perhaps I had lost the opportunity to be with this man in this lifetime. However, looking at the Psyche story, it occurs to me that the woman in the dream (with whom I had an ambivalent relationship in waking life) may well have been fulfilling the part of Aphrodite, discouraging my quest for love.

Psyche's second task is to obtain some fleece of the fierce Golden Rams of the Sun. Robert Johnson in *She: Understanding Female Psychology* (Harper & Row, 1977) postulates that Psyche gains here, through a roundabout route, the element of the masculine she needs to make herself whole.

My work with the Fellowship of Isis continued throughout this difficult time and Olivia Robertson had been immensely supportive, writing letters that encouraged me to work through and integrate the heart of the experience. The Centre of Babalon ran a nine-month training programme for several members seeking ordination and initiated 'Aquarian Aid', a linked meditation event for world-healing in July 1986, timed to coincide with the anniversary of 'Live Aid'.

In the spring of 1986, the College of Isis was formally inaugurated by the Fellowship of Isis and I was invited at the summer solstice to take initiation as Priestess-Hierophant. It felt appropriate to found a new Centre for the College, a lyceum, dedicated to Isis-Sophia of the Stars. To likewise reflect on my own growth and working through of the archetypes of the 'Scarlet Woman', I re-stated my vows of ordination. I did this without abandoning Babalon but instead acknowledged her as Sophia Achamoth and resonated to the higher octave of Divine Wisdom as Priestess of Sophia.

Taking on the designation of Priestess-Hierophant meant, in the terms of the Fellowship's teaching, that I was now capable of mediating all aspects of Deity including the Male. Here I gained inwardly the Golden Fleece. During the period of integrating this solar initiation, I found my relationship with the Male Principle, especially as expressed through the archetypes of Father and Mentor, healing and developing. Through this I gained a much truer independence than I had previously known. This period also saw the completion of my 'shamanistic' death/rebirth experience as I re-entered a time of powerful visionary experiences when I continued the journey of the previous summer. This time I had a better support system and was lucky enough to find a doctor with knowledge of religious experience.

A chance remark to a friend on how bees featured as a symbol throughout my experience led to him recommending the novel *The Beekepers* (Routledge & Kegan Paul, 1986) by Peter Redgrove that touches on the link between bees and states of oracular and ecstatic trance. I could not find the book, but did discover *The Wise Wound* by Peter Redgrove and his partner Penelope Shuttle (Paladin, 1986). After reading this, I looked at my episodes and found that, in each case, they had occurred just before the onset of menstruation. I observed my dreams as my menstrual cycle reached the same point and began to externalize the visionary elements first as poetry and then channelled writing. This eased the inner pressure as I was feeling as I creatively gave 'voice' to

my oracular impulse. The result was a radical transformation of
my entire experience. A book cited in an article by Jay Kinney
on the 'revelations of science fiction writer Philip K. Dick' in the
journal *Gnosis* (No. 1, winter, 1985) has relevance here. The book
mentioned was *The Exploration of the Inner World* by psychologist Anton Boisen (Harper & Row, 1936) examines schizophre-
nia and religious experience. Finding no clear line of demarcation
between these, Boisen's conclusion was that '. . .what ultimately
distinguishes madness from mysticism is the direction the affected
individual's life takes. For the insane, the experience leads to further disintegration; for the mystic, it leads to unification and
healing'.

To return to the myth, Psyche's third task was to fill a crystal
goblet with the Waters of Life, which were to be found on a mountain guarded by dragons. She is aided in the fulfilment of this
by Zeus' Eagle. Both Johnson and Houston seem unsure as to the
psychological meaning of this task, though they note that Psyche
is moving ever forward in her integration of masculine and feminine powers.

The richly symbolic flavour of the task, as stated in the ancient
texts, was reflected both in the writing I was doing and in my
active participation in a wide variety of ritual work. Certainly the
links made with 'Zeus-like' men in my magical mileau provided
much inspiration and support during this phase. Also, there was,
towards the end of this time, a wave of healing with a number
of those colleagues with whom I had fallen out during 1984 and
1985, which proved to be mutually fertilizing on many levels.

A meeting with one of these old friends who was in deep turmoil over the loss of his partner, led to my sharing with him my
dream of 1986 and the fear that I had, in this lifetime, missed
the opportunity for such a partnership. We wondered which of
us had had the harder path — to have found that special someone and lost them or to have metaphorically missed the ice floe!

The next night, I had another numinous dream. In this I passed
a doorway in the same house as before and was suddenly aware
of an intense mental link with a man in the room, but I could
not see him. There was a great sense of relief that we had found
one another at long last. We quickly caught up with what the
other had been doing, as well as a sharing plans for the future.
This was followed by subsequent dreams wherein I was betrothed
and about to marry. This new cycle of dreams indicated that, at
long last, the inner union was taking place. Yet, without knowing
it I still had to undertake the Underworld journey — to which

I had been so resistant from the time of the original seeding of the initiation in 1982.

There is a tremendous wealth of symbolism contained in Psyche's final task. As Jean Houston points out, in this sequence alone '. . . is encoded an entire guide to initiation'. In the myth, Psyche believes that the only way she can reach Hades to obtain some of Persephone's beauty is by dying and she climbs a tower in order to throw herself off. The tower speaks to her and tells her of a secret way to Hades that involves very precise and complex instructions to be followed both going and returning, including the injunction that, once obtained, she must not, under any circumstances, look within the casket.

In the spring of 1988, I had been invited to join a project wherein a small group of women were to work together to channel healing to the earth and to assist in the regeneration of an aspect of the Goddess banished to the Underworld realms. This was to take place in mid-August. Shortly after these plans were made, I attended a weekend workshop on the Tarot. One of the meditations contained a tower. I continued to work with the symbol and it provided a wealth of information with respect to the coming work.

Just before this ritual ended in August, I spent a week in Ireland with a fellow-priestess with whom I shared a deep sister bond that had recently been healed after an estrangement of some years. She had been stuck in her own Underworld experience for some time and often been perceived as a Nephtys (Isis' dark sister) or a Persephone figure.

Neither of us knew what to expect at Clonegal — each visit yields its own treasures. However, our experiences during the week in the form of structured and spontaneous workings exceeded all expectations. Among other things she emerged from her long-period within the Underworld and gained her wings through a transcendant experience of Isis-Urania. I was stuck with a strong identification with the Light aspect of the Goddess, just as my friend was with the Underworld Goddess. Like Inanna when, as Queen of Heaven, she '. . . set her ear to the Great Below. . .' to make her descent, I would remain unfulfilled, as woman and priestess, until I too could enter the Underworld realms.

While we journey through life in linear time, our inner and psychological lives are experienced through cyclical and spriralling time. We had long been perceived almost as twin sisters — two peas in a pod— and perhaps both of our cycles could only be fulfilled when we had, in a sense 'swapped places'. Who knows? Certainly her experience of the winged Isis and emergence from the Underworld was real and has continued to have relevance to her inner and outer life, as my own intense phase of Underworld journeying also has since that time.

Just before leaving, I decided what my contribution would be to the forthcoming ritual work. I was to be handed a chalice by a priestess robed and veiled in black. I decided to begin with the statement, 'From the hands of the Dark Queen I receive the Grail'. Even in this simple statement, I had taken another step as Psyche to receive Persephone's beauty.

I returned to Britain in high spirits and plunged into a virtual maelstrom of misunderstandings and rows for which there seemed no rhyme or reason and received quite a nasty kickback from the long-prepared for ritual of earth healing. Also, I suddenly seemed to be on the receiving end of other women's 'dark sister' projections and anything I did to try and sort things out led me into deeper muddiness.

The Lyceum was affected by one such row as a few members left to set up their own Centre. This inevitably created a wobbly atmosphere for a time. Other changes fostered a feeling of isolation despite my friends, worthwhile career, and so on. Certainly if the Lughnasad workings in Ireland on 2 August marked the beginning of my Underworld journey, then, for the first month or so, I was being affected strongly, but unconscious of it.

In late September I made a further trip to Ireland with a colleague to meet with two priestesses who ran lyceums in America. Our intention was to share ideas about methods of training and do experiential work as a group with Olivia and others. On our second day there, it was decided that we enact the Mystery of Demeter and Persephone and I was offered the part of Persephone. I was resistant to the idea.

This sense of discomfort was actually marking the onset of change. Certainly I did not feel very Persephone-like, just annoyed. A few weeks previously I had visited with friends in Cambridge who celebrated the Equinox with an enactment of the Fellowship of Isis' Mystery of Demeter and Persephone. I had been inspired by the woman who had so intensely mediated Persephone at that gathering and so used the memory of this as a benchmark for what I wanted to bring to my own participation in the same rite. I allowed my body, through dance and mine, to supplement the written material and led a spontaneous meditation into the Underworld based on my perceptions in that moment of being in the thick of it.

I was very unhappy immediately following the ritual. My

behaviour on that day and in the days following was moody and petulant. I began to feel confronted by the Americans' approach to the mysteries and, rather than allowing this to be a starting point for a creative discussion between us, I lost all sense of my own 'centre' and ended up quarrelling with everyone. When it was pointed out that all this was symptomatic of my falling into Persephone's passivity, I refused to admit it. I had obviously had a very deep experience of the Goddess, but I was resisting it, somewhat vehemently. So, I left without my usual 'fix' of inspiration, refreshment and dreaming from Clonegal — coming away feeling unsettled and convinced by my conscious mind that I had been untouched by the experiences. What I had not fully realized was how deeply the ritual had stirred me — even if everyone else present had done!

The day after I returned to Britain, I plunged into an intense three-day workshop on shamanistic dance led by Gabrielle Roth. Gabrielle uses free-form dance as a gateway experience to ecstasy. The non-stop dancing and lack of emphasis upon performance allows for spontaneous expression of emotions. Throughout the workshop — in the poetry I wrote and the dance — I found that I was expressing themes of entombment in the Underworld.

The sense of being under the earth — without resource to the ordinary means of communication — was very strong. A curious passivity prevailed, as though I was waiting for someone or something. This was quite alien to my ego as I have a tendency to be a compulsive 'doer', preferring when dealing with people or situations to act rather than to 'wait and see', even if that action is ultimately disruptive or caustic. Patience and allowing things to develop in their own time deeply frustrated me, yet, now, my energy had shifted and I was slowly becoming more comfortable with 'being'.

It seemed that wherever I turned I was confronted by Persephone! A group based in North London, which I had worked with extensively in 1987, were enacting a ritual based on the story of Persephone. It was set after her mother, Demeter, had secured her return to the world above, though at the point when the seasons are once again turning. Ravensong, who had written the ritual, asked that I take the part of Kore (Persephone) to his Hades. As I had so often taken major ritual roles during my active phase in the group, I initially declined. However, he felt in this instance that I was the right choice, so I agreed.

Anyone who has ever been through resistance to change or rejected a path yet found themselves coming round and round to the same place time and again like a tape loop will recognize the internal shift that occurs at that moment when 'no' becomes 'yes'. Perhaps there are enlightened people out there who have the capabability of 'going with things' to the extent that they never hang themselves up in this way, but for most of us working at the slow processes of self-transformation there is a constant struggle with inertia and old patterns of behaviour and being. Initially, I found it almost impossible to identify with Persephone, although I was certainly capable of recognizing her in others. I only needed to look at many of the women who I had been drawn to throughout recent years as a significant number of them resonated with this energy.

The ritual was scheduled for the first day of December and I found that my ambivalence faded and was replaced with a strong desire to mediate Persephone as consciously as possible. Just after this commitment was made, I dreamed ' . . . of being taken to a vast Underground world. I found myself before a chamber which had my name over the door. Inside was a tall, slender young man with dark hair. Something was said about my "becoming" Miriam, the teacher.' This dream indicated, as had others, that what I sought lay within the Underworld.

During the weeks before the ritual, I undertook to take on Persephone as fully as possible. I hand-sewed a special robe as I learned my part, as well as meditating and seeping myself in Underworld lore. The work gained a definite impetus and a strange thing began to happen in the week leading up to the rite — I began to forget the dreams about my partner. It was not just a matter of losing sight of the dream but a sense of unconsciousness. What I had so strongly held to — that these feelings and dreams were indicative of a living man with whom I was destined to share this life seemed trivial, unreal and without substance. This was more than just becoming 'sensible', it was fading from my mind, but there was also a part of me that knew this narcotic feeling as a real loss, a death-in-life I could not prevent.

On the day of the ritual, this feeling was very intense and, as I travelled home from work I suddenly found that I was writing an open letter in the form of a semi-poem. That this occurred on the London Underground was a little joke certainly not lost on myself or the others with whom I later shared the offering. As I wrote, it was as though, in expressing these words, a veil dropped from my eyes and I suddenly understood the process I had been engaged in.

Before the ritual my consciousness was intently focused and

I held myself much more in reserve than usual. When it began, I found that I was swept along, as though my actions and the words spoken were the most natural thing in the world for me to be expressing.

In the rite, offerings of flowers, fruit and sweetmeats were made to the three Eleusinian Goddesses — Kore (Persephone), Demeter and Hecate — and among these was a single rose. Kore stoops to pick up this rose and, as She speaks of its beauty, the disembodied voice of Hades is heard, as though emerging from the depths of the earth, calling Her name. It is significant that the rose is the symbol of Aphrodite, for indeed, it is Her love that calls to Persephone.

At first the voice seems unfamiliar to Her, but, as he declares His love for Her and His intention to fashion from the light of the stars a crown and make Her once again His queen, She awakens to Her other life. She sets aside Her maiden's circlet of flowers to take up willingly the serpent crown of the Underworld and star-bedecked black veil. As Kore regains Her throne, Zeus, Her Father, pronounces the justness of Her having '. . . chosen that which mortals call death'. The Priest of the Eleusinian Mysteries speaks to the companions present of '. . . a little of the mysteries: that Kore, having sought Her death, hath found Her true fulfilment and Her dominion over life'. He salutes Her with the Sword of Light and hands it to the darkly veiled figure. Its naked blade is held upright, the image reminiscent of the Justice trump of the Tarot.

Two cups are brought forward by a priest and priestess. The Bitter Cup is charged '. . . with all the powers of light and darkness, that whosoever drinks shall have knowledge of me'. The second cup, containing the Wine of Forgetfulness, is charged with '. . . the might and wisdom of the Serpent . . . that in having knowledge of the Kore shall thou obtain true knowledge of death'.

After the priest and priestess had drunk from these cups, a final statement was made by Kore that strongly emphasized Her role as Queen of the Underworld and Her essential nature as 'everlasting and alone'. Ritually saying these words was like pronouncing a doom upon myself.

I read my open letter/poem folllwing the ritual in the time set aside for such sharing.

'Golden Aphrodite — I have feared thee —
feared the passion you bestow and the blindness of the touch.
I sought refuge in the deear grey eyes of Athena

and in the independence of silver Artemis.
Yet you, I feared and fled from.
Drawn unconsciously to enact within my life Psyche's tale.
Beholding Love I betrayed him breaking my vow of silence and
blindness,
losing forever the essence of love.
Likened to Psyche, I called on the Gods,
wept for the chance to prove myself worthy of your son.
Tasks were given — seemingly impossible — yet one by one
attained.
Without knowing why I found myself seeing the dark queen's
beauty.
I would have died to find my true love,
yet, again, I was aided and a way shown to her Underworld
kingdom.
I first sought Persephone in those like her — her priestesses in life.
Drawn to them I faced my shadow time and again,
yet the cycle remained incomplete.
I hoped to avoid Psyche's error as she returned with the casket,
to gaze on that beauty and fall into sleep.
I remained conscious and yet no movement or completion,
no Eros regained.
I should have known . . .
And so, finally, change — rather than my sister it is I who am
become priestess of Persephone, once unwillingly —
once unconsciously as upwelling dreams inspired dance.
Yet tonight I entered Hades willingly and consciously.
Thus to be Persephone is to have beheld her beauty.
And I, like Psyche, have opened the casket.
Falling into this sleep I remain with Persephone'

When I had penned it on the Underground, I had been surprised
that it was dedicated to Aphrodite, but now it made sense.

One proof of the effectiveness of any magical ritual is the changes
experienced in the consciousness of the participants and their
lives (thanks to the co-operation of a universe that believes in
magic even if the anthropologists don't!) Immediately following
this ritual and the awareness that I had been playing out Psyche's
tale 'for real', a great wave of change was initiated in my life.

The week after, I met a man who seemed the very embodiment
of the Hades archetype. We found an instant rapport and quickly
were relating like long-time friends. Because of this psychic
intimacy, barriers came down very quickly and I shared with him
my turmoil over the Underworld material as well as my sense of
loss over the unrealized relationship. He made it clear from the
outset that he would not fulfil me as such a partner, but that he

was willing to assist in my working through the Underworld experience. This contract being made, we entered into an intense period through which much was stirred, raised and healed of the past seven years. As important as this healing work was, just as transformative was his encouragement that I take myself less seriously and the laughter and play we shared as a result.

Given the mythic theme underlying the relationship, it is not surprising that, as the spring equinox, approached we ran into severe difficulties. We had worked together in the ritual of Space Magic that opened this chapter and on that occasion he had comforted me for many hours afterwards. However, his instinctive awareness was that I needed to face this final stage on my own.

Long before our problems began, we had planned to spend May Day week on a structured retreat on the sacred island of Iona. We arrived feeling stirred up and trapped by each other. My first night was horrendous, as I experienced him as deliberately pushing me straight into the jaws of the Underworld with no hope of his being my rescuer.

The next day, I felt that I loathed him and stormed off to a lonely beach on the island where I proceeded to work through many things. To be fair, this was as much about dealing with my own 'ghosts' of relationships past as anything about him. I moved from anger through to tears and finally lay peacefully in a hollow of sand, watching the sea and, as I lay there, I had an experience of earth as my Mother — the Goddess who had given me life, holding her child ever so gently. I was cradled, loved, honoured, protected and enpowered by Her. I stayed there for many hours, communing with the elements, feeling a growing sense of peace and transformative energy. Most of all I felt liberated from the Underworld, free to make choices, free to love and be loved — I knew I had awoken.

In strength, I returned to my friend with a healed and open heart, able to accept and love him, perhaps more completely than I ever have any man. We had long hugs and proceeded to find, once more, a way of sharing what was unfolding for each of us there. Yet, this work was complete and so we symbolically parted on Iona. Our friendship endures and I extend to him my thanks for assisting me in the process.

I have not yet completed the Psyche tale, for her sacred marriage is celebrated on Olympus beyond the eyes of mortals, so this is an unfinished story — freezing at a moment in time between the fulfilment of an inner quest and its actualization. Perhaps, then, this is the proper place to draw a veil.

I am readying myself to move from London this summer and, in anticipation, have been relinquishing the administration of the Lyceum to others as new cycles of work begin. Through these past months, I have explored the Underworld and discovered its treasures — I fear it no more. This work goes on as I am learning to dance with measured steps the sacred maze between the worlds, that I might mediate both the Dark and Light Goddesses.

I am a mortal woman who has been granted the honour of being a handmaiden of the Goddess. My work with Her and with those drawn to the mysteries continues. The written word may not be my forte, but I hope that through this account I have conveyed some sense of my relationship with the Goddess and the paths we have travelled together.

Mine is a dreaming and dancing path — my muse, Terpischore of the Dance. Let me close this chapter with a dream that I had a short time ago. I was in a classroom with a number of friends and colleagues — some were known and others unknown, though we all shared the same purpose. As we sat there, one man got up and drew a butterfly, in all the delicate colours of the dawn, on the blackboard. I gazed on this and slowly made the connection, for the butterfly is Psyche's prime symbol. The scene shifted from the classroom to an open space as music began to play. The man who had drawn the butterfly began to dance, expressing himself through the music. I watched and knew that, if I also let the music flow through me, we could be drawn together as it if were the most natural thing in the world.

I woke, poised at that moment, still holding back, yet knowing that in a moment I would begin to move and allow that union to be.

# 9
# Consecration
## Diana L. Paxson

In the confusion of finding our vocation as a priestess, it is heartening to read Diana Paxson's chapter and meet such practical determination to mediate and manifest the Goddess. She has confronted the problem of who teaches and initiates the priestess head-on and without apology. Her work within Darkmoon Circle and the Covenant of the Goddess is an inspiration to all who are struggling to find a framework or theatre in which to express their vocation. The kinds of contemporary problems that trouble Western society seldom equate with what is known of ancient societies on the face of it, but there is a mythic scenario which accords with every problem.

Working as a ritualist, Diana Paxson has been forced to find appropriate mythic scenarios, helpful and protecting deities and solid modern ways of counselling those in difficulty. The challenge that priestesshood exacts is well signposted on page 203 of this chapter. If you are wondering about the depths of your own commitment to the Goddess and whether the vocation of priestess might be for you, answer these points honestly — they will tell you everything you need to know.

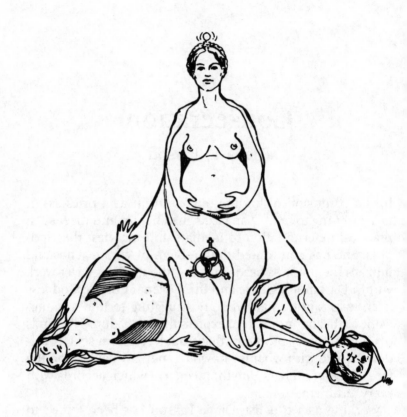

Diana Paxson is *active as a priestess, teacher and writer. She is one of the founders of Darkmoon Circle a Women's Mystery Tradition and the first director of the Fellowship of the Spiral Path, a Northern California organization that includes Darkmoon Circle and a number of other women's and mixed groups and which sponsors public religious services and classes. One of these is the mixed Equinox Circle, in which she is active. She also coordinates a group that is exploring the practice of seithyr, the old Norse shamanic tradition, and co-teaches the Old Religion class. She is currently completing her second term as First Officer of the Covenant of the Goddess, an international federation of Wiccan covens.*

*As a writer Diana Paxson is known for her novels of mythic fantasy, including the Chronicles of Westria. This series is set in a post-cataclysmic world in which the powers of nature have resumed their sovereignty, a series of contemporary fantasies that explore the varieties of mythic experience possible in today's world. She has also written several historical fantasies, of which the latest is The White Raven (New English Library, 1988). She has also had numerous short stories and essays published.*

# Consecration

'The mists are shadowing the hills,
The night is dark, I have no star.
I journey with no light but hope,
Not knowing if I'm near or far
From You —
For I see the path behind,
But not where You are leading me . . .'*

Diana L. Paxson, *The Liturgy of the Lady: The Fellowship of the Spiral
Path* (MZB Enterprises, USA).

Fog had rolled in from the San Francisco Bay the night before,
laying a thick blanket of cloud across the hills, but those hills
were where I wanted to spend my consecration vigil and so,
equipped with my medicine bag, a notebook, and a bottle of water,
I escaped from my family and headed up the mountain road.

The ridges of the Berkeley hills are wild parkland, criss-crossed
by hiking trails, but, though I have walked those paths regularly
in the years since then, I do not know exactly where I went that
day, when the mists came down between the worlds.

Perhaps that was appropriate. Since I set my feet upon this path,
I have never been quite sure just where I was going. The Mysteries of the Goddess have been suppressed for 2,000 years. Where
can one learn how to be a priestess today? There are no guide-
books, no road signs here, only a faint and much-eroded trail to
show that once the feet of other women trod this way, and that
the Temple to which it led them is still there. The temple I found
in the Berkeley hills was only a bit of dry grass beneath a bay
laurel tree, but it was enough. Gaia is one of Her names too. And
so I set up my altar with incense and votive candle, water in a
seashell and a few grains of salt on a stone. I controlled my breathing and tried to link into the power in the earth, let awareness
float free to touch the power beyond, sought the stillness at the
centre where the Goddess speaks to me. At the end of that day
I was going to be consecrated as Her priestess. During the
ceremony they would ask me why I sat with notebook in hand,
wondering what I was going to say.

'A thousand moments, one by one,
Have brought me to this place, this vow.

*Other quotations dotted through this chapter are also from *The Liturgy of
the Lady.*

Each one a small and simple thing
Until they are converge on now
And You —
For I see the path behind,
But not where You are leading me.. .'

When the late afternoon sun began to slant below the mists, I
drove down from the hills, sunburned by light I had not seen,
my spirit whirling with insights for which I had no words. I
changed into my robes with Shirine and Elfrida, who were being
consecrated at the same time, still wondering whether I dared to
take these vows, but at least a day of meditation had helped me
to understand how I got there.

I have never known just why my mother gave me the name of
a Goddess. Perhaps she didn't know either, but she encouraged
me to read mythology from an early age and pretended that she
did not hear when I climbed on to the roof at night to gaze at
the moon. My formal religious upbringing was varied, from the
Apollonian spirituality of Christian Science when I was a child
and the bourgeois sociability of the Presbyterians during my teens,
to an enthusiastic conversion to high church Episcopalianism
(American Anglican) in college when I discovered symbol and
liturgy. However, for all my devotion, when I washed the chalice
for the altar guild I felt as if I were treading on forbidden ground.
These were not my mysteries and, when the Christian churches
began to divest themselves of whatever sense of the sacramental
had survived the Middle Ages, I lost interest. For some, those founts
still hold living water, but for me they had run dry.

The man I married belonged to a small ceremonial magical order
based primarily on the teachings of Dion Fortune. I was initiated,
and I learned that it was possible to create new ceremonies that
would be as fulfilling as the old. The Order did not require any
rejection of Christianity. Instead, it taught that all paths lead to
the same Source, and that rite and symbol can be powerful aids
to making contact with the Divine. Here I learned the balancing
power of the four elements and grasped the concept that Divinity is both male and female — and more than either. Part of my
training was to take responsibility for creating one of the seasonal
festivals, and, in the process, I discovered that I had a knack for
writing ritual.

In 1979, a young friend asked me to create a rite of passage for
her, and a new period in my life began as well. For most of the
women I knew, the arrival of physical puberty had been traumatic

or, at best, anticlimactic. None of us had found it to be a sacred celebration. We envied the women of pagan cultures in their rites of passage, and those of us with daughters wanted to start a tradition that would give them better memories of coming to womanhood. Because there was no one else to do it, I wrote a ceremony and, because the archetype of the Goddess as Maiden, Mother, and Crone seemed appropriate to a rite of passage, in the ritual we invoked the Triple Goddess.

For the first time I put on a robe the colour of the night sky and led my sisters as a priestess. We were all priestesses together, welcoming our friend into the women's mysteries, and the Goddess came. What had we expected? A social occasion, perhaps, enriched by ceremony? Rites of passage are not unknown in our times, despite the erosion of community culture, but how rare it is to do more than share the emotions of the primary participants, such as the joy of the couple being married, the grief of a bereaved family. Certainly we had no high expectations of our own ersatz ritual — we had only our need. I think, though, that that ceremony was as powerful for the women who participated as it was for the girl for whom we were performing it. As we welcomed her into the Circle of Women, we became sisters, and, as we invoked the Goddess, we had the sense that something greater than ourselves was present in the room.

The debate regarding whether the Goddess (or God) is an external Power or a projection of our own personalities will never be resolved. The answer to that question should probably be 'All of the above'. Some experience Her as a force from outside, others as an awareness from within. Some experience Her in different ways at different times. *Where* She is does not matter, what is important is the fact that for us, on that evening, something that felt distinctly feminine in personality was present and, for too long, most of us had not felt the presence of anything spiritual — call it God or Goddess — at all.

When one has touched the Divine it is natural to try and repeat the experience. The thirst of the spirit is as compelling as that of the body and those who, for whatever reason, can find no nourishment in the traditions of their childhoods will seek elsewhere. For us, the old springs had dried up. But in our ritual we found living water. From an anciet well, for centuries forgotten, life was springing anew. Who, having tasted such water, will go back to the desert? We decided to continue meeting to seek that experience again.

From the ceremony came Darkmoon Circle, which, ten years

later, has budded several daughter circles and is still going strong. Some of the women who began it had previous experience in various Wiccan or ceremonial traditions, others had none. We had been brought up Catholic or Jewish or Protestant or nothing at all. Some of our members have stayed with us for a while and then moved on to other things. Others from the original group are still part of the circle and the tradition we began continues to evolve while remaining identifiably the same.

In the circle, every woman is a priestess of the Goddess and her womanhood gives her the right to perform the mysteries. We are mothers and daughters and sisters to one another. We worship the Goddess in all Her aspects and we see Her mirrored in each other — that vision validating us as priestesses. For me the circle has been a place of love and sometimes frustration. It has been a place to grow. The circle, though, was not the world.

Presently it began to seem to me that there was a need for a public worship service that would provide an opporturty for both men and women to relate to the Goddess. I wrote a formal liturgy to be performed by women acting as priestesses, and we began to present it publicly as a service to the community. At the time I am writing this chapter, it has been performed monthly for eight years and at conferences and festivals for congregations of from two to two hundred.

When my novels started selling and I became a regular panellist at science fiction conventions, I found that any panel that mentioned magic would usually lead to conversations with people who were desperately seeking a spiritual path and wanted counselling. This went well beyond the sisterhood of the circle. Once more I was exploring new territory and once more I began to wonder what right I had to act as a priestess in the world. I was not alone. Some of the other women in the Darkmoon Circle were finding themselves in similar situations. One had been asked to perform a wedding, others were doing counselling. We had already incorporated several of our activities as a religious corporation under the laws of the State of California and we began to explore the possibility of ordaining our own ministers. Once more the need came from others, but it was my own need, too, compelling me to make a commitment, to decide myself, to seek validation from the community and the Goddess I served, since there were no human masters from whom to seek authorization. So it was that I came to my consecration.

Sunset light was slanting through the windows, golden as the candle flames on the altar. There were flowers on the altar too, and images of the Goddess as Maiden, Mother and Crone. I waited with the others, listening as my sister, who was serving as high priestess, began:

'For millenia the Goddess has been denied. If She is to be served today, someone must stand forth to lead the services, but we do not need popes or gurus, we need helpers, explorers of the Way and witnesses that the Lady lives! Yet, how can any one of us take upon herself the right to proclaim the Lady? Who can consecrate a priestess of the Goddess now? We have no hierarcy of initiates, no apostolic succession from which to pass on the power. I cannot do this. As the people have required priestesses, it is through the people that consecration must come. Therefore, I ask if you are willing to be channels through which the power of the Goddess can flow to consecrate those who stand before you today?'

From all around us the affirmation came. Our own circle sisters were there, with friends and family and initiates of several traditions in the pagan community. They were calling and the response rose within us. 'Hear now the charge that is laid upon you and seek the answers to these questions in your hearts', said the high priestess. 'This congregation represents all those who will see you as the servants of the Goddess. As you answer them, know that the Lady also hears what you say'.

Once more, it was everyone who was asking the question, but, as I assented to each pledge. I began to understand what I was doing and why. I was called:

- to serve the Goddess for Her glory, not my gain
- to remember that I am only the channel, not the source of power
- to continue to search for Wisdom even when I seem to make no progress on the path
- to remember that any deed done may react upon the doer again
- to give whatever help I can to whoever comes to me to learn
- to hold all women to be my sisters and all men to be my brothers and look for the Lady and the Lord within them, even when they have forgotten Them themselves
- to remember that my body is the Temple of the Goddess, and my spirit is the voice of the Goddess, and honour and listen to them
- to remember that there are those who love me.

There was only one hitch to this. Since it was the people and the Goddess who were doing the consecrating, there was no

mechanism by which the priestessing could be undone. The high
priestess made sure we knew that, too, she said,

> 'Once you have bound yourself to serve the Goddess, we cannot
> predict what use She will make of you. Her service may bring you
> unexpected rewards and great joy, but it may also bring weariness
> or danger. The Goddess will enrich you with the gifts of the spirit
> and the love of your sisters, but if you abuse the power She gives
> you Her vengeance may be terrible. Do you therefore willingly con-
> sent to serve Her, not according to your own desires, but accord-
> ing to Hers? Do you enter into this service in full understanding
> and commitment to what you do?'

This, also, we vowed, knowing that in this life or another the pledge
must be fulfilled.

> 'So many years have veiled Your face
> Made You a legend or a song —
> Is it a dream I'm following?
> Can You still speak after so long?
> Will You?
> For I see the path behind,
> But not where You are leading me...'

Is She a dream indeed? How could I tell? I stared around me in
sudden panic, wondering if we were all deluding ourselves, playing a dressing up game with our robes and candles, indulging
in meaningless mummery.

Our culture is dominated by the cult of expertise. The religions
in which we were brought up are based on sacred writings, said
to be Divinely inspired, guided by the teachings of saints and
rabbis from the past and, in the present, by ordained ministers
with seminary degrees. We have been conditioned to distrust those
who do not have the proper licences and credentials, and, con-
versely, a man with a doctorate or better still a Nobel prize, is
considered an expert (whether or not he is speaking on matters
within his area of expertise). Very often, those who warn us against
the self-taught of self-aggrandizing have only too much reason
on their side.

'Beware of self-taught occultists', said Dion Fortune. For years
those words made me shake in my shoes every time I got up to
lead a ritual. But, even doubting, I did it — and for the same reason that other leaders in the neo-pagan movement with whom
I have spoken have kept on. People seemed to need what we had

to give, and there was nowhere else that they could go. Could I be sure that the Goddess was not a dream? Of course not — nor could I be *sure* that She had called me to Her service. It may be *hubris* to claim the name of priestess, or at least *chutzpah*, but it seems to be necessary.*

I cling to the awareness of my own temerity in striking out into this wilderness. Sometimes I can only discern the path when I turn to survey the way I've come, but, in retrospect, so many things seem obvious that I must conclude that She knows what She's doing. Looking back on what I have done gives me the courage to continue, but the possibility of error is ever present, and all the more terrifying because of the thought that, if I get lost, I may lead others astray. We have seen too many examples of spiritual leaders who begin to confuse their own desires with divine sanction, so I cultivate a healthy scepticism and treasure those sisters whom I can trust to tell me if I get out of line. It is a question of balance. If I am deluded, I may be dangerous or at least ridiculous, but I will fail my calling if such fears keep me from acting at all. To function as a priestess, I must learn to tune my awareness to hear what the Goddess has to say — and then step back and use my common sense to evaluate and interpret it.

Our respect for authenticity sometimes leads us to ascribe an antiquity to beliefs and practices that may be wishful thinking. I believe that both tradition *and* innovation are valuable. Just because a belief or practice is ancient does not mean that it will work for us today. Blood sacrifice, which was universal in the ancient world, is not psychologically (much less legally) functional for First World peoples. We, on the other hand, can combine myths and practices from cultures that never heard of each other in order to enrich our rituals, or make up new ones. At one Darkmoon meeting, the woman acting as high priestess invented a deity called 'Round Woman', who functioned perfectly well as the focus of a ritual intended to put us in touch with something greater than any single name, ancient or modern, that we could find for Her. I believe that it is legitimate to invent mythology, but I also believe that it is essential to know when we are doing so.

Those of us who are re-discovering the Old Religion in the twentieth century are faced with the problem of laying the groundwork for a new polytheism. The work of writers on religious pluralism offers some promising approaches. There are instructive possibilities in the writings of the Renaissance cabbalists, folklore, archaeology, anthropology and Jungian psychology can all contribute and it may well be worthwhile to examine the writings of Hinduism (especially those relating to the Shakti cult). Tibetan Buddhism and Shinto, but in the end, our thealogy will be developed by twentieth-century writers for a twentieth-century audience. How, indeed, does the Goddess speak to us today?

The religion of the Goddess is currently experiencing what one might call its 'matriarchal' period. Certainly most of the major writers on feminist spirituality are women. Some come from a background of psychology or counselling, others are blazing new trails by their own research or through their work with groups or covens. Many of these works are meticulously researched and many draw from the unarguable facts of the writer's own experience. A difficulty with some feminist scholarship, however, has been a tendency to dismiss any facts that do not support the writer's thesis as sexist or lies of the patriarchy.

It is certainly true that, until recently, most books of mythology or folklore gave scant honour to the Goddesses. One of the major tasks of our times has been to uncover or re-evaluate the evidence for the great respect in which Goddesses were held in antiquity. Unfortunately the relationship between Goddess-cults, matriarchy and sexual equality is not nearly as consistent as we would prefer. Historically, cultures that worship Goddesses do not necessarily honour women (for example, modern India and Japan). Scholarship that tries to force all evidence to fit the matriarchal good/patriarchal bad model succeeds only in calling into question the credibility of *all* feminist scholarship.

However, the myth of the matriarchal golden age may be useful, whether or not it can be proved to be historical. In a paper called 'Cultural Fashions and the History of Religions', Mircea Eliade analyses the phenomenon of Freud's book, *Totem and Taboo* (AR Publishers, 1983) that became wildly popular despite the fact that the ethnologists of his time were able to prove that its premises were unsupported by history. He concludes that cultural fashions may be important regardless of their objective value, and that the success of a mythology tells us something significant about those who believe in it. The matriarchal golden age may or may not have been a fact in neolithic times, but it is a myth with great meaning for us today. It provides a model of a peaceful society in which men and women can live together as equals, and in which the feminine, earth-valuing, qualities of the divine are given pre-eminence.

Certainly, some drastic redirection of human awareness is necessary. There is only too much evidence for the perilous condition of the environment and the fragility of the social order. All over the world, people are hearing the desperate appeal of *something* whose personality is perceived as feminine. An interesting but relatively unknown environmental theory caught the imagination of millions once it was named the 'Gaia hypothesis'. Even the messages of the Virgin Mary at Fatima and elsewhere, stripped off their sectarian coloration, can be heard as pleas to humankind to change its ways while there's still time. I hear the voice of the Goddess in these things, as I hear it in the voices of my sisters and in my own heart. Better to run the risk of being a fool, even of being wrong, than to refuse to hear that appeal.

Still trying to listen, I stood with the other two candidates for consecration as the elemental priestesses came forward. 'May you never lack inspiration', said the Priestess of Air, and I breathed deeply of the sage smoke with which she was smudging me 'and may your words carry both wisdom and truth'.

'May the fires of life and love burn brightly within you, and may you both see clearly, and become as a lantern by which the beauty of the Goddess may be clearly seen' said the Priestess of Fire, and I was dazzled by the radiance of the candle flame.

'May you never thirst in body or in spirit, and may you always move in harmony with the currents of the universe'. Drops from the chalice that the Priestess of Water carried blessed me like rain.

'May you always stand firm, and may the gifts of the earth always be sufficient for your needs'. I bowed as the Priestess of Earth anointed me on the brow, hands and feet with the holy oil.

I received the blessings of the elements gratefully, knowing that I was going to need them. In the years since then, the needs that those blessings have helped me to meet have been many and various. It is true that I have done a great deal of reading and research as well as training in various fields and that there are many areas in which I know I have expertise, but the problems that are brought to me as a priestess are different. There is, always, the priestly function of listening, of simply being there for someone with attention, with concern, with love. There are those moments, too, when a question brings forth answers I had no idea I knew, times when someone else's need stimulates my unconscious to pattern chance-found bits of lore into amazing structures of ritual and spell. It is my unconscious or the Goddess speaking through me. Three examples from the past month come to mind.

A young man, living on food handouts and sleeping in shelters for the homeless, came to one of our celebrations of the Liturgy. He wanted help, he said, because he was being attacked by demons. I agreed to talk with him, and we spent all one spring afternoon in a Berkeley park while he told his story.

In our clergy training we try to teach our trainees to distinguish between physical, psychological and spiritual or psychic problems and refer all but the latter to the appropriate professionals, but to whom could this young man go? He had no money, he was not even settled enough to make use of public services and, in any case, the average state psychologists would simply start from the assumption that he was crazy without trying to speak his language at all. All I could do was provide spiritual first aid.

He was convinced that the demons were draining him of his vitality. If I had denied their existence he would not have believed me. Instead, I suggested that he draw on a source of strength that is inexhaustible, so that no matter how much they took, there would still be energy left for him. We practised drawing up strength from the earth together, breathing it in from the air, tapping energy from the trees. He said he had not been able to get food down for three days because the demons kept him from swallowing. We bought food and ate it in the park together, blessing each bite, appreciating the sacrifice made by each plant and animal, consciously accepting the gift of energy.

I have not seen him since then, though he phones regularly for more advice. Did I help him? He says so and perhaps, at least for a time, it is true. At least he ate that day. I learned something from him, too.

At about the same time, a friend of mine came for help because her neighbour was trapping and destroying her cats. The police informed her that unless she actually caught her neighbour in the act, there was nothing they could do. The problem was dual — first to protect the cats and, second, to help my friend cope with her fear for them. The procedures I suggested to her were intended to work on both levels.

For the cats, I recommended making flea collars out of linen stuffed with a mixture of vervain, powerful against evil, and pennyroyal, which is a repellent of fleas on the mundane level and, on the symbolic level, of all danger. To this was added a little salt, since crystalline structures hold and amplify psychic impressions, to programme the spell. I advised writing a protective spell on the inside of each collar, in runes rather than letters, because the use of an unusual script or language impresses the magical nature of the act upon the psyche.

To dedicate the flea collars I proposed a ritual to Bast, the Egyptian Cat Goddess, along with Sekhmet, the lion-headed Goddess whose name is derived from the root meaning 'to be strong, mightly, violent' and who was renowned for casting fiery darts to consume her foes. According to tradition, she could only be propitiated with beer. Just to be eclectic, to this Egyptian duo was added the Norse Goddess Freyja, whose chariot was drawn by cats and who is a pretty effective protector in her own right. Since the problem was an ongoing one, I suggested making a permanent altar that could be used on a daily basis for brief rituals in which she was to invoke the Goddesses and visualize them watching over her pets. Whether all this activity will protect cats remains to be seen, but it has certainly given my friend something to occupy her mind.

A third example that comes to mind was a ritual performed to help a friend whose teenage daughter had run away from home. My friend had called me when the girl was first missing and asked for prayer and support while she searched for her. I was reminded of Demeter's search for Persephone and used that as the focus of my meditations, visualizing Demeter comforting my friend, and Persephone finding the girl and leading her out of the darkness.

Fortunately the daughter was located quickly, unharmed, but my friend was still undergoing a greal deal of psychological stress needing treatment, finding a new living situation for the girl, and re-evaluating the whole mother-daughter relationship. The immediate danger was over, but the pain continued and it seemed as if something more were needed to help the mother deal with the emotions that had been stirred up.

The rest of Darkmoon Circle were also concerned about this situation, and one of the other priestesses and I planned a ritual in which we would take the mother through Demeter's search in a ritual psycho-drama, followed by an evocation of Persephone's experience in the Underworld, performed vicariously for the daughter and with her for all other lost children, and for the lost and despairing child within us all. In the ancient poem of the Descent of Inanna to the Underworld, Ereshkigal is at length persuaded to release the captive Goddess by two androgynous beings, the kurgarra and the galatur, who win her favour by participating in her sufferings. Like those beings, the women in our circle echoed the pain of the sorrowing mother and, in sharing her emotion, she found ease.

This is the work of the priestess — to open herself to the knowledge of the Goddess and to give to whoever comes to her whatever help she can. In addition to helping in crises, we do weddings and work with mothers through pregnancy and birth, perform puberty rituals for young women, and wisewoman ceremonies for women after menopause and, when necessary,

memorial services as well. Each kind of problem elicits a different response. My expertise is in ritual and so I tend to use it to
deal with problems. Other priestesses in our group are skilled
in divination or herblore or trance and work in these ways. The
voice of the Goddess speaks through us all.

> 'And though I fear Your enemies
> may strike me if I dare proclaim
> you live, yet sisters I have found
> and brothers who will shout the name
> that's You!
> Still I see the path behind,
> but not where You are leading me . . .'

The responsibility of becoming a priestess is frightening enough
from the personal point of view, but as I sat on my hillside before
the ceremony I could not help reflecting that becoming a public
priestess was not without external dangers as well.

Hypatia of Alexandria was torn apart by a Christian mob because
she, a woman, continued to teach philosophy and refused to con-
vert to the new religion. In Northern Europe, those who practised the skills inherited from their foremothers were likely to
be accused of *maleficium* (the original Latin term for the practice
of destructive magic) and burned. In Italy, women who worshipped
the Goddess walked over a cliff into the sea rather than give up
their faith. I know a Wiccan priestess in Sacramento, California,
who had a fiery cross burned on her lawn and a priestess in Ohio
who received threats on the phone after her identity became
known. In the San Francisco area, a cosmopolitan and tolerant
social setting makes it possible to worship the Goddess in public
quite safely, but even here, people living in certain suburban neigh-
bourhoods or in some kinds of jobs are careful what religious
preferences they reveal.

In the Fellowship of the Spiral Path the major difference between
those who are priests or priestesses by natural birthright and those
who are consecrated comes from the fact that our consecrated
clergy take their vows publicly. Everyone has the right to approach
the Gods and to help others spiritually, but the consecrated
priestess has the *duty* to do so to the limits of her ability, for friends
or strangers and, having taken on that responsibility, she sacrifices
to some extent her right to privacy. In accepting consecration,
I knew that I was putting myself in a position where I might some-
day be required to choose between my faith and my safety.

In 1988 the pagan community in the United States was startled to learn of the existence of a newsletter called *File 18*, published by a police chaplain in Idaho. It was a badly printed and some-times incoherent compilation of material on the purported con-spiracy of Witches and Satanists to attack law, order and the American way of life. This publication contained lurid fantasies of human sacrifice and orgiastic rituals that were quite astonish-ing to actual practitioners of Wicca. Reading it, one suddenly understood how the inquisitors developed their concept of Witch-craft, for the fantasies evolved from issue to issue as imagination embroidered upon surmise. Since then we have learned that responsible police experts in occult crime do not take this material seriously, but the first reaction for many was to look frantically about for a closet to scurry back into. My vows as a priestess do not leave me that option and, even if they did, Wicca and the Old Religion have become too widespread and well-known to hide. The only other option is to become even more public — to make so many people aware of who we really are and what we really do that when the fanatics start ranting they will not be believed. When there is no safety in darkness, one must seek it in the light.

One step in that direction is to develop a training programme that will prepare our priestesses to function on equal terms with other clergy. Spiral's Clergy Collegium is still evolving, but the programme (which is now open to prospective priests as well) covers not only those skills special to our religion, but a ground-ing in comparative religion and apologetics and some training in pastoral counselling and the use of community resources. The group meets bi-monthly, and programmes have covered every-thing from the technology of initiation to a talk by a social wor-ker on the problem of child abuse. We struggle with the need to develop leadership without falling into the trap of hierarchy. We explore different strategies for decision-making and organizational development, balancing the need to use the skills and commit-ment of the consecrated clergy against the need for input from the organization as a whole. The current system is based on col-legiality and consensus. For our current size and growth rate it is appropriate, but we are committed to remaining flexible. There is no one true way for church government, any more than there is a single path to salvation.

A second step is to ally ourselves with other pagan groups for purposes of sharing information, moral support and legal pro-tection. For this reason, Darkmoon Circle and some of the other circles that are part of the Fellowship of the Spiral Path have also become members of the Covenant of the Goddess, a federation of Wiccan covens. The Covenant is open to those groups that worship the Goddess and the Gods and which are willing to subscribe to the Wiccan Rede — 'And it harm none, do as ye will'. Where there are sufficient numbers in a geographical area Covenant member covens are organized into local councils, or they might belong to the national coven-at-large. Individuals may also join as solitaries.

The Covenant newsletter enables these groups to keep in touch between annual Grand Council meetings and provides a means of mustering support when, for instance, a letter-writing campaign to oppose a repressive law is required. As an incorporated religious organization, Covenant provides its members with legal standing an enables Wiccan covens to retain the advantages of being small, intimate and independent while belonging to a nationally recognized group.

My own involvement with and appreciation for Covenant has increased considerably since I have had the priviledge of serving for two years as National First Officer, a job requiring the endurance of Gaia, the negotiating skill of Hermes and the wisdom of Athena. Chairing lengthy and convoluted meetings may not be part of the *stereotype* of the pagan priestess, but when I was nominated, I realized that this, too, was part of the job.

To some extent I have become known through my books already and I find myself in a position in which I can and must at times speak out publicly to educate or, if necessary, defend. The educational opportunities resulting from being a public priestess are more attractive — representing Spiral on the Berkeley Area Interfaith Council has brought me into contact with enlightened people from a variety of religions, as has giving papers on pagan theology at conferences of the American Academy of Religious Studies, but there are times, even now, when I am afraid. I was afraid at my consecration, too, but then the high priestess came to each of us with a braided blue and silver cord, saying, 'Priestess of the Goddess, as this cord is tied around you, may you be girded with Her power'.

It was a simple symbol, but a very ancient archetype. The girdle of the Goddess encompasses its wearer with Her energy. It serves the same psychological function as a ritual robe, but is much more convenient to carry around. The cord I received that day is getting rather worn, but when I tie it, I take on the persona of the priestess even if I am feeling discouraged or tired.

The woman representing the Maiden aspect of the Goddess followed the high priestess and hung around my neck a small mirror suspended from a ribbon, saying 'Priestess of the Maiden, as you are the Mirror of the Goddess, receive this mirror in which you may show men and women their souls'. After her came the Mother, carrying our chalices, saying 'Priestess of the Mother, as you are the Vessel of the Goddess, receive this grail in which you may bear Her blessings to humankind'.

Finally came the Crone priestess with the small sickles (grape knives, actually, very useful for cutting herbs) that in our Tradition substitute at times for athames. She said, 'Priestess of the Wisewoman, as you are the weapon of the Goddess, receive this sickle with which to cut away evil in order that good may grow'.

An old watchword of our faith is the statement that the symbol is nothing and the reality is all. What power have a mirror, or a cup, or a knife in reality? But in the world of the spirit they are potent indeed, bearing the power to defend, nourish and reveal the divinity that lies within. When our circle sisters and the representatives of other traditions in the pagan community came forward to give us their blessings, I knew that even though the road might be perilous, I would not have to follow it alone.

> 'But in my mirror's shining depths
> I find a light to fight the fear
> and in the stillness of my heart
> a Voice that whispers, 'I am here',
> And You
> See both the path behind,
> and where You're leading me'.

The vows had been taken, the blessing of the people received, but even those were not enough to make us priestesses. In the end, the dedication must be made at the altar of the spirit, in the sanctum of the Temple of She who has many faces and who is called by many names. No human had the authority to receive such vows. It was to the Goddess Herself that they must be offered. We closed our eyes, breathed in and out in the slow rhythm that signals the shift in consciousness and, as the high priestess led us into meditation, let the outer world fall away.

The first image was a familiar door that led to a bare passageway. At its end, thick curtains of black velvet. Those curtains obliterated sight and sound as I passed through them. Only the sensuous soft feel of them overwhelmed awareness and the faintest scent of incense clung to their folds.

The second image was a smooth floor of black and white squares beneath a ceiling of painted stars. Rows of columns lined each wall and I heard women's voices chanting a hymn of praise. Slowly I moved forward. The light grew brighter and I saw women from every time and land: I saw priestesses of Isis, gleaming with gold, Vestals of Rome, grave with responsibility, a Norse seithyr seeress in her catskin cap, a white-clad Yoruba priestess of Oshun, the sovereign priestesses of Sumer were there too, and a medicine woman of the Northern California Pome tribe, I saw witches from medieval Europe, and nuns who served the Virgin Mother, Tibetan servants of Tara and a Machi shamaness from South America, I saw feminist leaders in sloganed T-shirts and Wiccan priestesses clad only in their coloured cords. They were all singing, a mighty chorus of women united in praise. They were welcoming me.

The third image was that in the middle of the Temple was an altar that bore a statue of the Goddess. The altar was ablaze with many candles, so many that it was hard to focus on the features of the image there. As I stared, trying to focus, the brilliance of the candles dazzled vision. The painted stars were whirling, the floor blurring, the face of the Goddess flickering in and out of sight.

In the fourth image I stood in a meadow under a sky ablaze with stars. Around me the priestesses were dancing and before me stood the Goddess Herself, limbed in light. Her radiance was incandescent, but now my vision was strong enough for me to look upon Her face. She smiled and I took courage. I offered Her my service and asked Her what She wanted of me.

The fifth image was after a time beyond time and I found myself back in the Temple again. The other priestesses had gone already. I saluted the image on the altar and retraced my steps across the polished floor. Then the black velvet curtains were enfolding me. I came back to awareness of my body again, and saw the people around me, faces still luminous with memory in the flickering candle-light.

The Fellowship has consecrated a dozen priestesses since then. Each time we seek the Temple together, and each time it seems brighter and bigger. With every visit, more priestesses are waiting there. Once more I renew my vows and the Goddess speaks to me. Also, the way has become much clearer since that day. The goal may still be uncertain, but I go forward with more confidence now, knowing that what matters most is staying on the path.

Are we blazing the trail for a religion that will dominate the Age of Aquarius as Christianity ruled the Piscean Age, or is the neo-pagan movement destined to become a quaintly romantic dead-end? Is there some power — the long-suppressed feminine

aspect of deity, or perhaps the suffering spirit of Gaia Herself —
who has decided that the time has come to assert Herself and
is summoning all those who have ears to hear Her call? or has
our desperate need for a spirituality that will transform the sepa-
rations of man and nature, flesh and spirit, and present and past,
simply deluded us?

After many years I have begun to have faith that, however unexpected each turn in the road may be, someone is showing me
the way. It is not mine to decide the future, but, as long as there
is need in the present, the vows that I took at my consecration
will compel me to serve as a priestess.

# 10
# The Garments of Isis

## Naomi Ozaniec

'Every woman who finds the way makes it easier for others to follow', writes Naomi Ozaniec. It is only by perseverence and faith that the door to the Goddess opens, yet there is no one 'right' way. Each woman must find her own path, but for those who follow, their spiritual vocations will never be the same lonesome journey.

The experience of initiation here described is heartening for all women alone who wonder where their training is going to come from. As Naomi Ozaniec shows here, when a woman opens herself to the Goddess, so the answers and the help come. In times to come, many will look back upon the latter half of the twentieth century and speculate about the courage of women of this generation, who have recovered the ancient memories at such cost. The Goddess gives remembrance to all women. She awaits to be reborn in every heart.

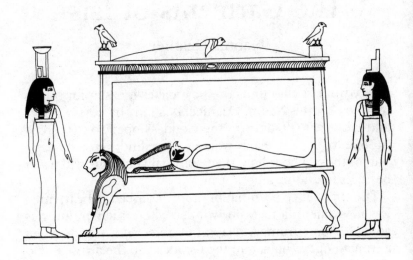

Naomi Ozaniec is *a student of the Western Mysteries. She has a long-standing interest in esoteric disciplines as avenues towards enlightenment. She is a writer and hynotherapist. Her first book,* Meditation: the Inner Way, *written as Naomi Humphrey (Aquarian, 1987) has been translated into three languages and she is currently writing a book on the chakras. She believes in the value of clear, practical teaching in all occult disciplines — a feature that is reflected in her workshops on meditation and the chakras. She is a member of the Fellowship of Isis and is working on an induction course into the Mysteries of the Goddess that will offer training to women who aspire to serve in the capacity of priestess. She is currently at work on a book entitled* Priestess *that will be an extensive study of women as priestesses in world history.*

# The Garments of Isis

'Isis is the All-woman and all women are Isis'.

Dion Fortune

There is little doubt that this often-quoted statement is perfectly true. In reality, however, only a handful of women in each generation make this discovery and proceed to live by it. It is difficult to say what factors lead a woman to this inner realization. Every woman who consciously finds herself standing at the portal of the Temple has her own story to tell. She has found her way by trial and tribulation, for the path to the Temple is hidden and obscured in the times in which we live. Nevertheless, women still discover the path and make the journey and every woman who finds the way makes it easier for others to follow.

I would suggest that karmic factors outweigh all other contributing impulses, even when they are not consciously acknowledged. The incidents or circumstances that actually bring a woman to face the Goddess serve as triggers for a deep and instinctive knowledge which is already present. I am sure that many feminists would disagree with my explanation, but, it is possible to argue that the mythologies and images of the Goddess serve to exemplify the natural state of womanhood, untainted by patriarchal conditioning. The moment of realization comes not with the force of a long hidden memory, but with the realization of the social, cultural and political forces that have shaped the condition of womanhood until a woman can no longer recognize herself in the Mirror of Isis.

It is possible to disagree about the forces, that precipitate the awakening of the Goddess within, but the process itself cannot be denied. When this point of realization comes, it frequently brings its own angst. Like the butterfly newly emerged from the chrysalis, there is no going back, yet where is the path?

The process that impels a woman to search out her own nature — takes both inner and outer forms. Inwardly there is conflict between competing value systems, between the old and the new, the radical and the accepted images of womanhood. There is a keen sense of questing for the Goddess, of actively searching for Her. Just as Isis searched for Osiris and Demeter searched for Persephone, so a woman must search for the Goddess. Outwardly the personal search takes many forms — seeking like minds in groups and acquiring new ways of thinking, extending personal knowledge through studying literature, psychology, mythology and the expansion of personal consciousness through the application of esoteric disciplines. All these many avenues have but one focus — the Goddess Herself.

Every would-be priestess has to find her own way using the circumstances and opportunities available to her. Speaking personally, my path was solitary and tortuous. I walked alone for a long time. Once I had inwardly discovered the Goddess, my search revolved around the ways of establishing contact. In the absence of any teaching I was forced back on my own intuition, instinct and intention, driven on by an inner restless compulsion. My only teacher and initiator was Isis.

'I am She who I am She who is black.
I am She who is white.
I am She who is No-thing.
I am She who is All thing.
I am She who contains Everything.
I am She.
She is me.
She and I are one.'

With this somewhat amateurish invocation, I made a space in myself for the Goddess to enter. I sat alone in a darkened room wondering what on earth I was doing. A single candle quivered in front of me. My altar was the top of a chest of drawers. It was perfectly empty apart from the candle, not by some grand design, but because I simply had no knowledge of ritual objects. I found myself intoning out loud. 'How ridiculous you are', repeated the left side of my brain over and over again until it was like a competing backgroud chant. As the invocation continued and rose in power, so my skin began to prickle, the candle flame appeared, to my inner vision at least, to grow taller. I seemed to sense a presence enveloping me. What had I done? Had I done anything other than sit in a darkened room and make myself ridiculous?

I repeated this over a period of weeks. I still felt ridiculous, but I was also magnetized by the process. On one particular occasion, the sense of presence was so overwhelming that I stopped. I cannot remember whether I became nervous or quite convinced that I had actually achieved something. In either case I no longer felt the need to perform my own ritual of identification.

It is only hindsight that has enabled me to rationally understand my own actions. I could not explain what I was doing, even to myself. I had plenty of good intentions but little else. Intent, however, carried the day and enabled me to open a doorway in myself to renew a very old relationship between myself and the Goddess. That was over 12 years ago. The door has never been shut since.

At that time I was a new member of an esoteric study group. We met for talks regularly, as a lot of groups still do, but it was not a magical working group, though it had pretensions to be one. For me, contact with esoteric teaching was like exposing potassium to air — the effect was instant, explosive and devastating. I began to remember a distant life, I recalled spiritual practices long since passed away, but above all I began to remember Isis, or perhaps She began to remember me.

My religious upbringing had been a very mixed affair. My father's family were Jewish and orthodox, but he had abandoned the religion and hated all things that smacked of ritual observance, so I never knew my Jewish grandparents nor any of my father's family. I have never been inside a synagogue nor mixed with Jewish people in any religious setting. Rationality was paramount in my father's eyes. My mother was nominally Church of England, but I cannot remember ever being taken to church with my parents. In fact, we grew up in a spiritual vacuum in many ways. I have often called it 'splendid isolation'. We were brought up, instead, to value humanitarian principles and live by an ethical code. I was also brought up to be sceptical, questioning and slightly cynical and I was encouraged to read and think for myself. I was always interested in people's belief systems, though, and made an effort to acquaint myself with those with a religious commitment and engaged in many deep conversations, especially with Christians, but they could never answer my questions. In time, my questions inevitably led me to a more esoteric standpoint and I discovered for myself that rationality was *not* paramount.

As a child I had loved myths and the stories of the many gods and goddesses. I read them all avidly and, I especially loved historical novels set in ancient times. I particularly loved one tale set in Crete. Part of the story revolved around the training of a young priestess and I still especially remember one incident. As she walked across a courtyard, she was stopped by a group of rough and slightly drunk soldiers. One barred her way and began to show off before his friends. He began to taunt her and lifted her skirt slowly and deliberately. She stood perfectly still as he continued. The atmosphere tensed. She looked up at him and said, 'Do you dare to life the veil of the Great Goddess?' He stopped and let the hem of her skirt fall — he had been humiliated before his friends. The crowd parted for her and she walked on.

This incident remained with me for many years as a symbol of the mysterious power that a woman possesses when she walks in the light of the Goddess. I was struck by the confidence and inner strength of the young girl in the face of brute force.

In those tales of ancient places, becoming a priestess was considered to be honourable. The route was straightforward, though the training was long and arduous. I had read how suitable girls were taken to the Temple, usually at the age of seven. Such girls were often discovered by their visionary ability to dream true dreams. Temple life was ordered and strict with ritual observances and cermonial duties. There were classes and many new skills to learn. The Temple was an important place in the life of the state and the people. Those days are long gone, yet the Goddess remains, even though her schools and Temples have disappeared.

When I took the decision to open myself up to the power of the Goddess, I had been involved in esotericism for no more than a few months. I had little conscious understanding of what I had spontaneously written and it took me many years to discover that I had generated a charge to the Goddess. A charge enables the priestess to draw upon the power of the Goddess and become one with Her and usually takes place within a ritual. The priestess may then be inspired to speak as an oracle, give teaching or just bless the assembled with the presence of deity. My invocations were held in private for myself alone. At that time I would not have dared to 'become the Goddess' for anyone but myself — it seemed so presumptive.

I continued with my studies and began to work hard at learning how to shift my own levels of consciousness. I took up meditation as part of my general studies and I set an evening aside each week for esoteric study. I read a great deal and, for a while, fell under the spell of *Moon Magic* and *The Sea Priestess* by Dion Fortune (both published by Aquarian Press, 1989). I then embarked on another series of small rituals and used an invocation that I hoped would admit me into the service of Isis:

'I am Isis,
Wife of Osiris,
Daughter of Ra,
Mother of Horus,
Mistress of Magic,
Queen of Heaven,
Lady of the Stars.

Come unto me,
Be with me here,
Take me as daughter.
Show me thy ways.
Teach me thy secrets.
I am again your servant.'

I sat much as before, I lit my single candle and entered a meditative state. When I felt ready I began my invocation (I felt a little less ridiculous by now) and when I felt that that power had died away, I closed with thanks.

The conscious decision to serve as a priestess and dedicate myself quite spontaneously to the Goddess simply felt like the most natural thing in the world to do, even though at that time I had no contact whatsoever with other women who might also be described as serving priestesses. I was working purely alone, guided by instinct and the crumbs I might glean from some esoteric writings.

Offering oneself to the Goddess is a serious undertaking and it should be the culmination of a long period of preparation and inner searching. Ideally such an event should take place within a working group as a ritual of initiation. The ceremony links the individual with the chosen Goddess and marks the beginning of an intense and personal relationship between the two. When the ritual aspect of the event is over, the group usually celebrates. The whole event marks a turning point in an individual life.

Initiation is much misunderstood. It is perhaps most easily grasped if one thinks of it as a rite of passage that represents death to the old life and birth into the new — it is an inner transformation, not an outer event. There are many initiations as we travel the path and encompass new levels of our being. I was not fortunate to have the support of a group and the certainty of collected knowledge as I journeyed and so I stumbled along feeling my way intuitively. My initiation came through a series of inner experiences. In one extremely deep meditation I found myself among a group of people who were robed and I was not. I was called forward and stood in the centre of the group. I was given my own robe and a figure stepped forward to put it over me. The experience had an intensity that I could not forget. When I surfaced I was shaking and in tears. I knew that something had happened to me, but I did not know what it was. I began to remember initiation in another place and time. It was fiercely demanding, requiring every particle of self-control, discipline and courage. I have always felt that such initiations mark the soul eternally.

I continued to work after this primarily on my own, but I did meet someone who was a priestess and this eased my feeling of isolation. My dreams or meditations took the place of a group and inner teachers appeared instead of outer ones. I can still recall my first encounter with the Goddess through meditation — it took place at a public festival. The scenario is now familiar to me, but then it was completely new. We descended into the meditation and travelled through a wooded landscape until we reached a clearing amidst the trees. In the middle there was a well. As we stepped towards it, the Goddess came forward to greet us. She held a chalice in Her hands and She offered us a drink according to our needs. I can still recall my utter amazement at Her image in my mind. When I stepped forwards, Her gaze was penetrating. 'Drink deep, my child, drink deep', she said, and I did.

I was so shaken by the encounter that neither the hall nor the people seemed in the slightest bit real. It actually took me several days to recover and to get my physical bearings again. Part of my total disorientation was doubtless caused by my own lack of experience, but everyone has to start somewhere. The *reality* of the experience came as a psychological shock and brought me face to face with perennial questions. Where had this experience really come from? Was it an external event that I was experiencing inwardly? Was it an internal experience that I was externalizing? Above all came the question, why did the experience shake me to the very roots of my being?

I have always dreamed vividly and in bright colour, but my dreams became especially vivid and often frightening, indicating a tremendous release of power and the discovery of hidden places. Throughout my life I had the recurring dream of being in a huge house with many rooms. In the dream I would go exploring and would always eventually discover that my way was blocked with a pile of rubbish or debris. I could never get into the room that I wanted to visit and I knew that this was a 'secret' room. During this period, I found, to my amazement that I was able to find this secret place with no difficulty at all. The house became Tardis-like, apparently ordinary from the outside but vast within. It took many forms in my dreams and still reappears from time to time now. I made an effort to remember my dreams and now make this a part of my daily routine, my dreams having become a rich source of personal inspiration and information. For example, I knew when I was pregnant with my first daughter and, much later, with my son through my inner life.

In the case of my daughter I had the following dream: I was standing in a hall, much like a school hall. The doors burst open and in came a procession of women. The leader of the group held a chalice aloft and the group sang as they walked. Someone then said to me, 'The children are coming back now'. I took this to refer to the fact that I had previously miscarried twice. The chalice symbolized the vessel that contains the waters of life. It was held high in celebration because it contained the beginnings of new life. Some years later I was leading a male student through a meditation and we encountered a woman robed in green in a circular hall filled with greenery and climbing plants. She addressed him and then to my surprise she turned to me and smiled. She handed me a single white arum lily. I knew that it meant that I would have a child. I was, in fact, already pregnant, though I could not have known it at the time as it was too soon for physical confirmation. I still smile at the classical annunciation image.

I am always amazed at the knowledge that dreams are able to convey to the intuitive mind and I am still fascinated by the dream state. I consciously put myself into an altered state before sleeping and use the sleep state to actively open myself up to inner teaching and experience. This, of course, as I discovered later, was part of the work of a priestess in the ancient schools of Egypt and other places. The naturally intuitive feminine function was refined through training to produce reliable dreams. The dream life, when under some degree of control, becomes another altered state of consciousness that serves as a tool for realizations. The priestess of old was trained to attain a wide range of altered states: deep trance, waking sleep (hypnosis), conscious dreaming, meditation, astral travel and identification with deity among others. Such states not only permit the development of clairvoyance, telepathy, precognition and other psychic skills, but also demonstrate the workings of the human mind from the inside. I found the study of the mind so fascinating that I trained as a hypnotherapist. This enabled me to put my own ideas into practice and to work directly with people.

The study and application of altered states of consciousness remains a major personal interest of mine. I see the conscious control of altered states of mind as playing a major part in the training of a priestess. After all, when the priestess is mediating the Goddess, she is certainly not in her usual state of mind. The assumption of the Goddess by the priestess remains perhaps the most sacred mental state of all. I don't think it can be taught, it can only be experienced. It can be described as a moment when the priestess 'makes way' for the Goddess to enter and empower her. It is not mediumship, which is often unconscious, and it is not possession, which takes over individuality. It is sometimes called mediation, that is, the priestess opens a channel within herself that enables a power to flow throught her and out into the assembly. The priestess is fully conscious of herself, of the power entering and later departing and of the surroundings, and there is no loss of consciousness, even if the priestess speaks as a channel. I can best describe the whole process as a moment of transfiguration — the priestess becomes 'a garment of Isis' and she may seem to alter very subtly in appearance and can seem to be suffused with a radiating energy. It is perhaps this personal contact with energies of a very high vibration that gives a functioning priestess an extraordinary quality of vitality.

As time passed, I met other women who were like myself and I discovered that there were groups that offered esoteric training. I joined a well-established training school and found security in being in a group. I enjoyed, too, the opportunities that arose to meet people at lectures, group meditations and the exchange of ideas these activities brought about.

I became involved in ritual workings for the first time and once again this seemed the most natural thing in the world. Ritual work cannot be taught, it can only be experienced. It is an extraordinary meeting place of trained minds, heightened sensitivities and patterns of force. Each ritual creates its own ripples, sometimes even shock waves, as inner plane dynamics emanate into the outer world.

The success of a ritual, that is whether it achieves its intention, depends upon a complex web of balanced dynamics between the forces brought into the group through the conscious activation of the participants. In ritual everyone participates — there are no onlookers. Each individual brings a different force into the arena, like a carefully orchestrated symphony of vibrations. It is of the utmost importance that each person has a working and integrated knowledge of the forces that they individually bring to the group. In practice this means that individuals usually work with God(ess)-forms that they have familiarized themselves with through their own study and meditation. Esoteric students invariably discover a God(ess)-form that draws them very powerfully and with whom they develop a close and intimate relationship. Over a period of time students extend this relationship to other forms, but one usually predominates. Close identification even brings subtle changes in appearance and bearing so that students can and do resemble their chosen God- or Goddess-form. The relationship between the individual and the God(ess)-form is very subtle.

During this time I found myself frequently ritually cast in the role of Nephthys, the dark sister of Isis. As the priestess moves more deeply into the service of the chosen deity, parallels between the life of the individual and the mythology of the Goddess seem to appear so that the two somehow become conjoined and I have seen this happen in many lives. I am not in a position to say whether it 'should' happen, I simply know that it does and I say choose your archetype with care.

Nephthys is sister to Isis, partner to Set and mother Anubis, the jackal-headed God. She is the opposite to Isis in every way — passive, ruling over the darkness and the processes of decay that leads into regeneration through death. Hers is the twilight realm of the things yet to come. She escorted Osiris into the Underworld and helped Isis to swathe the body of Osiris in His funeral wrappings. She stands behind Osiris when the hearts of the dead are weighed and is one of the Goddesses who take care of the mummified organs in the canopic jars.

Nephthys was not a Goddess that I had worked with in any depth, but I can only report that, during this period in my therapeutic practice, I seemed to have an undue number of clients who came for help as a result of bereavement. In several cases the cause was not initially apparent, but eventually came to light as the therapy deepened. A man came to me who kept passing out in the street and experiencing uncontrollable panic attacks. He had no idea what was causing this. He had received treatment at the local hospital, but this had not led to any improvement. Our sessions eventually revealed that his close friend had been killed while operating a fork-lift truck. My client had trained his friend in this job and felt that he was responsible in some way. He had consciously put this incident to the back of his mind and had never been able to release his inner feelings at the time.

Another young man came to me suffering from an irritating cough. He was always clearing his throat and felt as if he had a permanent lump there. I asked him to spontaneously draw for me. He drew using only black throughout. His picture showed a stark single figure on a barren landscape. He had drawn a sun, but his figure had no shadow. 'Looking for my shadow?' he said. I looked at the picture and asked him who had died. He was amazed. His twin brother had choked to death — no one had been able to save him. This was the key to the problem. He had only two sessions with me, the symptons just disappearing once he had recognized the problem and was able to talk about his twin.

I seemed to spend a great deal of time exploring the possibility of an after-life state with several clients. It just seems to keep cropping up quite unexpectedly. I have always thought it very important to talk about death openly. When I was in my late teens I underwent a series of experiences that convinced me of the reality of life after death. I became interested in the pioneering work of Elizabeth Kubler-Ross in this area and I was able to refer several people to her books. In this rather indirect way I hope that I was of service to people with a particular need. The work with Nephthys seemed to reinforce a part of my nature and seemed inexplicably to draw people who needed what Nephthys had to offer through me. I also seemed to have some memories of being trained to travel in consciousness with a person to the point of death and then return to the living. I have never been able to corroborate this in any way but the feeling remains very strong.

In my practice as a hypnotherapist I sought to help my clients help themselves through their own realizations. I frequently used symbols and path-working techniques to explore problems and I often had intuitive flashes or insights that proved to be significant. I had dedicated my practice to the Goddess and I always felt that I was a channel for a wisdom that was not mine.

My practice slowed down after my daughter was born. My practice was fulfilling up to a point and I learned a great deal from my clients, but I could never be open about my orientation. I found this frustrating and knew that I needed to work with people who specifically wanted to explore esoteric teachings, both theoretically and practically. Meanwhile, I slaked my thirst for magical involvement by attending one of a series of what proved to be extremely highly charged weekends. It was at one of these weekends that I recognized a friendly face from London. Although I did not know it, he was to become my magical partner and my future second husband. Sometimes it is better not to know one's future and I am glad that I could not see what lay ahead.

In time we formed a small esoteric group. We gave courses in cabala and tarot as basic symbols systems and taught the discipline of meditation. We later moved on to ritual work. We celebrated the quarterly rituals and, during one season, we enacted the descent of Persephone at the winter solstice and her re-emergence at the Spring equinox. I took the part of Persephone on both occasions. Looking back on this period, I seemed to be unduly mediating Underworld figures. The group remained remarkably cohesive over a long period of time and we had, in fact, created a very stable group mind that persisted even after we eventually withdrew. I found my work in the group totally fulfilling as it provided me with the opportunity, at last, to serve as a priestess. For me the role of priestess encompassed all aspects of group work — it was not limited to purely ritual functions. I drew on my powers as a priestess when lecturing, leading a group meditation, writing a ritual, planning a course of work or just helping someone solve a problem. I was at last free to be myself.

I also shared some workshops with a friend who is an extremely experienced magical practitioner. I remember one course especially that had far more men attending than women and that included a small ritual. We served at the altar, two priestesses jointly presiding over the communion of bread and wine. It was a rare event — women administering communion to men and each of the men commented on this fact afterwards. One man had been a monk for 17 years and had finally emerged, not just to minister to the outside world, but also to find the Divine Feminine, which was absent within the monastery walls. For him, communion from a woman as a mediator of the Goddess was a very special event. It was also very special for me.

I have always worked with men and women, having never felt the need to work exclusively with women, though I can envisage circumstances in which that might take place. I have always felt that a priestess has something to offer men, too, for where else can a man find a conscious reflection of the face of the Goddess? To deny a man contact with the Goddess is simply to force him back into the prison that patriarchy has created, and patriarchy does imprison men too. It is when a man comes to this realization that he most needs to reach out for a feminine image of divinity. I am aware of men who have made a dedication to the Goddess and this can only continue to happen if priestesses are willing to awaken men to the feminine aspect of deity.

My time as a priestess has not been easy. It is a great mistake to think that service to the Goddess somehow brings protection from the hardships and sorrows of life, because if anything, it does the reverse. We will not learn what it is to serve life it we are cocooned and protected from it. I have had my share of pain: my second daughter was still-born, I have felt alone, I have been physically and emotionally exhausted, I have felt close to madness. There was even a time when I wished to cut off my long hair as a conscious act of severing my service to the Goddess as I felt unworthy to serve Her — I no longer trusted my inner guidance, inspiration or dreams.

It was during a particularly unhappy period in my life that a close priestess friend suggested that I went to Ireland to the Fellowship of Isis and so we travelled together with my chidren in tow. There I was renewed and re-discovered myself after a long period of estrangement. In a meditation that was the culmination of my stay. I experienced Isis as Queen of the Heavens, crowned with a thousand stars. We were deep in the heart of cosmic space, dark blue and silent. It suddenly struck me that I had no gift to give her. Tears streamed down my face — I had nothing left to give her. 'I give you my tears', I said. 'Every tear will be a crystal', was Her reply and a necklace of crystal was placed over my head. In that single moment I understood more about the pain I had been through than I could ever explain in words. I had been lifted out of the Underworld and restored to myself.

The women I know and respect as priestesses are quite different from any other women that I have ever met. As individuals they are each true to themselves and as a group they possess keen minds and are independent thinkers. They are highly creative and accomplished scholars in their own right, each having a commitment to serve the Mysteries. Each has a timeless and ageless quality. Some are wives and mothers, others are independent and free. Every one has discovered her own womanhood and each presents a face of the Goddess to the world.

As for me, I shall continue to be but one garment of Isis. I cannot think of a higher or more honourable calling. I am now resolved to offer help to those who would also tread the same path by preparing an induction course into the Mysteries of Isis.

May Isis grant you the powers to hear the inner voice and the courage to follow where it leads.

# Oracle For a New Priestess

Be opened to Me,
Follow My sending,
Enclose Me,
That I may be born anew.

Keep kythe with Me,
That you be kindled.
Become My self,
That all be safe-kept.

Be My garment
And My temple:
Heart, womb and all —
A shrine of My worship.

Be My voice
Sounding in silence,
Echoing in lost hearts
And in empty places.

Be My blazon
For the world to know
That My hand is about you
Wherever you go.

## Blessing For All Who Seek Her

May your steps be led!
May your faith strengthen you!
May your vision burn bright!

May your words become bread!
May your blessings embue!
May your songs turn to light!

In your turnings and yearnings
In your half-rememberings
In all your forgettings

In your shrinings and twinings
In your self-dissemblings
In all your bequestings

May She be the brightness
That blessedly brings you
That questingly quires you

That lastingly leads you
That never denies you
The heart of Her homing.

Reverend Caitlín Matthews, priestess of Rhiannon

# Bibliography

**Woman as Priestess**

Adler, Margot, *Drawing Down the Moon* (Beacon Press, 1986)

Allione, Tsultrim, *Women of Wisdom* (Routledge & Kegan Paul, 1984)

Andrews, Lynne, *The Flight of the Seventh Moon* (Routledge & Kegan Paul, 1981)
*Medicine Woman* (Routledge & Kegan Paul, 1981)

Cameron, Anne, *Daughters of Copper Woman* (Women's Press, 1987)

Craighead, Meinrad, 'Immanent Mother' in *The Feminist Mystic*, edited by Mary E. Giles, (Crossroad, 1982)

Crowley, Vivianne, *Wicca: the Old Religion in the New Age* (Aquarian Press, 1989)

Dowman, Keith, *Sky Dancer: the Secret of Life and Songs of the Lady Yeshe Tsogyel* (Routledge & Kegan Paul, 1984)

Durden-Robertson, Lawrence, *Priestesses* (Cesara Publications, 1976)

Fortune, Dion, *Moon Magic* (Aquarian Press, 1989)
*The Sea Priestess* (Aquarian Press, 1989)
'The Worship of Isis' in her *Aspects of Occultism* (Aquarian Press, 1962)

Gilchrist, Cherry, *The Circle of Nine* (Dryad Press, 1988)

Jamal, Michele, *Shape Shifters: Shaman Women in Contemporary Society* (Arkana, 1987)

Mariechild, Diane, *Mother Wit* (Crossing Press, 1981)

Nicholson, Shirley, editor, *The Goddess Re-Awakening* (Theosophical Publishing House, 1989)

O'Brien, Theresa King, editor *The Spiral Path* (Yes, 1988)

Perera, Sylvia Brinton, *Descent to the Goddess: A Way of Initiation for Women* (Inner City Books, 1981)

Robertson, Olivia, *The Call of Isis* (Cesara Publications, 1975)
Starhawk, *The Spiral Dance* (Harper & Row, 1987)
   *Truth or Dare* (Harper & Row, 1987)
Stein, Diane, *Stroking the Python: Women's Psychic Lives* (Llewellyn
   Publications, 1988)

## The Goddess Herself

Anderson, Jorgen, *The Witch on the Wall: Medieval Erotic Sculp-
   ture in the British Isles* (Rosenkilde & Bagger, 1977)
Begg, Ean, *The Black Virgin* (Arkana, 1985)
Blofield, John, *Compassion Yoga: the Mystical Cult of Kuan Yin* (Allen
   & Unwin, 1977)
Canan, Janine, editor, *She Rises Like the Sun* (Crossing Press, 1989)
Craighead, Meinrad, *The Mother's Songs: Images of God the Mother*
   (Paulist Press, 1986)
Durdin-Robertson, Lawrence, *Juno Covella: Perpetual Calendar of
   the Fellowship of Isis* (Cesara Publications, 1982)
Goddess Guide Group, *Goddesses of the British Museum* (Goddess
   Guide Group, c/o Matriarchy Research and Reclaim Network,
   14 Hill Crest, Sevenoaks, Kent TN13 3HN, 1988)
Grian, Sinead, *Sula Brighde: Goddess of Fire* (Brighde's Fire, 1985)
   *The Sun Goddess* (Brighde's Fire, 1986)
Grigson, Geoffrey, *The Goddess of Love* (Quartet, 1978)
Hart, George, *A Dictionary of Egyptian Gods and Goddesses* (Rout-
   ledge & Kegan Paul, 1986)
Johnson, Buffie, *Lady of the Beasts: Ancient Images of the Goddess
   and Her Sacred Animals* (Harper & Row, 1988)
Luke, Helen, M., *Woman, Earth and Spirit* (Crossroads, 1981)
Matthews, Caitlín, *The Elements of the Goddess* (Element Books,
   1990)
   *The Search for Rhiannon* (Hunting Raven Press, 1981)
   *Sophia, Goddess of Wisdom* (Unwin & Hyman, 1990)
Mookerjee, Ajit, *Kali: the Feminine Force* (Thames & Hudson, 1988)
Neuman, Erich, *Amor and Psyche* (Princeton University Press, 1956)
Olson, Carl, *The Book of the Goddess* (Crossroad, 1987)
St George, E. A., *Under Regulus: Invocations to Sekhmet* (Spook
   Enterprises, 1985)
Sjöö, Monica, and Mor, Barbara, *The Great Cosmic Mother* (Harper
   & Row, 1987)
Stewart, Bob, *The Waters of the Gap* (Bath City Council, 1981)
Vermaseren, Maarten J., *Cybele and Attis* (Thames & Hudson,
   1977)

Wolkstein, Diane and Kramer, Samuel Noah, *Inanna: Queen of Earth and Heaven* (Rider, 1984)

Woodruffe, J., *Hymns to the Goddess and Hymn to Kali* (Madras, Ganesh & Co., 1982)

## General

Arden, John and D'Arcy, Margaretta, *Awkward Corners* (Methuen, 1988)

*Whose is the Kingdom?* (Methuen, 1988)

Burland, G., *Echoes of Magic* (Peter Davies, 1972)

Claremont de Castillejo, Irene, *Knowing Woman* (Harper & Row, 1973

Crowley, Aleister, *Magick in Theory and Practice* (Dover Books, 1976)

Cunningham, S., *Earth Power* (Llewellyn Publications, 1985)

Daly, Mary, with Caputi, Jane, *Websters' First New Intergalactic Wickedary of the English Language* (Women's Press, 1988)

de Pizan, Christine, *The Book of the City of Ladies*, translated by Earl Jeffrey Richards, (Picador, 1983)

Glidow, E., *Sapphic Songs* (Druid Heights Books, 1982)

Hall, Nor, *The Moon and the Virgin* (Women's Press, 1980)

Harding, M. Esther, *The Way of All Women* (Harper & Row, 1970)

*Women's Mysteries* (Harper & Row, 1971)

Harner, Michael, *The Way of the Shaman* (Harper & Row, 1980)

Harrison, Jane, *Prolegomena to the Study of Greek Religion* (Merlin Press, 1961)

Hess, Helene, *The Zodiac Explorer's Handbook* (Aquarian Press, 1986)

Jones, Prudence and Matthews, Caitlín, *Voices From the Circle: The Heritage of Western Paganism* (Aquarian Press, 1990)

Kalveit, H., *Dreamtime and Inner Space* (Shamballah, 1988)

Lamie, Lucie, *Egyptian Mysteries* (Thames & Hudson, 1988)

Lemesurier, Peter, *Healing of the Gods: the Magic of Symbols and the Practice of Theotheraphy* (Element Books, 1988)

Lovelock, James, *The Ages of Gaia: a Biography of Our Living Earth* (Oxford University Press, 1988)

Matthews, Caitlín, *Arthur and the Sovereignty of Britain: King and Goddess in the Mabinogion* (Arkana, 1989)

*Mabon and the Mysteries of Britain: An Exploration of the Mabinogion* (Arkana, 1987)

Matthews, John and Caitlín, *The Arthurian Book of Days* (Sidgewick & Jackson, 1990)

*The Arthurian Tarot: A Hallowquest Handbook* (Aquarian Press, 1990)

*Hallowquest: Tarot Magic and the Arthurian Mysteries* (Aquarian Press, 1990)

*The Western Way*, Volume I (Arkana, 1987)

Matthews, John, *Gawain, Knight of the Goddess* (Aquarian Press, 1990)

Matthews, John, with additional material by Caitlín Matthews, *Taliesin: the Shamanic Mysteries of Britain* (Unwin Hyman, 1990)

Matthews, John and Potter, Chesca, *The Aquarian Guide to Legendary London* (Aquarian Press, 1990)

Ngakpa Chögyam, *Rainbow of Liberated Energy* (Element Books, 1986)

Owen, T.M., *Welsh Folk Customs* (Gomer Press, 1987)

Paxson, Diana, *The White Raven* (Hodder & Stoughton, 1988)

Pollack, Rachel and Matthews, Caitlín, *Tarot Tales* (Century, 1989)

Rawson, Philip, *Tantra: the Indian Cult of Ecstasy*, (Thames & Hudson 1973)

Ross, A., *Pagan Celtic Britain* (Sphere Books, 1974)

St George, E. A., *Cat Worship, Ancient and Modern* (Spook Enterprises, 1985)

Savary, Louis and Berne, Patricia H., *Kything: the Art of Spiritual Presence* (Paulist Press, 1988)

Shuttle, Penelope and Redgrove, Peter, *The Wise Wound* (Gollancz, 1978)

Stewart, R.J., *Advanced Magical Arts* (Element Books, 1988)
*Living Magical Arts* (Blandford Press, 1987)

Wolfe, A., *In the Shadow of the Shaman* (Llewellyn, 1988)


## Goddess Liturgy

Laura, Judith, *She Lives: the Return of Our Great Mother* (The Crossing Press, 1989)

Paxson, Diana, *The Liturgy of the Lady: the Fellowship of the Spiral Path* (MZB Enterprises, PO Box 72, Berkeley, CA 94701, USA)

Robertson, Olivia, *Dea: Rites and Mysteries of the Goddess: Liturgy of the Fellowship of Isis* (Cesara Publications)
*Pantheia: Initiations and Festivals of the Goddess* (Cesara Publications, 1988)
*Sybil: Oracles of the Goddess* (Cesara Publications, 1989)
*Sophia:Cosmic Consciousness of the Goddess* (Cesara Publications, 1986)

*Urania: Ceremonial Magic of the Goddess* (Cesara Publications, 1983)

Winter, Miriam Therese, *Woman Prayer: Woman Song: Resources for Ritual* (Oak Park, 1987) Christian feminist rituals.

## Journals

*Arachne Magazine*, 14 Hill Crest, Sevenoaks, Kent
A magazine of matriarchal and Goddess studies.

*Matriarchy Newsletter*, 14 Hill Crest, Sevenoaks, Kent
A feminist newsletter about the Goddess and Goddess groups in Britain. Produced at the eight festivals.

*Woman of Power*, PO Box 827, Cambridge, MASS 02238, USA
A magazine of feminism, spirituality and politics. Four issues at $28 a year for overseas subscribers to be paid for in US currency only.

*Snake Power*, 5856 College Avenue, 138 Oakland, CA 94618.
A quartely magazine edited by Vicki Noble, dedicated to contemporary female shamanism. $28 a year for overseas subscribers to be paid in US currency only.

# Useful Addresses

**The Covenant of the Goddess**, PO Box 1226, Berkeley, CA 94704, USA.

A national organization of cross-traditional Wiccan and other Goddess-worshipping groups. It has won recognition of the Craft as a legally-recognized religion. Covens that have been operative for over six continuous months may join.

**Domus Sophiae Terrae et Sanctae Gradalae**, BCM Hallowquest, London WC1N 3XX

For more information about training and weekend courses given by Caitlín and John Matthews in the British Mysteries, Celtic and Goddess traditions, write for details enclosing four first class stamps (within UK) or two international reply paid coupons (overseas).

**The Fellowship of Isis**, Clonegal Castle, Enniscorthy, Eire

The Fellowship welcomes all — men and women — who love and venerate the Goddess in her many forms. Branches, temples and shrines worldwide. It publishes a quarterly newsletter and produces many other publications from the Cesara Press (see above under Olivia Robertson and Lawrence Durdin-Robertson).

**Fellowship of the Spiral Path**, PO Box 5521, Berkeley, CA 94705, USA

This association, open to women and men, has a clergy-training programme (not currently operating a correspondence course). The Fellowship considers itself to be a modern tradition of the worldwide Old Religion that also includes tribal religions. It celebrates the Liturgy of the Lady every month.

**The House of Net**, BCM Box 6812, London WC1N 3XX

A priestess-training programme that combines a correspondence course with periodic workshops and weekend courses. For more details write to Naomi Ozaniec at the above address.

**Monica Sjöö** c/o BCM-Hallowquest, London WC1N 3XX

For details of Monica's slideshows and exhibitions, or to commission original artwork from her, please send 3 first-class stamps or 2 international reply-paid coupons to the above address.

**Mystery Workshops**, Felicity Wombwell, 1 Ravenstone Road, London N8 0JT

Felicity Wombwell offers day courses about the Goddess, using the sacred creative arts of music, drama, dance and image, for finding your sacred self and exploring the cycle of the feminine within. For more details and latest leaflet, please write to the above address.

**The Nine Ladies Association**, 115d Pepys Road, London SE14

This association of women studies many aspects of myth and its practical application in daily life. It runs occasional courses and study groups.

**Order of Bards, Ovates and Druids**, 260 Kew Road, Richmond, Surrey TW9 3EG

The Order is open to women and men who have an interest in native earth spirituality and ecology. It offers a correspondence course and runs a tree-planting programme.

**Sulis Music and Tapes**, BCM 3721, London WC1N 6XX

Issues many musical, magical and meditation tapes by such artists as Bob Stewart, John and Caitlín Matthews among others.

**Wicca**

For more information about Wicca please write to Vivianne Crowley, BM Deosil, London WC1N 3XX, enclosing three first class stamps (within UK) or an international reply paid coupon (overseas).